The
Great Western
&
Great Central
Joint Railway

by
Stanley C. Jenkins MA

THE OAKWOOD PRESS

First Edition published 1978
Second Revised Edition 2006

British Library Cataloguing in Publication Data
A Record for this book is available from the British Library
ISBN 0 85361 653 1
ISBN 978 0 85361 653 5

Typeset by Oakwood Graphics.
Repro by Pkmediaworks, Cranborne, Dorset.
Printed by Cambrian Printers, Aberystwyth, Ceredigion.

Great Western 'King' class 4-6-0 No. 6016 *King Edward V* rushes through Princes Risborough with the 8.55 am Birkenhead to Paddington express on 19th July, 1952.

H.C. Casserley

Title page: An 'L1' class 2-6-4T draws into Beaconsfield with an up local train to Marylebone in 1958. Notice the former Great Central Railway coach immediately behind the locomotive. *Brian W. Leslie*

Front cover: Ex-GWR 'King' class 4-6-0 No. 6012 *King Edward VI* with the 7.40 am Birkenhead-Paddington service near Beaconsfield in April 1962. *J.P. Mullett/Colour-Rail*

Rear cover, top: Peppercorn 'A1' class 4-6-2 No. 60114 *W.P. Allen* at Beaconsfield having arrived with an excursion train of daytrippers destined for Bekonscot model village.

C. Leigh-Johnes/Colour-Rail

Rear cover, bottom: Class '165' diesel mutiple unit No. 165022 departs from Princes Risborough with a train for Marylebone on 12th May, 2002. *P.G. Barnes*

Published by The Oakwood Press (Usk), P.O. Box 13, Usk, Mon., NP15 1YS.
E-mail: sales@oakwoodpress.co.uk
Website: www.oakwoodpress.co.uk

Contents

Introduction to First Edition

The Great Western & Great Central Joint Railway (GW&GC), together with its northwards extension through Bicester, was the very last main line railway to be opened in these islands. For this reason alone, it should be of interest to the enthusiast yet, on reflection, it is clear that railway historians have ignored the 'New Line' to Birmingham. The reasons for this are twofold; perhaps an older generation of enthusiasts was unimpressed by a line opened as recently as 1910 - is it not true that the things which are 'old' appear 'romantic' whereas that which is new is commonplace? On the other hand, we are now in 1978, and, to younger enthusiasts, 1910 is a very long way away indeed!

When, all those years ago, the first trains appeared on the Bicester Cut-Off, they ran through a rural England in which motor cars were almost unknown, and in which the Anglican Church and the Squire were as powerful as ever before. To us, in the modern age, that world of 1910 is romantic, even archaic, and, for this reason, there should be no prejudice against a (relatively) modern railway; in any case, on examination, the pre-history of the GW&GC Joint Line stretches back to the 1840s, and so the route is perhaps not so modern after all!

The second reason why the 'New Line' has been ignored is, to the historian, more important. Many of the records relating to the period have not yet been opened up to public scrutiny, hence any history of the GW&GC Joint Line and its connections must inevitably rely heavily on secondary material; for this reason, the present monograph cannot hope to be an in-depth study - rather, it attempts to present the story of the GW&GC Railway as a readable, coherent narrative. It is hoped that something of the essential atmosphere of the 'Joint Line' will come over for, even if it is 'modern' the central section of the route, with its sharp curves and picturesque Chiltern scenery, certainly has character.

The story is taken up to the present day, and includes a 'Through the Window' guide section for the benefit of those wishing to discover the line for themselves. Motive power is covered in some detail, for as on all joint lines, engines of both owning companies appeared regularly on the route. Happily, the present-day GW&GC is still something of a 'joint' line as, although it is now part of the LMR, the few remaining locomotive-hauled services are worked from Paddington by the Western Region. It is hoped that the GW&GC remains in being as a 'joint' route for many years to come.

S.C. Jenkins
Witney
1978

A Note on Nomenclature

The term 'New Line' is used to describe the entire line from Old Oak to Aynho; the Great Western & Great Central main line is the 34 mile central section of this route, while the 'Bicester Cut-Off' denotes the northwards continuation from Ashendon Junction. The 'associated lines' are the Bicester Cut-Off and all other branch lines and connecting routes.

Introduction to New Edition

The present monograph was first published in 1978 and, although the book had been reprinted on at least one occasion, it was felt that the time had come for a new, enlarged edition to be prepared. Modern methods of printing and reproduction have enabled the original text to be re-arranged in some places and greatly expanded in others. There have, moreover, been many changes since 1978, the GW&GC route having been extensively modernised by the state-owned British Railways, and then handed over to private companies as a result of the policy of 'privatisation' that was then being pursued by the Conservative Government.

The introduction to the 1978 edition pointed out that, at that time, many of the records relating to the period had not been opened to public scrutiny. This observation generated considerable controversy after a certain hostile reviewer asserted that the claim was 'nonsense'. The person concerned (a railway signalman by occupation) seemed blissfully unaware of 'The Thirty Year Rule', under which the contents of certain classes of government records are kept secret for a period of 30 years. When these records are finally placed in the public domain, there is no guarantee that vital evidence will not have been 'lost', suppressed, or deliberately tampered with.

The writing of recent history can therefore present many problems - particularly when dealing with controversial matters such as the Beeching closures or railway privatisation. Regarding the Beeching period, it appears that sensitive information relating to the closures has indeed been 'lost', while government files appertaining to rail privatisation will remain secret for many years.

For these reasons, the story of the GW&GC Joint Line will inevitably be slanted towards the earlier periods - evidence relating to the planning and construction of the line having survived in embarrassing profusion. Some of this material has been included in the revised text while, to provide a counter-balance, the 'route' section has been much-expanded, with many further details of the infrastructure at individual stations. Most of this new data has been obtained from plans and documents that are now in private collections as a result of the great 'clear out' of archival material that preceded rail privatisation.

In fact, as far as some locations were concerned, there was an over-abundance of new material - so much so, that the 'route' section has expanded to three lengthy chapters. On balance, it is perhaps only right and proper that this should be the case - after all, for the past 50 years railway historians have tended to concentrate on branch lines and light railways. The complex infrastructure of the great main lines has been largely ignored, and stations such as Denham, High Wycombe and Bicester North have not received the attention that they deserve. It is hoped that this new version of *The Great Western & Great Central Joint Railway* will help to rectify this deficiency.

Thanks are due to those who have contributed photographs or helped in other ways, including Chris Turner, Mike Marr, Ian Kennedy, Brian Leslie, W.K. Makenzie and the late John Strange.

Publisher's Note: The BR closure files for the Beeching period for the area covered by this book are at National Archives, Kew (LMR files) and County Records Office, Trowbridge, Wilts (WR files).

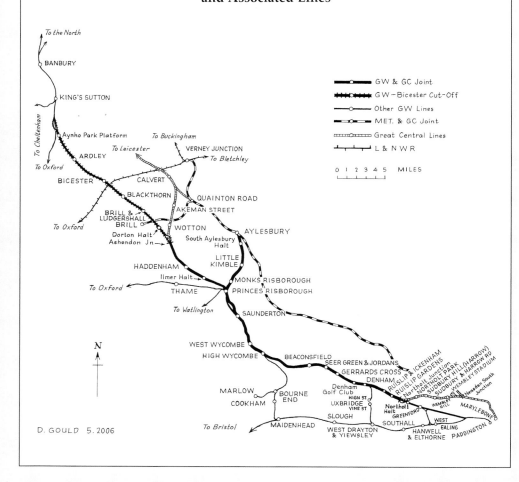

The Great Western & Great Central Joint Railway
and Associated Lines

To the North

BANBURY

KING'S SUTTON

To Cheltenham

Aynho Park Platform

To Oxford

ARDLEY

BICESTER

CALVERT

To Buckingham

To Leicester

VERNEY JUNCTION

To Bletchley

BLACKTHORN

QUAINTON ROAD

BRILL & LUDGERSHALL

AKEMAN STREET

BRILL

WOTTON

To Oxford

Dorton Halt

Ashendon Jn

South Aylesbury Halt

AYLESBURY

LITTLE KIMBLE

HADDENHAM

Ilmer Halt

To Oxford

THAME

MONKS RISBOROUGH

PRINCES RISBOROUGH

To Watlington

SAUNDERTON

N

WEST WYCOMBE

HIGH WYCOMBE

BEACONSFIELD

SEER GREEN & JORDANS

GERRARDS CROSS

DENHAM

RUISLIP & ICKENHAM

RUISLIP GARDENS

Northolt Junction

NORTHOLT PARK

SUDBURY HILL (HARROW)

SUDBURY & HARROW RD

WEMBLEY STADIUM

Neasden South Junction

MARLOW

COOKHAM

BOURNE END

Denham Golf Club

UXBRIDGE

HIGH ST

VINE ST

Northolt Halt

GREENFORD

WEMBLEY HILL

MARYLEBONE

To Bristol

MAIDENHEAD

WEST DRAYTON & YIEWSLEY

SLOUGH

SOUTHALL

HANWELL & ELTHORNE

WEST EALING

PADDINGTON

Legend:
- ━━●━━ GW & GC Joint
- ✕✕✕ GW — Bicester Cut-Off
- ━○━ Other GW Lines
- ━⊡━ MET. & GC Joint
- ⊡⊡⊡⊡ Great Central Lines
- ┴┴┴┴ L & N W R

0 1 2 3 4 5 MILES

D. GOULD 5. 2006

Chapter One

Pre-History and Origins of the Line
(1846-1901)

Buckinghamshire, one of the smallest English counties, was hardly the sort of place in which Victorian capitalists would rush to build a railway. A backward, conservative county, its main economic activity in the 19th century was agriculture. The northern half of the area - the clay plain known as the Vale of Aylesbury - was, and indeed still is, rich grazing land, but the southern parts of the county had only poor flinty and chalky soil. Moreover, the chalk hills which form the Chiltern range formed a barrier to communication, and made the prospect of building a railway between the Vale of Aylesbury and the markets of London a particularly expensive one. It is perhaps hardly surprising that Buckinghamshire should have been one of the very last English counties to be opened up by railways.

Pre-Railway Transport Facilities

Neighbouring Middlesex was, similarly, still a largely rural county, though it was already dotted with prosperous towns and villages; a 17th century topographer noted that the air was 'exceedingly healthful, and the soil fertile, the houses and villages everywhere neat and stately'. By pre-industrial standards, the road system in Middlesex was excellent - this being a natural concomitant of its geographical position on the western fringes of London.

The great highways of pre-industrial England radiated outwards from the metropolis, bringing trade and prosperity to roadside settlements such as Uxbridge, Beaconsfield and High Wycombe. All of these places were situated on the Oxford Road and, although they were too close to London to serve as major overnight stopping places, local traders and innkeepers were able to develop a flourishing trade from the travellers who passed through in stage coaches or in carrier's wagons.

Road traffic increased still further after the passing of a Turnpike Act in 1714 enabled tolls to be collected for the reconstruction and maintenance of the Oxford Highway. It was, nevertheless, several years before the turnpike trustees could implement any major road improvements, and long-distance roads were often poorly-maintained. As late as 1797-98, the Oxford Road became a treacherous quagmire after periods of heavy rain during the winter months. One contemporary writer described the atrocious conditions that then pertained as follows:

> There was but one passable track on this road; and that was less than six feet wide, and it was eight inches deep in fluid sludge. All the rest of the road was from a foot to eighteen inches deep in adhesive mud. This track was thronged with wagons (many of them drawn by ten horses and most of them having broad wheels, even to sixteen inches wide) and farmers' six-inch wheel carts, which occupied almost the whole of this confined space. It was, therefore, with great difficulty and some danger that horsemen and light carriages could pass.

Improved standards of highway maintenance and construction during the early 19th century lead to a huge upsurge in traffic on the Oxford Road, and by the 1830s this great artery of communication between London, High Wycombe, Oxford, Milford

Haven and Ireland had emerged as one of the most important stage coach routes in the country. Prestigious coaches such as *The Age* covered the 55 miles between London and Oxford in only 3 hours 40 minutes, and drivers such as Joe Tollit achieved legendary reputations in their own lifetimes. In 1834, *The Age* was driven between High Wycombe and London, a distance of 29 miles, in just 1 hour 40 minutes.

In retrospect, stage coach services were at their very peak during the 1820s and 1830s. This form of transport had several disadvantages; in particular, it was by definition a low speed system - the fastest stage coach being able to travel no faster than the speed of a horse. Moreover, the stage coaches were so expensive that ordinary people could not afford to travel on them - this mode of transport being used more or less exclusively by the gentry and professional classes. Under these circumstances, it is hardly surprising that the railways rapidly became the country's primary means of inland transport.

Origins of the Great Western Railway

The first tentative plans for a railway in the area to the west of London were formulated in the 1820s, when the pioneer railway promoter William James (1771-1837) suggested that his proposed 'Central Junction Railway or Tramroad' might pass through western Middlesex on its way from London to Stratford-upon-Avon. This project was hopelessly premature, but tangible progress was made in the following decade, the Great Western Railway Company (GWR) being incorporated by Act of Parliament on 31st August, 1835, with powers for the construction of a railway from Bristol to London.

The new railway was to commence 'at or near a certain Field called Temple Mead, within the Parish of Temple otherwise Holy Cross in the City and County of the City of Bristol' and terminate by 'a Junction with the London & Birmingham Railway in a certain Field lying between the Paddington Canal and the Turnpike Road leading from London to Harrow on the western side of the General Cemetery in the Parish or Township of Hammersmith in the ... County of Middlesex'. To pay for their 114 mile line, the promoters were empowered to raise no less than £2,500,000 in shares and a further £833,333 by loans - a total of £3,333,333, which was an incredible sum by the standards of the 1830s.

As originally proposed, the Great Western Railway would have been built as a standard gauge line, this assumption being implicit in the 1835 Act, which assumed that GWR trains would run over the London & Birmingham Railway between Kensal Green and Euston. However, Isambard Kingdom Brunel (1806-59), the Great Western Engineer, recommended that the line should be built to a broad gauge of 7 ft, and this suggestion was accepted by the GWR Directors.

In June 1836 the Great Western Directors decided that a contract would be awarded for construction of the line between Hanwell and Acton, and work was soon in progress. In the meantime, they had also agreed that the GWR would construct an independent terminus at Paddington - earlier ideas of using the London & Birmingham station at Euston having being abandoned. Parliamentary consent for the proposed deviation between Acton and Paddington was obtained on 3rd July, 1837, by which time the major earthworks between London and Maidenhead were substantially complete.

The first section of the Great Western main line was ceremonially opened from London to Maidenhead on 31st May, 1838, when a special train conveyed the

Directors and their invited guests from Paddington to a temporary station at Maidenhead. The line was extended westwards to Twyford on 1st July, 1839, and to Reading on 30th March, 1840. Further sections were opened at intervals, and the GWR main line was completed throughout its length from London to Bristol Temple Meads on 30th June, 1841.

Meanwhile, a variety of extensions were being projected, Oxford being reached by a branch from Didcot on 12th June, 1844, while on 2nd September, 1850 the Oxford & Rugby Railway was opened between Oxford and Banbury. Just two years later, on 1st October, 1852, the opening of a further extension enabled GWR trains to run to and from Birmingham.

The effects, as far as stage coach traffic was concerned, were catastrophic; long distance road services went into a swift and terminal decline, and former coaching towns such as Uxbridge and High Wycombe were relegated to the status of isolated rural backwaters. Indeed, a similar situation pertained in the case of Aylesbury, Princes Risborough, and throughout a huge swathe of central Buckinghamshire which was now entirely cut off from mainstream Victorian economic developments.

Nevertheless, the county was situated in a strategic position between London and the Midlands, and for this reason Buckinghamshire - or rather the eastern corner of it - found itself served by a major North-to-South trunk route as far back as the 1830s, when the London & Birmingham Railway opened its main line from Euston to Birmingham. The new line entered the county near Cheddington, and penetrated the Chilterns via Watford and Tring. By 1846, the London & Birmingham company had amalgamated with the Grand Junction Railway, and both companies had been re-born as a new undertaking known as the London & North Western Railway (LNWR).

The London & North Western company was soon planning new lines in the area. One of the earliest of these schemes was for a railway running westwards from Tring and serving the county town of Aylesbury. The Tring scheme - which was revived several times during the 1830s and 1840s - would have placed Aylesbury on a main line running west to Cheltenham and possibly South Wales. However, it is likely that the whole idea was nothing more than a gigantic 'bluff', designed to counteract various other projected lines which, if successful, would have linked London with Oxford, Cheltenham and the South Wales coal fields. The only tangible result was the construction of a short branch from Cheddington to Aylesbury, which was opened on 10th June, 1839.

The Buckinghamshire Railway

The Buckinghamshire Railway was a more concrete scheme although, needless to say, it was conceived for 'political' rather than purely economic reasons at a time when the London & Birmingham Railway was seeking to counteract the broad gauge Oxford & Rugby line. In 1847, two nebulous schemes - the Buckinghamshire & Brackley Railway and the Oxford & Bletchley Railway - were combined to form the Buckinghamshire Railway under the provisions of an Act obtained in that year (10 & 11 Vict. cap. 236). The promoters were thereby empowered to build a rail link running westwards across the Vale of Aylesbury from Bletchley to Banbury, together with a branch line from Claydon to Oxford.

The LNWR company was a substantial shareholder in the Buckinghamshire company, and had provided £450,000 to finance this two-pronged attack on the GWR.

Nevertheless, the Buckinghamshire Railway was built and opened by a nominally independent company, with Sir Harry Verney, a major local landowner, as its Chairman. The contractor for this 4 ft 8½ in. gauge line was Thomas Brassey (1805-1870), and the first sod was cut at Buckingham on 20th April, 1847.

Construction proceeded apace throughout 1848 and, at the half-yearly meeting held at Euston in 1849, the shareholders were informed that '£716,798 6s. 3d. had been spent on the works up to 31st December, 1848'. It is interesting to find that £200 had been expended to provide religious instruction for the navvies! At the next general meeting, Sir Harry Verney reported that the works were 'proceeding in a satisfactory manner on the line from Bletchley to Banbury', while the Oxford line was said to be in a 'forward state'. Work on the stations was under way although, as an economy measure, these new buildings would be 'reduced to the smallest scale consistent with efficient traffic accommodation'.

With support from the LNWR guaranteed, the Buckinghamshire Railway Company seemed destined for immediate success, but in the event external events intervened before this promising scheme could be completed. At the end of 1845 a series of catastrophic harvest failures threw the Victorian financial system into confusion at a time in which most of the nation's surplus capital had been invested in new railway schemes. The result was a long period of social and economic crisis, in which railway companies were unable to raise their authorized capital. Many railway schemes were abandoned in their entirety, while others were obliged to moderate their ambitions in the light of changing circumstances.

To their credit, the supporters of the Buckinghamshire Railway pressed on with their scheme, though in the first instance it was agreed that work would be concentrated on the section between Bletchley, Claydon Junction and Banbury. The Bletchley to Claydon Junction section was opened on 1st May, 1850, together with the branch line from Claydon Junction to Banbury. A further 16 miles of line, from the junction to Islip, were opened on 1st October. The Buckinghamshire Railway did not, as yet, reach Oxford, but on 2nd December, 1850 the opening of another 2½ miles of line between Islip and 'Oxford Road' brought the new railway within sight of its destination.

The Buckinghamshire Railway had originally intended to reach Oxford by means of running powers over the rival Great Western line, but when the latter company refused to allow access over its own property, the Buckinghamshire company was obliged to build an independent line, running parallel to the Great Western route as far as Rewley Road. Here, a small wooden terminus was opened on 20th May, 1851, and the completion of the line was celebrated in the usual way, with glowing speeches and a great banquet.

Meanwhile, the LNWR had agreed to lease the Buckinghamshire company for a period of 999 years, promising the Buckinghamshire Railway's shareholders a guaranteed dividend of four per cent per annum, and a half of the surplus profits. The Buckinghamshire company thereby became a purely LNWR venture, the whole scheme being designed to draw traffic from the rival Great Western Railway at Oxford and Banbury. Nevertheless, the Buckinghamshire Railway gave the Vale of Aylesbury a viable transport system, and thereby enabled the farmers of the area to send their products to London via Bletchley.

Some Other Early Schemes

The greater part of Buckinghamshire was, however, still without railways, and these LNWR routes remained the only lines to run through the central areas of the county. Then, in the 1850s, came a scheme which, if successful, would have made the later Great Western & Great Central Joint Line unnecessary. The Oxford, Worcester & Wolverhampton Railway (OW&WR) was originally a part of the Great Western system. Relations between the OW&WR and the GWR were, however, strained - mainly because the latter company had adopted the Banbury and Birmingham line as its main route from Paddington to the Midlands and North. The OW&WR Directors felt that this was a breach of faith, and broke away from the Great Western.

Struggling to operate its growing system with a handful of borrowed or second-hand engines, the Oxford, Worcester & Wolverhampton company saw the need for new alliances, and its own independent route to London. 'The Oxford & Brentford Railway' was the result; planned to leave the authorized route of the Oxford, Worcester & Wolverhampton main line near its junction with the Great Western at Wolvercot, this new line would have run down through Oxford, then turned east to reach Princes Risborough.

Following the route later taken by the Great Western & Great Central Joint Line, the OW&WR's 'London Extension' would have continued on down through High Wycombe and Denham, before turning south to reach Uxbridge and a junction with the London & South Western Railway near Brentford. A Bill for the new main line was sent up to Parliament in time for the 1852 session, but the Oxford & Brentford scheme aroused the hostility of both the Great Western and the LNWR companies, and the latter revived the earlier Tring & Oxford plans as a counter-measure. In the event, Parliament threw out the OW&WR Bill after a 15 day fight in the Commons, and the Tring scheme was allowed to drop once again.

The OW&WR sent a similar extension scheme - this time styled 'The London & Mid-Western Railway' - up to Parliament in the following year. The revised scheme would again have run via Princes Risborough and Uxbridge, crossing the Great Western main line at West Drayton and then running more or less parallel to it as far as Southall. Here the projected route would fork, with one line heading south-east to meet the London & South Western and the other running north to join the London & North Western Railway at Willesden Junction. Sadly, the London & Mid-Western scheme fared no better than the earlier Oxford & Brentford proposal, and Parliament rejected the scheme in its entirety.

The Wycombe Railway

Although the Mid-Western and Oxford & Brentford schemes had been unsuccessful, the very thought of the Oxford, Worcester & Wolverhampton Railway reaching London was a sobering reminder to the Great Western that small towns and villages to the north and south of the existing GWR main line needed rail links of their own. In the next few years the GWR company actively supported a number of branch line schemes, one of the most important of these projects being the Wycombe Railway.

As early as 1846, a branch had been projected from Maidenhead, across the county boundary in Berkshire, to High Wycombe. The Wycombe Railway Company was incorporated by Act of Parliament on 26th July, 1847 (9 & 10 Vict. cap. 147), but in the event the supporters of the Wycombe Railway were unable to implement their modest scheme, the economic crisis of the late 1840s having made it extremely difficult for small companies to raise their authorized capital.

The project was revived in the early 1850s and, on 30th June, 1852, the supporters of the scheme obtained a new Act of Parliament (15 & 16 Vict. cap. 147), providing consent for the proposed branch line from Maidenhead to High Wycombe. The authorized capital was £102,000 in shares, with an additional £33,600 by loans.

The Wycombe Railway was opened, as a 9 mile 47 chain broad gauge branch, on 1st August, 1854. The new line was single track throughout, with intermediate stations at Maidenhead (Boyne Hill), Cookham, Marlow Road, Wooburn Green, and Loudwater. The line was laid with Barlow rails, which had been invented by William Barlow (1812-1902), and were designed to be laid directly onto the ballast, without sleepers or other means of support. The principal engineering works included two timber viaducts near Marlow Road, while at High Wycombe the new railway terminated in a classic, 'Brunel' style station, with a barn-like wooden train shed.

Like the Buckinghamshire Railway, the Wycombe company was a nominally independent undertaking with its own Chairman and Board of Directors, although in reality the railway had been leased to the Great Western at a fixed annual rent of £3,600. On 17th August, 1857 the Wycombe Railway obtained a new Act permitting an extension of the line from High Wycombe to Princes Risborough and Thame. By that same Act, the company was authorized to raise a further £60,000 in shares and £20,000 by loan, the receipts from the extension to be applied in payment of debenture interest, while the remainder would be shared between the GWR and Wycombe companies, the Great Western receiving 60 per cent.

On 28th June, 1861, The Wycombe Railway obtained a further Act (24 & 25 Vict. cap. 87), authorizing the construction of an eastern extension from Princes Risborough to Aylesbury, and a westwards extension from Thame to Kennington, near Oxford. By that same Act, the company was permitted to raise an additional £260,000 in shares and £86,000 by loans, the GWR subscribing £100,000 towards this latest extension scheme.

The line from High Wycombe to Thame, a distance of 13 miles 72 chains, was brought into use on 1st August, 1862, and the Wycombe Railway 'main line' was completed throughout to Kennington Junction on 25th October, 1864. The Aylesbury branch was opened on 1st August, 1862, simultaneously with the line to Thame. The completed Wycombe Railway system formed a circuitous alternative route between Maidenhead and Oxford, but at the same time it brought the advantages of rail communication to towns and villages such as High Wycombe, West Wycombe, Princes Risborough and Thame.

The Wycombe line, serpentine, single track and heavily graded, was little more than a rural branch line, serving scattered agricultural communities; only High Wycombe, which boasted a chair industry based upon the surrounding beech woods, offered any source of goods traffic for the line. The Wycombe line - which was converted to standard gauge in 1870 - was destined to play a vital part in the subsequent history of the Great Western & Great Central Joint Line.

By this time, schemes for railways in the central Buckinghamshire area were coming thick and fast. In 1861, for example, the OW&WR (now known as The West Midland Railway) resurrected its Mid-Western extension scheme for the third and final time. The proposed new line - 'The London, Buckinghamshire & West Midland Junction Railway' - was to pass through Thame, Princes Risborough, Amersham, Beaconsfield and Uxbridge, and terminate at a new station in the vicinity of Sloane Square.

As before, the scheme was opposed by both the Great Western and the North Western companies but, just as the Parliamentary contest was about to begin, the West Midland dropped the Bill, and, to the surprise of all concerned, announced that it was to amalgamate - on favourable terms - with the Great Western Railway. Thus, round three of the 'Mid-Western' saga ended with the elimination of the major protagonist!

Three years later, another enemy of the GWR - the Midland Railway - entered the arena by backing a proposed 'London, Buckinghamshire & East Gloucestershire Railway'. This was to be a line running from the Midland main line at Hendon, through Amersham, Princes Risborough and Thame to Yarnton Junction, near Oxford. West of Yarnton, the tiny, single track Witney Railway would form the basis of a new trunk route to Cheltenham and the South Wales coal fields. This ambitious project, however, fared no better than the earlier Oxford, Worcester & Wolverhampton schemes, and it was thrown out by the Commons.

The Aylesbury & Rickmansworth Railway

In 1875 an independent company projected a line from London to High Wycombe, via Beaconsfield, but this also failed - mainly as a result of opposition from what today would be called 'conservation groups' in the Chiltern area. A similar scheme for a line from Ealing to High Wycombe was mooted in 1881, but this failed in the same way. The Great Western itself projected a line via Uxbridge, Denham and Aylesbury at around the same time - probably as a 'bluff' to counteract various rival proposals such as the Metropolitan-backed Aylesbury & Rickmansworth Railway and the independent Uxbridge & Rickmansworth Railway - both of which came before Parliament at the same time as the Great Western scheme.

Local newspapers such as *The Bucks Herald* took much interest in these diverse schemes, and on 2nd April, 1881 the *Herald* printed a very full report for the benefit of its readers. It is clear, from this evidence, that the Metropolitan Bill was well-supported by local residents, and it seems that there was a groundswell of popular opinion in favour of the Aylesbury & Rickmansworth Railway. As the paper pointed out, the Aylesbury & Rickmansworth Bill was supported by:

No fewer than nine Petitions ... the petitioners were the farmers and others attending Aylesbury market; the commoners of Chorley Wood Common; the commoners of Chesham Bois Commons; the inhabitants and ratepayers of Aylesbury and neighbourhood; the inhabitants of Amersham, Chesham, Chesham Bois, and neighbourhood; the inhabitants of Chenies, Chalfont St Giles and neighbourhood; the inhabitants of Wendover; the inhabitants of Great and Little Missenden and Neighbourhood.

The Metropolitan scheme was preferred for a number of reasons; it would, for instance, provide the hitherto-isolated Missenden Valley with much-needed transport facilities, while the approach to London via Harrow and St Johns Wood was regarded as a much better route than the suggested Great Western line through Uxbridge. Among the many advantages expected to accrue from the proposed Metropolitan line were cheaper supplies of coal, and manure for use on local farms (London's huge horse population produced vast quantities of manure, and this was substance was widely-used on the surrounding farm land).

The Great Western proposals, if implemented, would have created a useful, but circuitous outer-suburban line. In his evidence to the Select Committee appointed by

Parliament to examine the scheme, John Fowler (1817-1898), the Great Western Consulting Engineer, stated that there were 'no engineering difficulties in the way of its construction', whereas the rival schemes would have entailed heavy engineering, and considerable interference 'with house property in Uxbridge'. The proposed Great Western station at Denham would, he said, 'be about three-quarters of a mile' from the village.

The Metropolitan Bill was examined by the Select Committee on Wednesday 30th March, 1881, and it soon became clear to all concerned that this was the favoured option. One by one, a succession of powerful landed magnates gave evidence in support of the Aylesbury & Rickmansworth Bill and (by implication) against the Great Western scheme.

The Duke of Buckingham & Chandos stated that the district between Aylesbury and Rickmansworth was entirely without railway accommodation, and that the only means of transport between Aylesbury and London was via existing the London & Western and Great Western branch lines - neither of which offered fast or frequent services. When asked his opinion on the proposed Metropolitan line his Grace replied:

> For local purposes it would give all the inter-communication that could be desired by the county for the county business, and the markets and everything of that sort, and it would give the shortest through communication to London of any of the schemes which have been proposed for the accommodation of the district.

Sir Philip Rose, a landowner at Penn, was also in Favour of the Metropolitan line, and he added that his neighbours were all anxious to promote the Bill:

> In his opinion they preferred the Metropolitan line because they considered that it would accommodate the county the best, and would be more likely to be made. He thought that it would supply a want in the communication with Aylesbury. The Missenden Valley was at present without accommodation. The valley where he lived was considered one of the prettiest spots in Buckinghamshire, but at present it was inaccessible to a great many men who had work to do in London.
>
> As a resident, the railway would not confer any benefit on him, because he used Loudwater station at present. He thought that one of the greatest elements in favour of the Bill was that the Metropolitan Company would be certain to construct the line if they obtained the Bill. Taking into consideration the conveniences in London, there would be an enormous advantage in being able to get about to any part of London on the Metropolitan. The county was supplied with manure from London and coal from the North. It was perfectly obvious that the Metropolitan would provide proper accommodation for the goods traffic.

Sir Harry Verney - one of the most important landowners in north Buckinghamshire - agreed with the other witnesses, and added that the Metropolitan station at Baker Street 'was more convenient than either Euston or Paddington'. Another witness, Colonel Philip Smith, Lord of the Manor of Wendover, thought that the new line would do the area much good, whereas the Great Western line 'approached London at a great angle' and the journey 'involved a change of carriages and every kind of inconvenience'.

The outcome of the Parliamentary battles fought in 1881 was perhaps inevitable, and on 13th July the Aylesbury & Rickmansworth Railway was incorporated, with powers to construct what was, in effect, a northern extension of the Metropolitan

Railway, via Missenden and Wendover, to Aylesbury. The rival Great Western proposals were, meanwhile, quietly dropped - ostensibly because of the severe Winter of 1881 which had, it was claimed, caused a fall in revenue. The Metropolitan Railway finally reached Aylesbury on 1st September, 1892, and it seemed that this new line had finally solved the transport problems of a large part of central Buckinghamshire.

The London & South Wales Railway

It appeared that there was no need for the Great Western to consider further extensions in the area, but then, in 1895, came the ambitious 'London & South Wales' proposal, which envisaged the creation of a trunk route running along the Upper Thames Valley to Oxford, and striking east by way of Bledlow, from where the line would fork with a northern branch to Missenden and a southern arm through Beaconsfield. The scheme had the support of the LNWR, the Midland, and a newcomer - the Manchester, Sheffield & Lincolnshire Railway (later the Great Central Railway (GCR)).

The Great Western, as one might expect, was alarmed at this proposal; the company was, at this time, at a low ebb as a result of its great gauge conversion operations. Now, at the worst possible time, a powerful triumvirate of rival companies had decided to back yet another bid to steal the lucrative South Wales coal traffic away. It was clearly a 'darkest hour' for the Great Western, but in the end the company was able to save itself by splitting up the rival alliance; the Manchester, Sheffield & Lincolnshire backed down after the Great Western had offered certain concessions, and the GWR was then able to defeat the South Wales scheme with comparative ease.

The Great Western at this time was, in truth, rather lethargic, and made very little effort to compete with the rival LNWR Birmingham services. In the days of the broad gauge, Great Western expresses had covered the 129½ miles between Paddington and Birmingham in 2 hours 50 minutes - some 10 minutes faster than the best North Western trains. With the gradual elimination of the broad gauge, the GWR Birmingham trains were slowed one by one, and by the 1870s the few 'fast' services between London and Birmingham were allowed anything from 3 hours 20 minutes to 4 hours for their journeys!

However, at the end of the 19th century, came the so-called 'Great Awakening', and with the aid of a new generation of narrow gauge single-wheelers, the Great Western management at last began to challenge the rival London & North Western Railway. By 1898, the fastest train was covering the distance in 2 hours 27 minutes, and in July 1902 these faster timings were extended to more services, giving one up and three down workings timed to reach their destinations in 2 hours 20 minutes.

Having belatedly decided to speed things up, the Great Western soon saw the advantages of new, improved and shorter routes. Hence, at the end of the 19th century, the company projected three major 'cut-offs' in order to improve its services. The West of England route was shortened by means of a new straight link between the existing Berks & Hants line and Taunton, and to iron out the 'kink' in the South Wales route, a cut-off was provided between Wootton Bassett, near Swindon, and Patchway, near the Severn Tunnel. Both of these new lines (opened in 1906 and 1903 respectively) complemented rather than superseded the original Bristol route.

The third and final 'cut-off', on the other hand, was to be an entirely new venture. Leaving the Bristol main line just outside Paddington, it would branch off almost immediately, and then run north-westwards for a distance of 59 miles to join the earlier Oxford & Rugby line near Banbury. Although the old Wycombe Railway was to form part of the route, the line would for all intents and purposes be a 'New Line' - in fact it was to be the last new main line opened in Britain during the age of steam.

Origins of the New Line

Curiously, this new line to the North came about almost by chance. As we have seen, the area through which the line was to run was a veritable 'battle-ground' of rival companies. In 1897 the GWR obtained Parliamentary consent for a railway from Acton to High Wycombe, in response to a line to High Wycombe put forward by the Metropolitan District Railway. Parliament preferred the Great Western line, and decided that the rival scheme should be cut short at Uxbridge. Thus, quite by chance, the Great Western gained powers to build the first section of the 'New Line'.

Attention now switches to the Manchester, Sheffield & Lincolnshire Railway (MS&LR), which first appeared on the scene as a backer of the London & South Wales proposals, and had, as a result, already had dealings with the GWR. As its name implied, the Manchester, Sheffield & Lincolnshire was originally a purely northern line, its heartlands being firmly established in the bleak Pennine hills. The company was incorporated on 5th May, 1837 with powers for the construction of a railway from Sheffield to Manchester. After many vicissitudes, this spectacular trans-Pennine route was completed throughout from Sheffield Bridgehouses to Manchester on 22nd December, 1845.

The original Manchester to Sheffield line was soon extended to serve other destinations in the North of England. In 1844, for example, the Great Grimsby & Sheffield Junction Railway was empowered to construct 36 miles of railway from Gainsborough to Great Grimsby, with branches to New Holland and Market Rasen. The latter route was opened was opened between Grimsby and Habrough on 1st March, 1848, and from Habrough to Market Rasen and Brigg on 1st November, 1848.

These diverse lines had, by that time, been merged with the Sheffield to Manchester route to form the Manchester, Sheffield & Lincolnshire Railway. The MS&LR system continued to expand until, by the 1870s, it extended from Grimsby on the east coast to Liverpool and Chester in the west - the latter cities being reached via the jointly-owned Cheshire Lines Committee.

The MS&LR company carried an extensive coal traffic, while the suburban lines around Manchester were busy passenger routes. Still, however, the railway continued to expand, and under its ambitious Chairman Sir Edward Watkin (1819-1901) the MS&LR embarked upon a grandiose extension scheme involving the construction of over 90 miles of new railway between Annesley and London. When completed, the London Extension would transform the entire system into a major trunk route between Marylebone and the North of England. To underline this change of status the MS&LR company renamed itself the Great Central Railway - this more expansive title being adopted in 1897.

As originally planned, the London Extension would have run southwards through the Midlands to form an end-on junction with the recently opened Metropolitan Railway line to Aylesbury. As Sir Edward was also Chairman of the Metropolitan Railway, the idea of using 40 miles of existing line between Quainton Road and Neasden seemed at first to be a good one; the only alternative - since all three major gaps through the Chilterns were now occupied by railways - would have been the construction of major cuttings and tunnels through the chalk.

Unfortunately, Sir Edward, having arranged the alliance between the Metropolitan and the Great Central companies, had to retire through old age, and without his strong personality to unite the two Boards, the partners started to fall out. In 1898 (a year before the opening of the Great Central main line), they had indeed almost come to blows at the 'border' station at Quainton Road, when the General Manager of the Metropolitan Railway tried to stop the Great Central company from exercising its running powers into London.

Furthermore, even if relations between the main line railway and its 'Underground' partner had been easier, there would still have been a problem of congestion on the busy suburban route between Aylesbury and London once the Great Central main line was open to traffic. It was inevitable, therefore, that the Great Central should have looked towards the Great Western, which already reached out towards the new main line at Aylesbury.

The two companies had in fact already collaborated in the region to the north of Banbury, where an eight mile line had been planned to link the two systems (this line, which ran from Banbury to Culworth Junction on the GCR, was a result of the Great Western's efforts to 'buy-off' the Great Central during the London & South Wales crisis). Clearly, with these connections between the two companies, and the Great Western planning to build a line between Acton and the old Wycombe Railway, it would be possible to divert at least some Great Central traffic to London via either Banbury, Oxford and Thame, or Aylesbury and Princes Risborough. The two companies therefore decided to collaborate still further, and on 1st August, 1899, the Great Western & Great Central Railways Joint Committee was established by Act of Parliament.

The Joint Committee was empowered to take over the construction of the 1897 Wycombe and Acton line, and purchase from the Great Western the section of line between High Wycombe and Princes Risborough. North of Princes Risborough, the Joint Committee were to build an entirely new railway, running for 15 miles 25 chains via Haddenham to join the Great Central main line a few miles to the north of its 'junction' with the unco-operative Metropolitan Railway (in this way, there would be no problem of running over the short section of the Metropolitan route between Quainton Road and Aylesbury).

The whole of the capital required for the new scheme would be provided by the Great Western company, interest of four per cent per annum being paid until the line was open for traffic. When the line was open, the Great Central would repay the GWR one half of the capital expended on the undertaking, and pay interest at four per cent on the other half, as a first charge upon the GCR traffic receipts from the new line. It was also agreed that the cost of purchasing the portion of the former Wycombe Railway between High Wycombe and Princes Risborough would be £225,000, the cost of purchase being regarded as part of the final cost of the new line.

In all, the new scheme would involve the construction of $76\frac{1}{2}$ miles of track, and these $76\frac{1}{2}$ miles were to constitute the last major building operation of the Railway Age in Britain. There would, in addition to the main lines, be two connecting loops between the 'New Line' and the Paddington to Bristol route. One of these would run from Greenford to West Ealing, while the other was intended to connect Denham, Uxbridge and West Drayton. The lines to West Ealing and Uxbridge were regarded as integral parts of the planned new line, the construction of these two local routes being undertaken as an adjunct to the main civil engineering contracts.

GREAT WESTERN RAILWAY,

AUDIT OFFICE, PADDINGTON,

29th July, 1899.

GREAT WESTERN & GREAT CENTRAL JOINT LINE.

On and after the 1st August, 1899, all Passenger Traffic for HIGH WYCOMBE and WEST WYCOMBE, BY ALL ROUTES, and for PRINCES RISBORO', VIA HIGH WYCOMBE ONLY, also Traffic passing over the Line between HIGH WYCOMBE and PRINCES RISBORO', will be JOINT with the GREAT CENTRAL RAILWAY, and must be accounted for in the Railway Clearing House Classification.

GREAT CARE must be taken that all Tickets intended to be used over that Line are so routed.

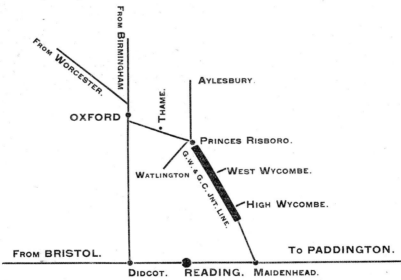

In cases where Printed Card Tickets are not in stock for that Route, R.C.H. Paper Tickets must be issued for traffic passing to and over the GREAT WESTERN and GREAT CENTRAL JOINT LINE.

Should you find that printed Tickets are necessary by that Route for any particular Station, please to forward to this office a Requisition for the Tickets which are required.

The Tickets which are in stock from Stations North of Oxford to Stations on the Line between Maidenhead and Paddington, and the Branches from that Line and *vice versa*, which do not clearly show the Route South of OXFORD must be issued only for Passengers travelling via Reading.

Please to acknowledge receipt of this Circular by an early Train.

J. FRYERS, *Audit Accountant.*

An official circular issued in connection with the transfer of the former Wycombe Railway to the Great Western & Great Central Joint Committee with effect from 1st August, 1899.

Chapter Two

Construction and Opening
(1901-1910)

The first portion of the 'New Line', as authorized by the Great Western (Additional Powers) Act 1897, was to commence by a junction with the Paddington to Bristol route at Old Oak Common West Junction, near Acton, and then run north-westwards for 6 miles 70 chains through the parishes of Twyford Abbey, Hanwell, Ealing, Harrow-on-the-Hill, Perivale and Greenford to Northolt; here, it would be joined by a Great Central line, 6 miles 30 chains in length, which would connect the Joint Line to the Great Central system at Neasden Junction.

Beyond Northolt, the Joint Line proper would begin, and it was originally intended that joint ownership would extend all the way to Grendon Underwood Junction, where the GW&GC line would rejoin the Great Central. The Great Western, however, decided to build a new line from Ashendon, a little under six miles to the south of Grendon Underwood, to Aynho near Banbury, rather than use the Princes Risborough to Oxford route for its 'Cut-Off'. Following this change of plan, joint ownership was terminated at Ashendon Junction, 34 miles from Northolt, and the Ashendon to Grendon Underwood section henceforth became the sole property of the Great Central.

Construction Begins: Work in the Park Royal Area

Construction began early in 1901, under the direction of the Great Western Railway engineering department; the Resident Engineer was Mr R.C. Sikes BA, AMICE. The authorized route would entail heavy earthworks and some major feats of civil engineering, with several river or canal crossings at the southern end of the line, and two tunnels and numerous cuttings and embankments in the Chiltern section between Gerrards Cross and Princes Risborough.

In addition, it was agreed that a major new locomotive depot would be erected near the starting point of the New Line at Old Oak Common, authorization for the 'removal of spoil from land ... on which locomotive sheds, etc., are proposed to be erected' having been given as early as July 1898. It was intended that a station would be built at Greenford, while on 4th December, 1901 the GWR Directors authorized the 'construction of goods and passenger stations at Park Royal, with accommodation necessary to serve the new permanent show yard of The Royal Agricultural Society'.

In connection with this new station, the Royal Agricultural Society agreed to contribute the sum of £1,000 towards the cost of an access road from Willesden Lane to the station and permanent show ground. The contract for construction of the southern end of the line, together with the connecting loop from Greenford to West Ealing and the stations at Greenford and Park Royal, was awarded to Messrs J.T. Firbank & Company.

The Great Western made good progress with the first section of the new route, and the first public trains were able to run on 15th June, 1903, in connection with a Royal Agricultural Show at Park Royal. Trains ran outwards via Old Oak Common and back to Paddington via Greenford and the Greenford Loop. In all, 3½ miles of

Two contemporary postcard views showing construction work in progress on the GW&GC Joint Line in the vicintiy of Haddenham; 'steam navvies' were extensively used during the construction of the route.   *Photographer unknown*

the New Line were involved. Services ceased west of Park Royal on 10th August, to allow the embankments to settle after heavy rainfall, but on 1st May, 1904, the line was able to reopen. There were halts at North Acton, Twyford Abbey and Perivale, in addition to the station and other facilities for agricultural traffic at Park Royal.

There was, at first, a certain amount of trouble with earth slips, and on 12th November 1903 the Directors agreed that 'Sir Thomas Firbank, the contractor for the line', would be paid £1,200 for 'work dealing with slips'. Interestingly, on 21st April, 1904, they authorized the payment of a gratuity of £200 'to Messrs Hadley & Sons in recognition of the efforts made by them to complete the construction of the station buildings at Park Royal in time for the opening of the Royal Agricultural Show in June last'.

The Great Central, meanwhile, was running into difficulties with the Neasden to Northolt line. Since obtaining Parliamentary sanction in 1898, the estimated cost of the line had risen from £168,200 to almost £300,000. The route involved some massive retaining walls and other works - including a 203 yds-long tunnel at South Harrow - so it is hardly surprising that this short link between the two partners was so expensive; the main contractors for this section were Messrs Thomas Oliver & Sons of Rugby, while Pattinson & Son of Westminster secured the station contracts.

Work around Denham and High Wycombe

The major contractors on the Great Western & Great Central Joint Line and associated lines were Messrs R.W. Pauling & Company of Westminster. Their contract - for the Northolt to High Wycombe section of the route - was worth £580,000. This part of the line was perhaps the most difficult of all; running in cuttings or on embankments for most of its 16½ mile length, the works included six large brick viaducts and the 343 yds-long Whitehouse Farm tunnel between Beaconsfield and High Wycombe.

In earlier days, railways had been hacked and blasted across the countryside with picks, shovels and dynamite but, by the early 1900s, the work was more mechanised, and Paulings' employed 16 steam-driven excavators together with an extensive light railway system, which included 34 locomotives and no less than 895 items of rolling stock! In November 1903, *The Locomotive Magazine* reported that, despite unfavourable weather conditions during the previous summer, 'rapid progress was being made on what was, in effect, an entire system of railways in the hitherto secluded districts of West Middlesex and Buckinghamshire'.

The report added that Messrs Pauling & Co. had set up their main centre of operations at Gerrards Cross, a 'shed for no less than 22 locomotives' having been established at this site, together with workshops, stables and other facilities. The locomotives are of particular interest to the enthusiast. Most were typical industrial saddle tanks, of simple, robust design, but there were also five ex-London, Brighton & South Coast Railway 'Terrier' 0-6-0Ts, that had been purchased from the Brighton line between May and September 1902. The engines involved in the deal were Nos. 36, *Bramley*; 39, *Denmark*; 49, *Bishopsgate*; 52 *Surrey*; and 57, *Thames*. Many of these engines were shedded in Paulings' locomotive depot at Gerrards Cross, and photographic evidence suggests that they were well looked after during their sojourn on the GW&GC line.

As former passenger engines, the five 'Terriers' were particularly suitable for use on workmen's trains, and indeed such trains were provided from an early date, one

A view of Denham station under construction, looking west towards High Wycombe, probably around 1905. Although the standard Great Western red brick station buildings appear to be more or less complete, the permanent way has not yet been installed – the roughly-laid trackwork visible here being a temporary contractor's line.   *Lens of Sutton Collection*

Construction work in progress on the site of Haddenham station, with a Hunslet 0-6-0ST visible in the foreground.   *John Alsop Collection*

Haddenham Station G. W. Ry.

of the 'regular' services being between Uxbridge (where many of Paulings' workforce lodged) and construction sites on the GW&GC main line. These trains were mentioned by *The Locomotive Magazine* in its November 1907 edition, which also included a photograph showing No. 49 *Bishopsgate* outside the temporary locomotive shed at Uxbridge, in company with one of Paulings' Manning, Wardle 0-6-0Ts. The trees visible behind the shed suggest that the photograph had probably been taken in the previous summer (i.e. 1905), and from this evidence, it seems that the short branch from Denham to Uxbridge High Street must have been substantially completed by that date.

North of High Wycombe, the up-grading of the existing line to Princes Risborough, together with 3¾ miles of new construction towards Haddenham, was undertaken by Messrs Mackay & Davies of Cardiff, while Mr L.P.Nott successfully tendered for the remaining 19½ miles to Grendon Underwood. All of the old Wycombe Railway stations were reconstructed, and High Wycombe and Princes Risborough stations were re-sited.

Between Saunderton and Princes Risborough, the Wycombe Railway's original single line had descended abruptly when leaving the scarp slope of the Chilterns. The gradient here was eased to 1 in 100 for some of the way, leaving a stretch of 1 in 87 at the lower end, but this was still considered to be too steep for southbound trains, and so the up line was deviated from the down for a distance of 2¼ miles.

Running through a deep chalk cutting and an 84 yds-long tunnel, the new up line was given a gradient of only 1 in 167. Situated in open downland, miles from roads, houses, or signs of habitation, the Saunderton gradients, burrowing in and out of the hills like a scenic railway, were one of the most interesting features of the Joint Line's construction. North of Princes Risborough, the line was carried on long embankments as far as Ashendon, where it turned due north to reach its junction with the Great Central; the River Thame was crossed by a brick viaduct with five 40 ft spans.

Some Further Details of Construction

The construction of over 70 miles of double track main line attracted considerable attention in railway and civil engineering circles, and specialist journals such as *The Engineer* and *The Railway Magazine* published several detailed progress reports. On 27th May, 1904, for example, *The Engineer* printed a comprehensive description of the new line, and some of this information is worth repeating in full. Having explained that the 'new system of railways' would carry both main line and suburban traffic, the report continued as follows:

The construction of the Acton and High Wycombe Railway is divided into two sections. The first extends from Acton to a point in the Parish of Northolt, a distance of 5 miles 11 chains, and also comprises a spur line from Greenford to West Ealing and Hanwell, 2.5 miles in length. This section belongs solely to the Great Western Railway.

The second extends from Northolt for 17 miles 65 chains, till a junction is effected with the existing Maidenhead-Wycombe line, at 32 chains east from Wycombe station, and for the major portion of the distance is the joint property of the Great Western and Great Central Railway Companies. The contractors for the first section are Messrs J.T. Firbank Ltd, and those for the second Messrs Pauling and Co. of Westminster.

The new railway branches off in a northerly direction from the Great Western main line at West London West Junction, which is 3 miles 30 chains from Paddington, and almost immediately enters a long straight cutting 2 miles in length and 38 ft deep at its deepest.

This cutting, in common with all other important cuttings, has been excavated to the width sufficient for a four-track road, whenever the increase of traffic demands two additional tracks, and with this object in view, throughout the line loftier banks have been tipped to a corresponding width, all over-bridges have been given a central arch of 51 ft span, and most of the underbridges provided with the abutments for widening.

Only one viaduct however, namely that across the River Colne, is constructed to accommodate four tracks. In this cutting is Park Royal Station - 4 miles 44 chains - whither a short line runs to a small goods station and large island platform adjoining the show ground of the Royal Agricultural Society. The Great Western Railway Company is now to construct a large electric power and light plant near Park Royal station, which will be needed for the electrical working of the suburban trains off the Metropolitan system after they leave and before they come to Bishop's Road station.

The cutting ends at Twyford Abbey Bridge, where the line curves to the west, and its course to Wycombe may be described as being due east and west. For two miles onwards the line is on an embankment, except where it is carried across the Brent Valley upon a four-arch brick viaduct, 320 ft in length, and with the rail level at an altitude of 38 ft.

The next station is Greenford - 7 miles 65 chains ... the first section is now practically finished, that portion between Acton and Greenford East Junction and the loop line having been passed for passenger traffic by the Board of Trade in June last. The main line permanent way consists of 97½ lb. steel rails, which will be used throughout. The line rises almost the whole way from Acton to Northolt, but the steepest gradient is only 1 in 225, while on the loop the steepest is 1 in 200. Except at loops and junctions there is no curve sharper than of two chains radius in the entire section.

The second section forms the most formidable undertaking, on account both of its greater length and engineering difficulties. Work on this section was begun two years ago, and as yet the track has been laid in only a few short stretches. Owing to last summer being wet, progress was much retarded, and the banks slipped in many places.

The section begins in a cutting extending for 1 mile, and at 10 miles 18 chains occurs the junction at Northolt with the new Great Central line from Neasden ... from Northolt Junction to High Wycombe the new railway is being jointly constructed by the Great Western and Great Central Companies, but under the aegis of the Great Western engineers ... the first of the joint stations is Ruislip, 12 miles 8 chains, which lies in a shallow cutting. Ruislip station is situated between the villages of Ruislip and Ikenham, being half-a-mile distant from either.

The report explained how the proposed Uxbridge branch would join the main line by means of a triangular junction, enabling the Great Western to provide 'a circular suburban service from Paddington' via Uxbridge and West Drayton; there would be a new station in Uxbridge at the bottom of the High Street, but the old GWR station at Vine Street would continue to be used by some local services. (As we shall see, the Uxbridge scheme was never completed, and the two GWR terminal stations at Uxbridge were never physically linked.)

Continuing its description of the GW&GC Joint Line, *The Engineer* stated that the route passed through Denham on a 25 ft high embankment, which was followed by shallow cuttings and a further embankment. There were four large viaducts on this section, all of them being built of brick - though the Colne viaduct at Denham had a concrete core. The Colne viaduct, an impressive structure incorporating five brick arches resting on concrete piers, was described as follows:

At 14½ miles is the important viaduct over the River Colne, which here forms the boundary between the counties of Middlesex and Bucks. The Colne viaduct - built for four tracks - consists of five arches, the largest, over the river, having a span of 80 ft, with a total length of 250 yards and a height of 36 ft. The structure has only a skin of brickwork, for the foundations, abutments and heartings of piers are of concrete.

The neighbouring Grand Union Canal viaduct, which was just 19 chains further east, was a similar structure, albeit with nine arches and a total length of 198 yards. Like the Colne viaduct, it is constructed mainly of concrete, though an outer skin of traditional brickwork masks the way in which modern materials had been used in its construction. The viaduct was described briefly in *The Great Western Railway Magazine* of August 1904:

This structure consists of nine elliptical spans, eight being of 47 ft and one, over the canal, of 60 ft. The abutments are built of concrete faced with brick. This facework was brought up in lifts of about 4 ft 6 in., the concrete hearting being put in layers of about 2 ft after allowing for the brickwork to set.

Denham station, to the west of the two viaducts, was evidently in a state of near completion by 1904, and *The Great Western Railway Magazine* was able to provide some useful details of this archetypal GW&GC Joint Line station. Two platforms were provided, each 400 ft long, while the red brick station buildings were said to be 'of the Great Western standard type' with the usual 'booking clerks and station master's offices, waiting and cloak rooms and ... offices'. The most interesting feature of the station was perhaps its high level site, and in this context *The GWR Magazine* was able to furnish some useful constructional notes:

Being on an embankment 25 ft high, the station buildings are carried on cast iron girders, supported on concrete and brick piers brought up from the original ground level. Access to the station is obtained both from the Rickmansworth road and a pathway from Denham village, the two approaches being connected by a subway, with access to the platforms by stairways.

Beyond Denham, the route entered another major cutting, and *The Engineer* added the following interesting details:

In this cutting, at 17 miles 35 chains, is Gerrards Cross station, and here is situated the contractors' head offices, workshops, store sheds, stables, and an engine-house for 22 locomotives, the whole being lit by electricity ... From the termination of the Gerrards Cross cutting to the next station at Beaconsfield, 21 miles 56 chains, the line successively runs on a bank, 60 ft high, and three-quarters of a mile long, through a cutting 50 ft deep, and half a mile long, and through Wilton Park for three-quarters of a mile, for most of which distance it is in a shallow cutting.

At 21 miles begins the second heaviest cutting on the line, one and half miles long, 48 ft deep, and representing three quarters of a million cubic yards. The steam navvies at work in this cutting have achieved what is believed to be a record rate of excavation, amounting to three wagon loads a day apiece ... Not far from the western extremity of the big cutting, the line is on the loftiest bank of any, 70 ft in height, and 16 chains long, which terminates in a short, deep cutting, leading up to a tunnel through the Chiltern Hills. White Horse [*sic*] Farm Tunnel, as it is called, is 16 chains long, chiefly through chalk and gravel, and on a curve of one mile radius. Emerging from another cutting at the western portal of the tunnel the Maidenhead to High Wycombe line is seen on the left, half a mile away, and at the foot of the valley.

It was originally intended to construct a loop from about this point to Loudwater station, on a low-level line, but the project has been abandoned. On the remaining 3 miles to Wycombe there are three cuttings, three banks, and an ornamental red and blue brick viaduct of three 62 ft spans over Sir Philip Roses's carriage drive. The new railway ends in a junction with the existing Maidenhead to High Wycombe line at 26 miles 26 chains from Paddington, thence into Wycombe station the distance is 32 chains.

From Northolt Junction to Denham the line runs practically level, from Denham to Beaconsfield it rises at 1 in 175, and from Beaconsfield to the western end of the tunnel falls at 1 in 225, whence it is level to Wycombe. Throughout this section, the sharpest curve, except at junctions, is one mile radius.

The station at High Wycombe is being entirely rebuilt upon the four-track principle, and the line between Wycombe and Princes Risborough, a distance of 8 miles 16 chains, doubled, and the gradients and curves remodelled … The new Great Western & Great Central Joint Railway from Princes Risborough to a place called Grendon Underwood, on the Great Central extension to London, was commenced later than the other sections.

The line is 15 miles 25 chains long, and with the exception of a three-arch brick viaduct across the River Thame possesses no engineering features worthy of noting. There will be three intermediate stations, namely, Haddenham, 9 miles from Princes Risborough; Wotton Park, and Akeman Street station.

At Wotton Park the line crosses over, and will give an interchange of traffic with the steam tramway from Quainton Road to Brill. There may also be a station at Grendon Underwood Junction, which lies 2 miles 4 chains north from Quainton Road.

When the Great Central Company's new route is completed, and it ought to be open for traffic in the Autumn of 1905, the distance from Marylebone to Grendon Underwood will be 51 miles 54 chains, instead of 46½ miles via Aylesbury. Consequently, the length of the Great Central journey will be increased by five miles, but the new route, though longer than the present one, will enable the trains be accelerated. As things are now, a great deal of time is wasted in toiling up the severe banks, and in slowing down for the awkward curves of the Metropolitan Line.

There will be no obstacles of this nature on the new route, which also will leave the company free to develop that which it cannot own in present circumstances, viz., a suburban and outer-suburban traffic.

Accidents during Construction

Generally speaking, the works proceeded without incident in the Uxbridge and Denham areas, although there were one or two accidents of varying severity. In January 1903, for example, the Manning, Wardle 0-6-0ST *Dunraget* was involved in a shunting incident near Denham in which an unfortunate navvy had his hand crushed. A few months earlier, another of Paulings' locomotives was derailed at Denham, and its driver was killed; the dead man - Richard Pilkington - was interred in Hillingdon cemetery.

A far worse accident took place in the unfinished Whitehouse Farm tunnel on 6th September, 1902, when a roof fall killed six men. Preliminary work on this 343 yds-long bore had commenced at the very end of 1901, and the 'bottom heading' was completed in May 1902. The work of lining the tunnel with brickwork commenced on 5th June, 1902, but it was unfinished at the time of the accident. Charles Morgan, the London, Brighton & South Coast Railway Engineer, was asked to investigate the accident on behalf of the Board of Trade, and after careful consideration of the evidence, he reported as follows:

The lining to the tunnel is of brick, faced with Staffordshire brindles, the arch being 18 inch, 20½ inch and 27 inch thick according to the nature of the material passed through, which is principally chalk, but by reason of the presence of 'pot holes' of gravel and clay, is of a somewhat treacherous nature. The tunnel is not at a great depth from the surface, only averaging about 69 ft to formation level, or 47 ft cover over the extrados of the arch.

The 'pot holes', or faults, are rather freely distributed throughout the length of the tunnel, some appearing as low down as the bottom heading, and others only being disclosed when excavating for the top heading. In all cases where pot holes were visible, it is stated additional timbering was used. By the accident, six men were killed and two rather seriously injured.

In the length where the accident happened, the evidence is very distinct that the material was sound and good chalk throughout, and no sign of any fault whatever was disclosed in the course of the excavation. Under these circumstances, the work was proceeding in the usual manner, and without any extra precautions.

At the time of the accident the 'nipper cill' and the 6 draw-bars, each of which, it is stated, were supported on the 'nipper cill' by the nipper props, and also by the back props, and in addition the eighth bars were in position, but the evidence is not definite whether these were propped on the 'nipper cill'. The excavation had proceeded to a depth of about 2 ft below the 'nipper cill', that is, to the top of the head-trees of the lower heading, and the tenth bars were in process of being fixed at the time of the collapse. Very fortunately, the ends of the bars resting on the last completed length of tunnel did not become displaced when the leading ends fell, thus forming a protection to some of the men. The 'nipper cill' upon which all the bars were propped, was a very vital part of the timbering. Each end had a bearing on the solid chalk, clear of the sides of the bottom heading of 18 inches, and between rested on a layer of about 2 ft thick of chalk throughout its length over the bottom heading.

The layer of chalk was in turn supported by the poling boards over the head-trees of the bottom heading, and further by additional liners fixed between the head-trees. It is highly probable, that in fixing the head-trees referred to, the chalk immediately above them would be disturbed.

Further, with the material excavated from the front of and below the level of the 'nipper cill', any excessive pressure brought on to the thin layer of chalk (about 2 ft thick) lying under and between the 'nipper cill' and the head-trees of the bottom heading would be liable to become displaced, and leave the 'nipper cill' imperfectly supported, and bring about the failure of the same, followed by the collapse of the other timbering carried by it.

The layer of chalk upon which the 'nipper cill' is generally bedded has in practice proved unreliable for the purpose of transmitting the pressure from the 'nipper cill' to the head-trees below, and has actually worked out as stated by Arnold in his evidence; but in these cases it was observed, and the 'nipper cill' packed with timber on to the head-trees below. The timbering ordinarily in use is not of sufficient strength for dealing with any additional pressure arising from undisclosed 'pot holes', or other like causes, but it appears to be sufficient under normal conditions where the work passes through sound chalk.

He concluded that the collapse had been caused by the breaking of the 'nipper cill' beneath the weight of a hitherto undiscovered 'pot hole' immediately above it. He recommended that 'having regard to the undoubtedly treacherous and uncertain nature of the ground', each length should be treated as if faults existed, the head-trees and other timber supports used during construction being strengthened accordingly so that 'the weight would be properly transmitted from the "nipper cill" to the supports below it'.

The Wycombe Railway station at West Wycombe, photographed during the construction of the GW&GC Line. The new platforms and footbridge have been installed, but the original Brunelian station building is still *in situ*.   *John Alsop Collection*

Opening of the GW&GC Joint Line

On Saturday 1st October, 1904, a further 53 chains of the Great Western & Great Central main line was brought into use, when trains began running between Greenford East Junction and Greenford station, and on 20th November, 1905 the entire main line was opened for freight traffic between Greenford and Grendon Underwood. At the same time, the Great Central Railway commenced running goods trains between Neasden Junction and Northolt.

Three months later, on 1st March, 1906, the Great Central opened the Neasden to Northolt line to passenger traffic, using a steam railmotor car for the new service. Stations were provided at Wembley Hill, Sudbury & Harrow Road, and South Harrow, and the line was quadruple for the first 1¾ miles from Neasden and double thereafter. Sudbury & Harrow Road and South Harrow were provided with 4-road stations, with the platforms on the outer loops and the fast lines in the middle, while Wembley Hill, being on the quadruple track section, had a similar quadruple-track layout.

A description of the bridges and other major civil engineering features on the new section of Great Central line appeared in the March 1906 edition of *The Railway Engineer* while, in the following July, the same magazine described the stations in considerable detail. As all three stations were built to the same basic plan, the article confined itself to a detailed examination of Sudbury & Harrow Road. The article makes it clear that the Great Central Railway had purposely designed a show-piece that would stand comparison with the Great Western-style stations found on the Northolt Junction to High Wycombe line.

Opening Northolt Junction to Grendon Underwood Junction to passengers

The main sections of the GW&GC route were, by this time, well advanced, and the entire line was opened for passenger traffic on 2nd April, 1906. To celebrate the occasion, railway officials from both companies attended a public luncheon given by the High Wycombe & District Chamber of Commerce, and held in High Wycombe Town Hall. Stations opened or re-opened on 2nd April included Ruislip & Ickenham, Denham, Gerrards Cross, Beaconsfield, High Wycombe, Saunderton, Princes Risborough and Haddenham. All were built on a lavish scale, and the final cost of the completed line worked out at an average of £40,000 per mile.

The new stations tended to follow the same plan, both in layout and architecture. The more important places *en route* - such as Greenford, Denham, Gerrards Cross and Beaconsfield - were provided with quadruple-tracked stations in which the platforms were situated on loops laid parallel to the main up and down running lines. This arrangement enabled expresses to run through non-stop and at high speed.

On the other hand, although local stopping trains could stand safely in the platform roads while they were overtaken by faster services, there was a problem of speed restrictions when entering and leaving the loops, and for this reason, local trains on the Joint Line were destined to be rather slower than those on the neighbouring Metropolitan route.

The quadruple track station layouts provided on the Great Western & Great Central Joint Line and on the Northolt to Neasden line were designed to accommodate through freight traffic an well as suburban passenger trains, and for this reason the up and down loops were equipped with dead-end spurs at each end so that 80 wagon freight trains could be held clear of the main running lines. In July 1906, *The Railway Engineer* outlined the operational theory behind these 4-track stations:

> The platform lines are extended at both the facing and the trailing ends - this is quite a novel feature, and, is and economical method of providing for long trains, such as are now run on English railways. A train of 80 wagons requires a length of loop with the facing and trailing connections with the fast lines so far apart as to be beyond the distance allowed by the Board of Trade to be worked from one signal box, thus two boxes are required.
>
> But by the arrangement provided ... a long train runs into the loop and up the extension at the facing end - thus clearing the trailing points - these are then pulled over, and the train sets back along the extension at the other end until clear of the outlet points, which operation is done during the time the main through line is being occupied by an express train; as soon as this has cleared the section the facing points in the loop are put over, and the long goods train can proceed on its journey, the points being kept within Board of Trade limits for working from one signal box.

In practice, the Great Western employed two signal boxes at most of the stations between Northolt and High Wycombe, whereas the purely Great Central stations such as Sudbury & Harrow Road had just one cabin. On the other hand, the dead-end extensions provided at each of the loops added an additional element of safety in that unfitted goods trains could be completely isolated from the running lines - thereby obviating the danger of breakaways.

Architecturally, the stations on the Great Western & Great Central Joint Line were of Great Western design, and followed that company's established house-style; built of

Two views of Haddenham station on opening day, 2nd April, 1906; the ladder that can be seen leaning against the footbridge suggests that painting and decorating work is still in progress!

(Both) John Alsop Collection

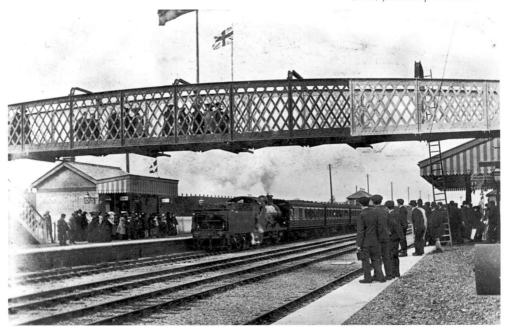

red brick, with trimmings executed in purple-black engineer's brick, the station buildings were long, low, single-storey structures. Stations nearer London, such as Denham and Greenford, had hipped roofs, tall chimneys, and projecting platform canopies, but away from London the style changed, and a simplified building, in which the roof was cantilevered out over the platforms was provided. Stations with the 'simplified' design included High Wycombe, Princes Risborough, and Haddenham.

Signals and signal boxes were again of standard Great Western design. The latter were large, hip-roofed structures of brick or wooden construction; most of the intermediate stations had two such boxes, but some locations were equipped with three or more cabins. High Wycombe, for example, had three signal boxes, while Greenford had four (including Greenford South Junction signal box on the connecting line to West Ealing).

Additionally, some of the longer block sections were provided with intermediate boxes as a means of increasing line capacity - examples being the isolated cabins at Tylers Green, between Beaconsfield and High Wycombe, and Wilton Park, between Gerrards Cross and Beaconsfield. (Both of these boxes were later replaced by intermediate block signals - a refinement made possible by the introduction of track-circuiting.)

A peculiarity of the line was its relatively sparse local goods facilities, and in this context it is worth noting that the familiar large goods sheds were rare on the GW&GC Joint Line. Instead, most of the Joint Line stations had rather smaller brick-built lock-ups; High Wycombe was the only station with a large goods yard. This suggests that the Joint Committee realised that the New Line would be primarily a passenger route, and held out little hope of establishing a busy freight business.

North of Ashendon Junction, the Great Central constructed two further stations at Wotton and Akeman Street. These were opened at the same time as the stations on the GW&GC proper, and again were built on a grand scale in anticipation of a busy passenger business (which in the event never materialised). Signalling on this section followed the Great Central pattern and the signal box at Ashendon Junction was of Great Central design.

Engineering works on the Great Central line between Ashendon Junction and Grendon Underwood included two steel girder bridges under the line near Wotton. One of these carried the railway over a public road, while the other spanned the Brill steam tramway. The road bridge had a single span of 25 ft and measured 56 ft 6 in. between its parapets, while the tramway bridge had a span of 58 ft. A cutting near Akeman Street station extended for 76 chains, and its excavation had entailed the removal of 137,258 cubic yards of spoil.

Trackwork on the Ashendon Junction to Grendon Underwood section was formed of standard Great Central bull-headed rail weighing 98 lb. per linear yard, and laid in 30 ft sections (as opposed to the 44 ft 6 in. rail lengths favoured by the GWR).

In spite of the earlier speculation vis-à-vis a proposed junction station at Grendon Underwood, the Great Central decided that a station would have been superfluous in such a remote location, and on 14th July, 1905 *The Engineer* reported that it was 'unlikely' that there would be a station there, because Grendon Underwood village was three miles from the railway.

The initial service of Great Western trains provided workings from Paddington to either Aylesbury or Oxford, together with a few trains from Oxford to London and back via Princes Risborough, High Wycombe and the line to Maidenhead. In general, however, the Princes Risborough to Oxford and High Wycombe to Maidenhead sections were henceforth worked as separate branches, although

Gerrards Cross, the 'Junction' for Uxbridge services from 1909, showing a GCR local train in the down loop. Note the 'split level' station buildings.   *J.M. Strange*

A postcard view of Gerrards Cross station, looking towards Princes Risborough, *circa* 1912.
                                                                                        John Alsop Collection

through trains to or from London formed about half of the services between Princes Risborough and Oxford during the GWR's ownership.

The Great Central, meanwhile, provided main line as well as local services on the 'New Line' - particularly at peak periods, when the Metropolitan route was congested with suburban traffic. The quarrel with the latter company had for all intents and purposes been patched-up, and in 1906, the matter of running powers was finally settled by the creation of a second joint concern (the Metropolitan & Great Central Committee) to take over and administer the Metropolitan line between Harrow and Verney Junction.

Thus, the Great Central's need of the GW&GC Joint route was not as pressing as it had been back in 1899, and the High Wycombe route became something of a 'second string' line as far as the GCR was concerned. Nevertheless, as pointed out above, the Wycombe line was useful during the morning and evening rush hours, and some trains - such as the popular 6.20 pm express from Marylebone to Bradford - regularly worked over the Great Western route, in spite of the additional 4½ miles added to the journey.

The Bicester Cut-Off

The final section of the 'New Line' - the 'Bicester Cut-Off' was, as yet, unfinished. Powers to build this 18¼ mile link between Ashendon and Aynho were obtained in 1905, and the resulting Act enabled the Great Western to build a railway 18 miles 24 chains in length commencing:

> In the parish of Aynho, in the County of Northampton, by a junction with the Oxford and Birmingham Railway of the Company at a point thirty chains or thereabouts south of the bridge carrying the road leading from Banbury to Buckingham over that railway, and terminating in the parish of Ashendon .... in the rural district of Aylesbury, in the County of Buckingham, by a junction with the railway (now in course of construction) authorised by the Great Western and Great Central Companies Act of 1899.

The route was surveyed by W.W. Grierson, the Great Western's Chief Engineer, and Edward Perry, with J.C. Inglis (Grierson's predecessor) as consultant. Running north-west from Ashendon in an almost dead straight line across the Vale of Aylesbury and the flat, fox-hunting country of East Oxfordshire, the new railway entered a branch of the Cotswold Hills near Ardley, and approached its junction with the Oxford & Rugby line through rock cuttings and the 1,150 yds-long Ardley tunnel.

Other notable engineering works that would be required included two large brick viaducts between Ardley and Aynho, numerous long embankments, and flying junctions at both the Ashendon and Aynho ends of the line. The contractors on this final section of the 'New Line' were Messrs Scott & Middleton and, as before, the Resident Engineer was Mr R.C. Sikes. The gradients of the Bicester Cut-Off would be relatively easy, the steepest sections being no more than 1 in 200. The line would, moreover, be virtually dead-straight, the sharpest curves being of 40 chains radius at Ashendon Junction and 37½ chains radius at Aynho Junction.

Having obtained Parliamentary consent for the Bicester Cut-Off line, the Great Western Directors were eager to bring the line into existence without further delay. The route was soon staked-out and fenced throughout its length, and on 11th October, 1906 the construction of the 'Ashendon & Aynho Railway' was authorized

The site of Ardley station, around 1908, during the construction of the Bicester Cut-Off.
J.M. Strange

by the GWR Board. It was agreed, from the very inception, that stations would be built at Brill & Ludgershall, Blackthorn, Bicester, Ardley and Aynho Park, the facilities at each location being specified as follows:

Brill & Ludgershall Station (3¼ miles from Ashendon Junction) Up and Down platforms each 500 ft long. Station building, footbridge and accommodation for goods and cattle traffic. Station master's house and 4 cottages for traffic and engineering staffs.

Blackthorn Station (6¼ miles from Ashendon Junction) Up and Down platforms each 500 ft long. Station buildings, footbridge and provision for goods and cattle traffic. Provision of station master's house and 3 cottages for staff.

Bicester Station (9¼ miles from Ashendon Junction) Up and Down platforms each 600 ft long. Station buildings, footbridge and provision for goods and cattle traffic.

Ardley Station (13 miles from Ashendon Junction) Up and Down platforms each 500 ft long. Station buildings, footbridge and provision for goods and cattle traffic. Provision of station master's house and 4 cottages for staff.

Aynho Park New Station (17½ miles from Ashendon Junction) Up and Down platforms each 400 ft long with waiting rooms, and booking office on Up side adjoining public road. Provision of 5 cottages for the staff.

The estimated cost of the land, civil engineering and stations was £603,150, but as the work progressed, the Great Western Directors authorized various additional items of expenditure, including £6,600 for 'long loops at Bicester and at Brill & Ludgershall', £315 for a footbridge near Brill, and £470 for the 'provision of crossing places to enable the Bicester Hunt to use the Railway in connection with their hunting'. Other payments were agreed for signals & telegraph, a new 43-lever signal box at Aynho Junction and repairing earth slips, and by October 1909 the total cost of the Cut-Off had reached £642,725.

The construction of the line was rapid and straightforward - Ardley tunnel, for example, was completed and lined with brickwork in the short period of a year and a half! As on the Joint Line proper, steam navvies and other mechanical aids were widely used, and what would, in earlier days, have been a major railway building project was completed in around four years.

The completion of the Cut-Off was reported in a short article by F.C.Warren, which appeared in *The Great Western Railway Magazine* in April 1910. The article pointed out that:

> The effect of bringing into use the new route, taking it as a whole, will be to lessen the distance between London and places north of Aynho, including the important centres of Birmingham, Wolverhampton, Wellington, Shrewsbury, and Liverpool by eighteen and three quarter miles, in comparison with the route via Didcot ... The stations are of the usual Great Western patterns adopted in recent years, Bicester being, of course, the largest and most important.
>
> Nearly 3,000,000 cubic yards of clay and rock had to be excavated in the cuttings, practically all of which had been deposited in the embankment of the line. Twelve over-bridges and seven under-bridges, of which eleven are of girder work, seven brick arches and one with an arch and girderwork span also, are provided to accommodate public roads crossed by the railway. Twenty-two occupation bridges and one river bridge have also been built. The drainage of the district required to be accommodated by a number of culverts, large pipes, etc.
>
> The permanent way, which, including loops, has a total single track mileage of 42 miles of plain road, 108 switches and 128 crossings, is of the Company's heavy standard type for express routes, there being in addition over two miles of sidings. As the line is laid out in line and level for fast running, with the Company's highest standard type of permanent way, and with a ruling gradient of about 1 in 193 and wide curves, the enterprise of the Company should, on all reasonable anticipations, reap a full reward commensurate with its bid for enhanced favour from the travelling public in shortening the time occupied in transit.

The Bicester Cut-Off was opened for goods traffic on Monday 4th April, 1910, and for passengers on Friday 1st July. The majority of Great Western main line trains to the Midlands and North were immediately transferred to the new route, resulting in some spectacular speed-ups. Whereas the fastest London to Birmingham timing via Oxford and the Old Line had been 2 hours 20 minutes, the best trains on the 'New Line' reached their destination in two hours flat. Now, for the first time in many years, the Great Western was able to challenge its old rival the LNWR for the lucrative London to Birmingham traffic.

The opening of the cut-off was a relatively subdued affair, although the Great Western ran a special train from Birmingham to London. Opening Day was reported in the local press, and by *The Engineer*, which described the day's events as follows:

> In the future doubtless some historical interest will attach to the journey of the first passenger train from London to Birmingham by the Great Western Company's shortened route. But the trip itself was uneventful. The train was 1 minute behind time at High Wycombe, and 2 minutes late at Birmingham. The coach load at starting was 317 tons, subsequently reduced to 292 tons by the Princes Risborough slip, and further to 267 tons by the Leamington slip. The locomotive was No. 2916 *St Benedict*, of the 4-6-0 two-cylinder class.
>
> On the same day a special conveying officials and guests of the company was timed to start from Birmingham at 12.45 pm, and run to London without a stop in two hours. This train was much lighter than the down train, consisting of six coaches (three of them restaurant cars), which yielded a total weight behind tender of 160 tons.
>
> The locomotive was No. 2910 *Lady of Shalott*, also of the 4-6-0 two-cylinder type. However, the late arrival of the first through Manchester-Bournemouth express, which is due out of Snow Hill at 12.39 pm, not only delayed the start till 12.54 pm but was the cause of several slowings for signals as far as Leamington, which checks culminated in a dead stop at what would be the eighty-sixth mile post from London via Bicester.
>
> This spot, unfortunately situated at the foot of a six-mile long bank at 1 in 187 to Southam Road, was left at 1.28 pm, and there were no more extraordinary interruptions.

Aynho North Junction, through which the speed of 'up' trains should not exceed 50 miles per hour, was passed at 1.54 - 23½ miles in 26 minutes; speed 54 miles per hour. Notwithstanding the temporary speed restriction occasioned by the slip between Aynho Park station and Fritwell tunnel, Ashendon Junction was passed at 2.12 pm; hence the speed over the new line, 18.25 miles in length, averaged 68.4 miles per hour.

The forty-one miles from Ashendon to Old Oak Common were covered in 38 minutes, the rate of travelling being: 64 miles per hour, although the normal speed limit of 40 miles per hour round the reverse curve north of High Wycombe was scrupulously observed.

Paddington platform stop was made at 2.54 pm, so that in spite of the delays beyond Leamington, the two-hour schedule for the whole journey was fulfilled, while the intermediate distance of 86 miles reckoned from the halt for signals south of Leamington was accomplished in 86.5 minutes. From end to end of the new route proper, i.e. between Old Oak Common and Aynho North Junctions, the permanent way gave ideally smooth running.

The newly-opened Bicester Cut-Off had intermediate stations at Brill & Ludgershall, Blackthorn, Bicester and Ardley, together with a halt at Aynho Park. Strictly speaking, this last stopping place was a 'platform', and not a halt ('platforms' often had one or two staff, unlike halts, which were unstaffed). At Aynho Park, a red brick office was provided at ground level, although the up and down platforms, which were situated on an embankment, had small wooden waiting rooms. Blackthorn was a simple two-platform station, but Brill, Bicester and Ardley had quadruple-track layouts, identical to those on the Joint Line, with long platforms and standard Great Western red brick station buildings.

Bicester had a large, covered goods warehouse, but the other stations had only small brick-built lock-ups. Bicester, in fact, was the only place *en route* which offered any substantial traffic - passenger or freight. Unfortunately this small market town already had a railway station (on the LNWR Buckinghamshire branch) so there seemed little chance of winning any major traffic, even from there.

The other stations served mere villages; possibly the Great Western directorate hoped that the coming of the railway would encourage well-off business travellers to move out to villages such as Ardley and Blackthorn, but in the event, this part of Oxfordshire never became fashionable in the way that, for example, the Cotswolds or Thames Valley did, and the large stations provided handled only local traffic.

Thus, in the Summer of 1910 - nine years after the first construction work had commenced - the 'New Line' was completed throughout. Seventy-six and a half miles had been added to the railway system of Great Britain, of which, 34 miles were the property of the Great Western & Great Central Railways Joint Committee. The table given below will clarify matters concerning the full extent of joint ownership:

Ownership of the Line

Section of Line	Length	Ownership
Old Oak Common West Junction to Northolt Junction	7 miles	GWR
Greenford to West Ealing	2 ½ miles	GWR
Neasden Junction to Northolt Junction	6 ¼ miles	GCR
Northolt Junction to Ashendon Junction	34 miles	GW&GC Jt
Ashendon Junction to Grendon Underwood Junction	5 ¾ miles	GCR
Ashendon Junction to Aynho Junction	18 ¼ miles	GWR
Denham West Junction to Uxbridge High Street	2 ¾ miles	GWR
Grand total	76 ½ miles	

There were, in addition, the truncated remains of the Wycombe Railway, which now formed three separate branches to Oxford, Aylesbury, and Maidenhead, and a branch line from Princes Risborough to Watlington (opened in 1872). Of these, only the 7 mile 8 chain Aylesbury branch was subject to joint control - the rest were Great Western property. The total extent of the Great Western & Great Central Railways Joint Committee was therefore 41 miles including the Aylesbury line. (Further details of the New Line branches will be found in Chapter Eight.)

The Great Western & Great Central Joint Line was never a 'Joint Railway' in the sense that the Midland & Great Northern or Somerset & Dorset lines were jointly owned routes; it owned no locomotives or rolling stock of its own, and was not a system in its own right (a railway from Northolt to Ashendon would be completely useless without its vital links to the parent companies!).

Nevertheless, it is worth mentioning, before moving on to the subsequent history of the Great Western & Great Central Joint Line, that it did have some of the trappings of an independent concern. It had its own seal, for example, and the staff on the Joint section of the route sported the initials 'GW&GCJC' on their uniforms. Moreover (and perhaps of greatest interest to the enthusiast and collector) the Joint Line issued its own tickets, scrupulously lettered with the initials of the Joint Committee.

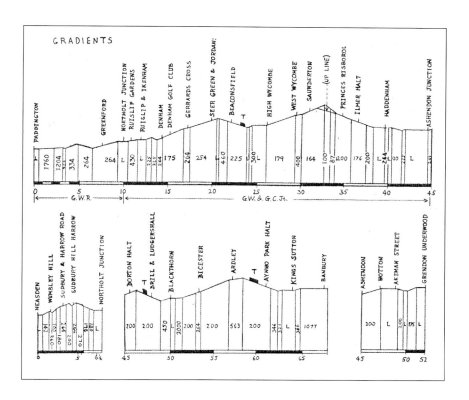

LIST OF SIGNAL BOXES.

Distance Box to Box M.C.	Name of Box	Week Days (Saturday nights excepted) From	To	Saturday Nights From	Sundays From	To	Monday Mornings Opened at	Whether provided with S'rich
—	Paddington Arrival	..	..	—	..	..	..	No
—	„ Departure	—	..	..	2.0 a.m.	6.0 a.m.	..	No
—	Royal Oak,	—	..	..			..	No
20	Westbourne Bridge				..	..		Yes
37	Subway Junction	10.0 p.m.	6.0 a.m.	10.0 p.m.	..		6.0 a.m.	Yes
17	Green Lane				10.0 p.m.		6.0 a.m.	Yes
18	Portobello	..	..	..			—	Yes
38	Ladbroke Bridge	..	..	—	6.0 a.m.		6.0 a.m.	No
—	West London	..	..	—	..		—	Yes
34	Kensal Green	..	..	..	..		..	No
43	Old Oak Common East Box	..	..	—				No
38	Old Oak Common West Box	..	..	—	{ 1.15 a.m. 12.15 ngt.	7.30 a.m.	} 5.30 a.m.	Yes
70	North Acton Junction	1.15 a.m.	5.30 a.m.	Opened as required.		—		Yes
14	Park Royal East	..			6.0 a.m.	—	6.0 a.m.	Yes
27	Park Royal West				..	—	—	Yes
1 87	Perivale	Closed until further notice.			6.0 a.m.	—	6.0 a.m.	Yes
74	Greenford, East Loop				{ 6.0 a.m. 10.45 p.m.	2.45 p.m. —	.. 6.0 a.m.	} Yes
24	Drayton Green	..	..	..	6.0 a.m.	—	6.0 a.m.	Yes
1 40	Greenford South Loop	..	..	..	{ 6.0 a.m. 10.50 a.m.	9.10 a.m. ..	6.0 a.m.	} Yes
29	Greenford East Station	..	..	..		11.0 a.m. —	6.0 a.m.	} Yes
30	Greenford West	10.0 p.m.	6.0 a.m.	10.0 p.m.	{ 10.45 p.m.		6.0 a.m.	} Yes
2 11	Northolt Junction East			Open when required.			..	No
1 83	Northolt Junction West	..			11.0 p.m.		4.0 a.m.	Yes
1 45	Ruislip and Ickenham	..	..	..		11. 0 a.m. 4. 45 p.m.		} Yes
48	Denham (East)	11.5 p.m.	6.40 a.m.	11.5 p.m.	{ 1.30 p.m. 9. 0 p.m.		6.40 a.m.	} Yes
42	„ Station	..	..	..	11.0 p.m.	11.0 a.m. —	4.15 a.m.	Yes
2 40	Gerrard's Cross (East)	11.0 p.m.	7.0 a.m.	11.0 p.m.	{ 1.30 p.m. 9. 0 p.m.	4.45 p.m.	7.0 a.m.	} Yes
26	„ (West)	6.0 p.m.	10.0 a.m.	6.0 p.m.	—	—	10.0 a.m.	Yes
2 80	Wilton Park				11.0 p.m.		5.15 a.m.	Yes
1 46	Beaconsfield (East)	..	..	..	—	11.0 a.m. —	..	Yes
24	„ (West)	10.0 p.m.	6.0 a.m.	10.0 p.m.	{ 1.30 p.m. 9. 0 p.m.	4.45 p.m.	6.0 a.m.	} Yes
2 25	Tyler's Green	6.35 p.m.	10.35 a.m.	6.35 p.m.	—	—	10.35 a.m.	Yes
2 14	High Wycombe (South)	..	..	..	{ 6. 0 a.m. 1.30 p.m. 11.15 p.m.	10.30 a.m. 3.15 p.m.	.. .. 6.0 a.m.	No
36	„ „ (Middle)	..	—	..			6.0 a.m.	Yes
24	„ „ (North)	10.0 p.m.	6.0 a.m.	10.0 p.m.	{ 6. 0 a.m. 12.45 p.m.	10.15 a.m. 6.15 p.m.	6.0 a.m.	} Yes
1 47	West Wycombe	..	..	..	{ 5. 0 a.m. 9. 0 p.m.	—	6.0 a.m.	} Yes
2 76	Saunderton	..	..	—	{ 1.15 p.m. 9. 0 p.m.	4.30 p.m.	5.30 a.m.	} Yes
2 72	Princes Risboro' (South)	—	—	—	—	—	—	No
81	„ „ (North)	..	..	..	{ 1. 0 p.m. 8.30 p.m.	4 15 p.m. 12.0 night	..	} Yes
5 32	Haddenham	..	..	..	8.30 p.m.	—	5.15 a.m.	Yes
77	Ashendon Junction				8.30 p.m.	—	5.15 a.m.	Yes
—	Ashendon North	Closed until further notice.			..	..	6.0 a.m.	Yes
2 86	Brill and Ludgershall	10.0 p.m.	6.0 a.m.	10.0 p.m.	..	..	pick up or	Yes
3 2	Blackthorn	Will only open when trains calling there have traffic to put off.			{ 6. 0 a.m. Z 1. 0 p.m. 8.30 p.m.	11.30 a.m. 6.30 p.m.	}	Yes
2 68	Bicester	..	..	..			5.0 a.m.	Yes
3 71	Ardley	10.0 p.m.	6.0 a.m.	10.0 p.m.			6.0 a.m.	Yes
2 3	Uxbridge (High Street) §	After day's service is completed.						Yes
31	Friars Junction	..	—	..	..	..		No
39	Acton, East	..	—	..	10.0 p.m.	..	6.0 a.m.	Yes
18	Acton Middle Box	..	—	..	2.0 p.m.	—	6.0 a.m.	Yes
36	Acton, West Box	..	—	..	..	..	..	Yes
66	Ealing	..	—	..	..	..		No
1 9	West Ealing	..	—	—				No
48	Hanwell East Box	..	—	..	12.0 night	—	5.0 a.m.	Yes
59	Hanwell West Box	..	—	..	2.0 p.m.	—	6.0 a.m.	Yes

§ No Block telegraph.   Z To close after day's service is completed and last down train has cleared Aynho Junction.

Complete list of New Line signal boxes, 1922.

Chapter Three

The First Forty Years
(1906-1947)

The newly-completed Great Western & Great Central Joint Railway (and its connecting branches) traversed a vast tract of open countryside, the county of Middlesex, at the southern end of the route, being as rural as neighbouring Buckinghamshire. The 1906 *Little Guide to Middlesex* reveals that Greenford was then a 'pleasant village between Southall and Harrow' that straggled, 'with intervals of fields, down the hill for a quarter of a mile from the picturesque cross-roads to the church', while Perivale was little more than 'a hamlet on the River Brent', with 'only seven houses and a population of about thirty souls'. Ruislip, a few miles further west, was similarly described as:

A pretty village, lying secluded in the level plain between Harrow and Uxbridge, with fine woods to the north between it and Northwood. It is an ancient place, once of some importance, for the parish was the second largest in Middlesex. The village now consists of a cluster of picturesque houses and inns at the cross roads, with the tower of the church showing above the roofs, and the big outbuildings of a large farm on the other side of the road.

These attractive country villages soon became popular among Londoners who travelled out on the new railway as day trippers, and older people still recall idyllic childhood picnics in deepest Middlesex. Mr W.K. MacKenzie remembered that:

Right up to 1914, the open country around Northolt and especially Ruislip was a great area for the Sunday School annual outings, which were a feature of Victorian and Edwardian life. Almost every church on the line to Baker Street had an annual 'treat' in the area. On arrival at Ruislip & Ickenham station (there was such an argument whether it should be pronounced 'Rew-slip' or 'Rice-slip') we felt that we were right out in the country - as indeed we were.

Cottagers sold great bunches of wild flowers (dog roses were the favourites) which seldom survived the journey home! Several farmers in the area around the small village of Ruislip apparently found it more profitable to let out their fields and provide teas for the hundreds of children who, for several weeks in the summer, took part in these church outings.

Unfortunately, the advent of cheap and efficient rail transport facilities encouraged speculative building in desirable villages such as Ruislip, Ickenham and Northolt, and this development ultimately destroyed the rural tranquillity that had lingered for so long in these hitherto remote places.

New Stations and Halts

It is difficult to appreciate that the area around Northolt and Ruislip was open country until the building of the GW&GC line and its connections opened up the region to settlers. Put in such crude terms, the idea sounds ludicrous, yet this is indeed what happened. Once the new railway was open, speculative builders moved in to exploit the Englishman's desire to live 'in the country', but at the same time be able to commute to and from his work in the City. Hence prosperous middle class suburbs grew up near the stations, and in time the whole area became one continuous built-up conurbation, stretching out towards Buckinghamshire.

'County' class 4-4-0 No. 3814 *County of Chester* heads an up express along the GW&GC main line near Gerrards Cross.   *John Alsop Collection*

Churchward '43XX' class 2-6-0 No. 6328 passes Ruislip & Ickenham with a lengthy freight working, probably around 1930.   *John Alsop Collection*

The Great Western and Great Central companies were of course only too glad to see rural Middlesex transformed into a sprawling suburb and, in the early years, several new stations and halts were opened to act as 'carrots' for potential developers. Northolt Junction for example - a full fledged station complete with full passenger facilities - was opened to the public on 1st July, 1908. Situated at the convergence of the Great Western and Great Central lines at Northolt, the new station was lost in acres of open farmland, and in the event it would be several years before the hoped-for suburban development actually appeared.

Nevertheless, the Joint Committee continued to open new stopping places, and Denham Golf Club Platform was brought into use on 7th August, 1912, followed by Beaconsfield Golf Links on 1st January, 1915; this last-named 'Platform' became Seer Green (For Beaconsfield Golf Links) in 1919, and is now Seer Green & Jordans. On the connecting line to Paddington, Old Oak Lane Halt appeared on 1st October, 1906, followed by Northolt Halt on 1st May, 1907, and Brentham on 1st May, 1911.

Pre-Grouping Motive Power

The new railway saw a great variety of motive power. In pre-Grouping days, the main Great Western expresses to Birmingham Snow Hill, Wolverhampton Low Level and Birkenhead were handled by Churchward's 'Saint' and 'Star' class 4-6-0s. Introduced in 1902 and 1906 respectively, the 'Saints' had two 18½-inch by 30-inch cylinders, whereas the 'Stars' were a four-cylinder design. In theory, the 115-ton 'Stars' were more powerful than the 112-ton 'Saints', but in practice the light loads of the early years were well within the capabilities of both classes.

After the Great War, when trains became longer and heavier, things became more interesting, as drivers had to contend, not only with the climb at Saunderton, but also, in the down direction, with a two mile stretch of 1 in 175 at Denham. On top of this, the curvature of the line in the High Wycombe area meant that the route has always carried a number of intermediate speed restrictions. Nevertheless, the 'Stars' and 'Saints' were always equal to the task, and indeed gave some of their finest performances over the Joint Line and the Bicester Cut-Off. (This last-named section, being straight and relatively flat, was considered a 'Racing Ground', and speeds of 80 mph or more were common once the newly-formed embankments had been given time to consolidate.)

Although the majority of Paddington to Birmingham expresses were handled by 4-6-0s, four-coupled locomotives of the 'Atbara', 'Flower', and 'County' classes also appeared in the early years, along with the De Glehn compound 4-4-2s and the 'City' class 4-4-0s. Another 4-4-0 type seen on the Great Western & Great Central Joint route in the pre-Grouping period were the four Dean 'Armstrong' class engines. Looking very much like four-coupled versions of the familiar Dean Singles, three of these old engines had started life as broad gauge locomotives. They tended to work long distance stopping services, such as those which ran between Oxford, Princes Risborough and Paddington via the Thame route.

Shorter distance Great Western locals were handled by tank engines, notably 'Metro' class 2-4-0Ts and '517' class 0-4-2Ts. The '517' class had originated as an 0-4-2 saddle tank design in the 1860s, but in 1870 a side tank version was introduced, and the earlier 0-4-2STs were subsequently rebuilt as side tank locomotives. These small, but attractive locomotives were constructed at Wolverhampton, and in their final form they had 5 ft 2 in. wheels and 16-inch by 24-inch inside cylinders. They were

Robinson 'Director' 4-4-0 No. 437 *Charles Stuart Wortley* speeds through Gerrards Cross with a northbound Great Central express.   *John Alsop Collection*

The first 10 'Directors' (Nos. 429-438) appeared in 1913, but a subsequent batch (Nos. 501-511) were added in 1920; No. 5501 *Mons*, seen here, was the first of the 'improved Directors' of 1920. 'Directors' worked the 12.15 pm Marylebone to Manchester express for many years. In London & North Eastern Railway (LNER) days the 'improved Directors' became class 'D11', whereas the original engines were designated class 'D10'.   *Real Photographs*

widely used on local passenger services throughout the GWR system, and numerous examples appeared on the 'New Line' and its branches at different times.

The 'Metro' tanks were introduced in 1869, and 140 were built during the next 30 years. Some examples were fitted with condensing apparatus for use on the Metropolitan line, and for this reason the entire class became known as 'Metros'. Although the 'Metro' class 2-4-0Ts worked all over the GWR, there was always a significant concentration in the London Division, Southall and Slough sheds being among their particular haunts.

In the Pre-Grouping era, many railway companies preferred 2-4-2T or 4-4-2T locomotives for suburban passenger work. The Great Western produced small numbers of both types - the 'Birdcage' class 2-4-2Ts and 'County Tank' 4-4-2Ts being employed in the London suburban area during the early 20th century. The '36XX' or 'Birdcage' class (so-called because of their large cabs) were an interesting design, dating from the early 1900s. They had 17-inch by 24-inch inside cylinders and 5 ft 2 in. coupled wheels; although the prototype had appeared in 1901, the two main batches were built in 1902 and 1903. They were numbered in sequence from 3600 to 3630, and lasted until the early 1930s.

The 'County' tanks, too, were extensively used on the Joint Line in its early years; basically tank engine versions of Churchward's 'County' class 4-4-0s, they were introduced in 1905, and lasted until replaced by newly-built '61XX' class 2-6-2Ts in the 1930s. These engines were numbered in the '22XX' series and, together with the 'Birdcage' 2-4-2Ts, they were responsible for most GWR long-distance suburban services over the GW&GC route until the post-Grouping period. At the same time, there were also a number of '31XX' class 2-6-2Ts - the forerunners of the highly-successful '61XX' class prairie tanks.

Great Western freight duties were undertaken by a range of classes, including 'Dean Goods' 0-6-0s, 'Aberdare' 2-6-0s, '43XX' class 2-6-0s and '28XX' class 2-8-0s. There were, in addition, large numbers of 0-6-0 tank locomotives for local freight and shunting work over all parts of the 'New Line' and its branches. Finally, mention must also be made of the steam railmotor cars, which were extensively used on local workings in the early days. First introduced in 1903, these vehicles worked many services at the London end of the line, including the Uxbridge High Street and Ealing to Greenford branches.

The first Great Central main line trains between Marylebone and the North were hauled by a range of newly-designed locomotives, which were remarkable for the elegance of their proportions, and the care lavished on their external appearance. The standard GCR main line engines in the earliest years were 4-4-0s built to the design of Harry Pollitt, the GCR locomotive engineer, and introduced in 1897. The first example of this type was No. 268, while sister engine No. 269 was chosen to haul the inaugural train over the London Extension in 1899.

In 1900 Harry Pollitt was replaced, as GCR locomotive engineer, by John G. Robinson, who joined the Great Central from the Waterford, Limerick & Western Railway of Ireland. J.G. Robinson soon began to develop a range of new engine classes, all of which were notable for their elegant appearance. In 1901, for example, he introduced the '1020' class 4-4-0s (later LNER class 'D9'), which soon replaced the Pollitt engines as top link motive power on the GCR main line. Other Robinson 4-4-0 classes, notably the famous 'Directors' (LNER class 'D10') subsequently appeared, and these powerful 4-4-0s were to enjoy a long association with the Great Western & Great Central route. The first 10 'Directors' emerged from Gorton works in 1913. Carrying the numbers 429-438 they were designated class '11E', and had two 20-inch by 26-inch inside cylinders, and 6 ft 9 in. coupled wheels.

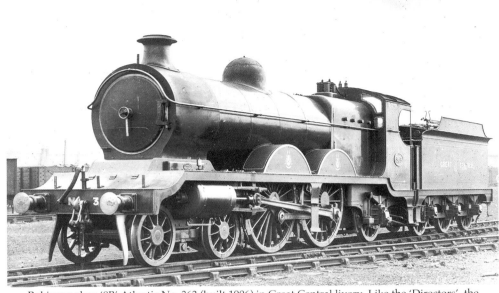

Robinson class '8B' Atlantic No. 363 (built 1906) in Great Central livery. Like the 'Directors', the Robinson 4-4-2s worked on the GW&GC line for many years. No. 363 was numbered 5363 during the LNER period, and it was initially painted in full apple green livery, although these handsome locomotives were later painted in lined black.   *Real Photographs*

Robinson class '8B' Atlantic No. 1089 leaves Marylebone with a down express during the early post-Grouping period, *circa* 1924. This locomotive, which had been built in 1905, subsequently became LNER 'C4' class 4-4-2 No. 6089.   *John Alsop Collection*

Robinson's most attractive locomotives were perhaps his '8B' and '8D' 4-4-2s (later LNER classes 'C4' and 'C5'). Known as 'Jersey Lillies', because their well-proportioned and elegantly curvaceous bodies were said to remind Edwardian gentlemen of the actress Lillie Langtry (1853-1929), the first Robinson Atlantics appeared in 1903. As top link motive power they soon appeared on the London Extension, 19 of the Atlantics being stationed at Manchester (Gorton) while the remaining 12 members of the 31-strong class were sent to Neasden. In 1907, No.192 was allocated to Leicester shed, which eventually housed 19 members of the class, while other 4-4-2s were sent to Woodford Halse.

With their graceful curved footplating, tapered chimneys, brass-beaded splashers, and rich Brunswick green livery, these engines were a superb travelling advertisement for the Great Central Railway, and even the most dyed-in-the-wool Great Western stalwarts had to admit that that, aesthetically, the GCR 4-4-2s compared favourably with anything that the GWR could offer at that time. Happily, the Robinson Atlantics worked over the GW&GC Joint Line for many years, often on the popular 6.20 pm Marylebone to Bradford express, which was 4-4-2-hauled until as late as 1936.

The relatively lightweight GCR trains allowed the Robinson Atlantics to surmount the gradients beyond Princes Risborough with steam to spare, although, by the LNER period, the train had become an 8-coach formation. Nevertheless, speeds of 48 mph or more were frequently recorded on the long climb to Saunderton. Interestingly, Robinson's 4-4-2s are generally said to have been better engines than the same designer's 4-6-0 classes - possibly because the Atlantics had deeper fireboxes, which were able to produce more steam than their 4-6-0 counterparts. On the level section beyond Princes Risborough, these engines could easily attain speeds of 85-88 mph.

Robinson's first 4-6-0s, the class '8' or 'Fish Engines' (LNER class 'B5'), were designed for mixed traffic duties, although in 1903 he introduced two '8C' class express passenger locomotives (LNER class 'B1', later 'B18'), followed in 1912 by the inside-cylindered 'Sir Sam Fay' class (LNER class 'B2', later 'B19') and in 1917 by the four-cylindered 'Lord Faringdon' class 4-6-0s (LNER class 'B3').

These impressive machines were employed on some of the best trains on the GCR route, but their performance in everyday service was disappointing, and perhaps for this reason the Great Central company constructed 11 'Improved Directors' in 1920 (LNER class 'D11'), the new engines being distinguished by their side window cabs and World War I names. Thus, by the end of the pre-Grouping period, the Great Central company seems to have decided that four-coupled express locomotives were perfectly adequate for use on its system, and the principal GCR expresses routed over the GW&GC Joint Line continued to be hauled by 'Jersey Lillie' 4-4-2s and sturdy 'Director' 4-4-0s.

Marylebone local workings were handled initially by '9K' and '9L' class tanks (later LNER classes 'C13' and 'C14'), but in 1911 the first members of a new class of 4-6-2 passenger tanks appeared on the line. Designated the '9N' class by the GCR, the engines were known colloquially as 'Coronation Tanks', because they appeared in Coronation year, and they were to work the arduous suburban services out of Marylebone for the next 40 years. Like the Atlantics, the 4-4-2Ts and 4-6-2Ts sported the full Great Central passenger livery of Brunswick green, lined in black and white, with purple-brown frames.

Great Central goods workings brought other locomotive types onto the line, notably Robinson's sturdy '8K' class 2-8-0s - which, in LNER days, became the 'O4' class - and

Robinson class '9K' 4-4-2T No.47 at South Harrow during the Edwardian period. When they were first introduced in 1903, *The Engineer* opined that these locomotives were of 'unusually handsome design'. *John Alsop Collection*

Great Central 4-4-2T No. 47 on a Marylebone suburban train at South Harrow (later Sudbury Hill Harrow). The station master's house can be seen behind the locomotive. *Real Photographs*

Robinson class '9L' 4-4-2T No. 1124 hurries along the GW&GC line with a Great Central local working, *circa* 1912. These locomotives were slightly larger than the earlier '9K' 4-4-2Ts, although the two classes were otherwise very similar.   *John Alsop Collection*

Robinson '9N' class 4-6-2 suburban tank No. 168; the GCR locomotive livery was Brunswick green with purple-brown frames.   *Real Photographs*

Robinson 2-8-0 class '8K' goods locomotive No. 1312 as LNER No. 6312.   *Real Photographs*

Robinson class '9N' 4-6-2T No. 5045 was one of a batch of 10 locomotives completed in 1923. These engines became LNER class 'A5'.   *Real Photographs*

the '1B' class 2-6-4Ts. The last-mentioned engines are of particular interest in that, when introduced in 1914, they were the first 2-6-4 tanks to appear in England; looking rather like lumbering misshapen versions of the 'Coronation Tanks', they were known to railwaymen as 'Crabs'. They could, however, travel at speed if required, and on rare occasions they worked passenger trains.

Other GCR goods services were worked by the equally-famous Robinson '9J' class 0-6-0s; the LNER called these hard-working engines the 'J11' class, but to railwaymen and enthusiasts alike they were invariably known as the 'Pom-Poms'. This was because their staccato exhaust beats were supposed to resemble the sound of a type of exploding machine gun shell that had been used against British forces during the Boer War.

C. Hamilton Ellis once remarked that 'the London Extension was the Great Central's showpiece', and as its trains were in competition with long-established lines such as the Midland and LNWR, the company used its newest and best locomotives on the Marylebone services. It was, in consequence unusual to find many Manchester, Sheffield & Lincolnshire locomotives at the southern end of the line. The only MS&LR engines present in any numbers were the Parker 'N5' 0-6-2T, which could be found at Neasden in considerable numbers as late as the 1950s.

Locomotives seen on the GW&GC Joint route came from a variety of depots, the main London sheds of the two partners being at Old Oak Common and Neasden respectively, but many GWR suburban engines were shedded at Southall or Slough. The GWR also had sheds at Banbury, Leamington Spa and Tyseley, but the main 'northern' shed at the Birmingham end was Wolverhampton Stafford Road. Similarly, Leicester was the 'northern' shed for Great Central services - which usually changed engines there. Both companies stationed local engines at a small joint depot at Aylesbury, and the Great Western had small branch sub-sheds at Marlow and Watlington.

Post-Grouping Developments

The Grouping of Railways in 1923 did not bring about any immediate changes, apart from the disappearance of the old Great Central Brunswick green passenger livery. Henceforth, ex-GCR locomotives with wheels larger than 6 ft 6 in. carried the lighter shade of green favoured by the newly-created London & North Eastern Railway. Other classes, such as the 4-6-2 and 4-4-2 tanks, appeared in black livery, while LNER passenger rolling stock was turned out in a 'varnished teak' livery. In practice, most LNER passenger rolling stock was painted, some main line vehicles having a simulated 'wood' finish, while other coaches were turned out in an unadorned mid-brown livery.

One small, but significant change concerned the introduction of an entirely new system of class notations for LNER engines. This new system was both logical and simple, in that 4-6-2s became 'As', 4-6-0s became 'Bs', 4-4-2s became 'C's, and so on. As there was usually more than one type of engine with a particular wheel arrangement these basic notations were further sub-divided by the addition of a numerical suffix. For example, the 'Coronation' tanks became class 'A5', while the 'Jersey Lillies' were designated class 'C4' (simple) or class 'C5' (compound versions).

The LNER also introduced a new numbering system for locomotives and rolling stock. In the case of locomotives, the former Great Central classes were renumbered in the '5XXX' series, the original GCR numbers being increased by 5,000, so that (for example), Robinson Atlantics Nos. 194 and 1083 became Nos. 5194 and 6083 respectively. Great Central goods wagons were renumbered in the 500,000 series, but passenger vehicles retained their GCR numbers, albeit prefixed by a letter 'C'.

Two views of Wembley Exhibition station on 4th July, 1915, showing a former Great Eastern Railway 'N7' class 0-6-2T locomotive on the Stadium loop line; note the 'Imperial Indian' style architecture. The 2 ft 8 in. gauge 'Never-Stop Railway' which can be glimpsed in the upper photograph, was worked by a revolving shaft of varying pitch situated in a continuous well beneath the 'Never-Stop' cars.   *(Both) H.C. Casserley*

Later, the 'C' was replaced by a digit to represent the appropriate operating section, and Great Central vehicles were then prefixed by a '5'.

Suburban development along the route of the GW&GC Joint Line - which had been halted by World War I - resumed with a vengeance after 1918. By the late 1920s and early 1930s the urban 'colonisation' of Middlesex was in full swing, and the once pleasant countryside was replaced by an endless sea of brick, slate and pebble dash. The new housing developments brought yet more halts into being - Harefield Halt appeared in the timetables in 1928, and Ruislip Gardens, between South Ruislip and Ruislip & Ickenham, was opened on 9th July, 1934. (The former had only a short life, however, and it was closed in 1931.)

Meanwhile, in an effort to attract more passengers to the rural northern sections of the route, the GWR opened a halt at Ilmer, between Princes Risborough and Haddenham, on 1st April, 1929. The 'halt' concept found much favour on GWR lines during the 1920s and 1930s, but the LNER was not averse to introducing new stations in suitable areas, and on 19th July, 1926 the company opened a passenger station with a 'a goods siding and cart roadway' at South Harrow & Roxeth, between the existing stations at South Harrow and Northolt Junction.

A further Great Western halt was opened to serve Dorton near Brill, on 21st June, 1937, but in general commuter traffic never developed north of High Wycombe - at least not on any large scale - and 'mass commuting' was confined to the new suburban areas at the London end of the route. Architecturally, most of the earlier GWR halts conformed to a distinct house style, and boasted corrugated iron 'pagoda' shelters, standing on sleeper- or cinder-built platforms. Seer Green, however, was provided with slightly larger wooden buildings which were designed to complement the nearby golf club house, whereas the later halts at Ilmer and Dorton were of utterly basic construction.

The British Empire Exhibition, held at a specially-created exhibition centre at Wembley, brought much extra traffic to the Neasden to Northolt line during the 1920s. A new station, known as 'Wembley Exhibition', was constructed on the site in order to deal with the heavy passenger traffic which was expected to develop. The exhibition station was situated on a loop from the main line at Neasden North Junction, and the new station was provided with a single platform, 600 ft long. The station buildings were built in an appropriate 'Imperial Indian' style, in order to blend-in with the nearby 'Palaces of Engineering and Industry'.

The Wembley Loop was first used on 28th April, 1923, on the occasion of the notorious 1923 Football Association (FA) Cup Final between West Ham United and Bolton Wanderers, in which a crowd of several thousand spectators invaded the pitch, and were dispersed by a lone policeman on a white horse called 'Billy'. It was later revealed that 126,000 football enthusiasts had passed through the turnstiles, while another 100,000 had managed to enter by other means - over a quarter of a million people having somehow crammed themselves into the Stadium.

The Exhibition itself began several months later, in April 1924, and lasted until 1925. The Exhibition station was busy throughout this 19-month period, with 20 trains an hour running out-and-back from Marylebone via the Stadium Loop. These services were worked by Great Central 4-6-2Ts, and later by 'N7' class 0-6-2Ts. The Exhibition station - renamed 'Wembley Stadium' - remained in use after 1925 in connection with FA Cup Finals and other sporting events held in Wembley Stadium, or the nearby Empire Pool (which was added in 1934).

Former Great Central class 'J11' Pom-Pom 0-6-0 No. 6082 heads an LNER freight working along the GW&GC route, probably near Denham, in 1934.   *John Alsop Collection*

Dean '2361' class double-framed goods locomotive No. 2368, passes beneath the Brill branch near Brill & Ludgershall on 22nd June, 1935. The '2361' series engines were built in 1885-86 as broad gauge 'convertibles' although, in the event, none ever ran on the broad gauge.

Real Photographs

The General Strike

The other major event of the mid-1920s - the 1926 General Strike - was a less happy occurrence. Called in support of the miners, the strike began on Tuesday 4th May. All railways were severely disrupted, but non-striking railwaymen and civilian volunteers managed to maintain an emergency service on the main lines. On 6th May, *The Oxford Mail* was able to report that some suburban trains had reached Aylesbury, while 'all long distance milk and fish trains on the GWR and LNER were running to schedule'.

The situation on the branch lines was more serious. The Thame line, for example, had no trains at all until Tuesday 11th May - thereafter a skeleton service of two up and two down workings ran to and from Princes Risborough.

By the middle of the second week, the strikers were starting to drift back to work- although the overall picture was confused. Indeed, in one or two places the strike petered out on a note of pure farce. At Ardley, for instance, a signalman, believing that he had to return to work on 12th May, cycled to the station as usual. On arrival he found his box locked and deserted, and so climbed-in through a window to telephone Bicester for further instructions; the station master at Bicester informed him that he was trespassing, and as a result he was taken to court on a charge of breaking and entering - and fined £3!

The General Strike ended officially on 13th May, but it was some days before the railways were back to normal; the first train from Watlington, for example, arrived at Princes Risborough driven by a volunteer from Chinnor Lime Works. Some strikers, refusing to accept that the great strike could end in defeat, 'stayed out' until the end of the week, while the unfortunate miners carried on alone till the Autumn - thereby creating a serious coal shortage.

New Motive Power

On a happier note, the next few years were to see the introduction of more modern motive power onto the GW&GC route. In 1936, the LNER introduced its impressive 'V2' class 2-6-2s, and these locomotives were to be associated with the route for many years. The Gresley 'V2's were large engines by any standards, and their use on the GW&GC Joint Line was confined strictly to the main and passenger platform lines. The new engines had three 18½ -inch by 26-inch cylinders, and 6 ft 2 in. coupled wheels; the first engine to appear was given the name *Green Arrow*. The 'V2' 2-6-2s were initially designed for fast freight work, although these mixed traffic engines were also used for main line passenger traffic.

In 1928, the LNER introduced the 'B17' class 4-6-0s, with three 17½-inch by 26-inch cylinders and 6 ft 8 in. coupled wheels. Known as the 'Sandringhams', they were initially sent to East Anglia for use on the Great Eastern section, they eventually appeared on the Great Central system. In August 1933, for instance, *The Railway Magazine* mentioned that several readers had commented on the use of 'three-cylinder Sandringham type locomotives on the Great Central main line to London of the LNER, numbers specially observed being 2816, 2834, and 2840 and 2841 of the latest batch'. The engines concerned were stationed at Gorton, from where they worked main line services to Marylebone.

The arrival of these new locomotives did not result in the wholesale extinction of the earlier engines, and for the next few years the GW&GC Joint route remained a

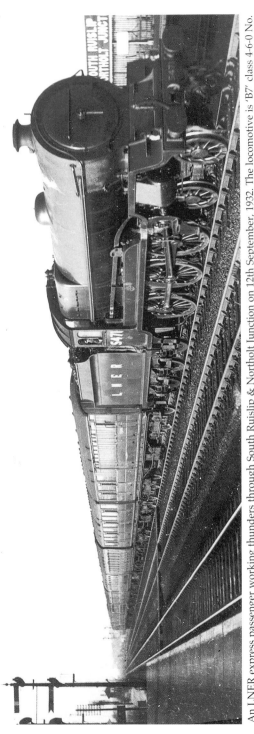

An LNER express passenger working thunders through South Ruislip & Northolt Junction on 12th September, 1932. The locomotive is 'B7' class 4-6-0 No. 5471.

H.C. Casserley

Gresley 'B17' class 4-6-0 No. 2816 *Fallodon* passes through Neasden with the 3.20 pm down service from Marylebone on 12th May, 1934.

H.C. Casserley

bastion of Great Central motive power. The familiar 'Director' class 4-4-0s were still well-established at Neasden, and they regularly worked over the GW&GC Joint Line with the main London to Manchester expresses, which left Marylebone at 10.00 am and 12.15 pm. Three 'Lord Faringdon' 4-6-0s were stationed at Neasden, and they appeared on the GW&GC line on a less regular basis, sharing their duties with the 'Director' 4-4-0s and 'Jersey Lillie' 4-4-2s.

Other ex-Great Central 4-6-0 classes worked over the Great Western & Great Central route on excursions and other special workings which, in LNER days, were invariably routed via High Wycombe and Princes Risborough. The 'Sir Sam Fay' class 4-6-0s, for example, were often used on the summer weekend 'Norway Cruise' boat trains between Marylebone and Immingham. Another ex-GCR type noted on these duties were the Robinson 'B4' or 'Immingham' class 4-6-0s; later, at the very end of the LNER era, a few of these engines were employed on long-distance stopping services, together with 'B8' class 4-6-0 No. 5004 *Glenalmond*.

The Great Western, meanwhile, had improved its own locomotive fleet, and by the 1930s, the 'Stars' and 'Saints' had largely given way to the 'Castles', and more especially, the 'King' class 4-6-0s. These two classes, introduced in 1923 and 1927 respectively, were to work on the line for three decades, and their introduction prompted the suggestion that the time for the Paddington to Birmingham run could be slashed to just 1¾ hours.

Sadly, although in 1935 the introduction of 'The Bristolian' had given Bristol travellers a 1¼ hour express service to Paddington, Birmingham passengers had to be content with the two-hour timings that had been introduced back in 1910. Indeed, in 1933, certain Birmingham expresses were actually decelerated.

Great Western enthusiasts found the management's attitude inexplicable but, to be fair, it must be pointed out that the physical characteristics of the Birmingham route are very different to those pertaining on the original GWR line to Bristol; whereas the latter is almost dead flat, the GW&GC Joint Line is, as we have seen, rather hilly in places. Nevertheless the fact remains that, if a special lightweight Paddington to Birmingham train had been introduced, it would have required an average speed of only 63.2 mph to achieve the desired 1¾ hour schedule.

The 1930s saw changes on the Great Western local services. More and more trains were passing into the hands of prairie tanks until, in the immediate pre-war years, the '61XX' class 2-6-2Ts emerged as the 'classic' GWR London area suburban locomotives. Although the company had favoured the employment of 4-4-2 and 2-4-2 tank engines on its longer distance suburban services from Paddington, operational experience with the pioneer '31XX' class and '3150' class prairie tanks had suggested that the 2-6-2T configuration was better-suited for work in the London suburban area, and in due course the GWR built large numbers of prairie tanks, notably the '61XX' class 2-6-2Ts, which first appeared in 1929.

The '61XX' class prairies were handsome locomotives, with 5 ft 8 in. coupled wheels and two 18-inch by 30-inch outside cylinders. Externally, the downward slope of their cutaway 2,000 gallon side tanks complemented the converging shape of the GWR tapered boilers, while their outward-curving bunkers seemed to visually balance the massive cylinder casing at the front end of the locomotives. In the minds of most enthusiasts, these elegant locomotives were the London Division suburban tank engines par excellence, and Southall normally had a large allocation.

Shorter distance locals were usually worked by push-and-pull auto-trains, and in 1930 the '54XX' class 0-6-0 pannier tanks were introduced especially for auto-train work. Two years later the Collett '48XX' (later '14XX') class 0-4-2Ts appeared, again

Great Western '54XX' class 0-6-0PT No. 5419, photographed near Brill & Ludgershall while working the 2.00 pm local service from Banbury to Princes Risborough on 22nd June, 1939. The auto-trailer appears to be No. 83.   *H.C. Casserley*

Collett '48XX' class 0-4-2T No. 4873 hauls a single auto-trailer along the GW&GC main line near Brill & Ludgershall on 13th May, 1939.   *H. C. Casserley*

for push-pull work, and the introduction of these new classes enabled many of the older engines, such as the '517' class 0-4-2Ts, to be withdrawn.

Freight services were worked by a number of different classes, 4-6-0s or 2-6-0s being employed on many long distance 'perishable' goods services, while 2-8-0s were typically used on heavy coal and mineral workings. A lineside observer at a GW&GC station such as Denham might, for example, have seen a succession of '63XX' class 2-6-0s, 'Aberdare' 2-6-0s and '28XX' class 2-8-0s during the mid- to late-1930s. Great Central goods services were headed by Robinson 'O4' class 2-8-0s, 'B7' class mixed traffic 4-6-0s, 'Pom-Pom' 0-6-0s and 'Crab' 2-6-4Ts.

For local freight and shunting work, the GWR introduced a new 0-6-0 pannier tank class in 1929. Known as the '57XX' class, many ex-Great Western drivers argued that, after the 'Castles', they were the best GWR engines of the lot! They were, in effect, modernised versions of earlier 'large' panniers such as the '2721' class 0-6-0PTs. There were two sub-groups - the earlier batches, such as the '57XX' and '77XX' series, having low-roofed cabs with circular windows, while later batches were given improved cabs with larger windows.

They occasionally appeared on passenger trains, and in 1931 the '97XX' class condensing variety were introduced for work through the Metropolitan Line tunnels; all 10 examples were based at Old Oak Common shed. Finally, at the very end of the Great Western period, the tapered-boilered '94XX' class panniers appeared, and these too could often be seen around the London end of the line; eight of the original 10 engines were allocated to Old Oak Common by December 1947.

Train Services in the 1930s

The last years of peace saw the GW&GC Joint Line well established as an important main line. Perhaps one should say a 'Great Western main line' as, in the three decades since the line's opening, a pattern of services had emerged in which the GWR provided main line trains, while the LNER, as successor to the Great Central Railway, operated most of the suburban services.

In general, the LNER ran 30 or so through suburban trains from Marylebone daily, while the Great Western provided about a dozen - some of which ran from either Oxford or Aylesbury. In 1939 for example, there were four trains from Oxford to Paddington via Princes Risborough, and four from Aylesbury. These services treated the discerning (or frustrated!) traveller to a roundabout tour of the Home Counties, which could be of up to three hours' duration.

Great Western local services north of Princes Risborough were confined mainly to auto-train workings - some of which were extended to High Wycombe. Both companies provided numerous short distance local services in the London area. The LNER trains terminated at Ruislip or Denham, while many GWR locals worked extremely complicated diagrams involving the Greenford to Ealing Loop. The Great Western also provided a circuitous service between High Wycombe and Paddington via Maidenhead, and this facility did much to make up for the paucity of GWR local trains on the Beaconsfield route.

Few LNER expresses now ran on the GW&GC line, but among the services which did travel the extra four miles via High Wycombe were the old-established 6.20 pm Marylebone to Bradford service, the 10.00 am Marylebone to Manchester and the 12.15 pm Marylebone to Manchester workings.

Great Western 'County' class 4-4-0 No. 3828 *County of Hereford* departs from Beaconsfield with a Great Western stopping service, *circa* 1930.   *John Alsop Collection*

'King' class 4-6-0 No. 6017 *King Edward IV* thunders northwards beneath the Brill branch overbridge while working the 2.15 pm express from Paddington to Wolverhampton on 22nd June, 1935.   *H.C. Casserley*

Gresley 'B17' class 4-6-0 No. 2854 *Sunderland* at the head of the 6.58 am Mansfield to Marylebone service near Saunderton summit in May 1936.   *H.K. Harman/Rail Archive Stephenson*

Great Western express services were lavish in comparison. In 1910, the original GWR express service over the Joint Line had provided six northbound and eight southbound workings. In the down direction, the principal departures from Paddington were at 9.10, 11.05 am, 2.35, 4.00 and 6.05 pm. All of these services ran through to Birkenhead via Birmingham Snow Hill, Shrewsbury and Chester. In the southbound direction, the main up services left Birkenhead at 6.15, 8.15, 9.10, 11.47 am, 12.55, 2.35 and 4.35 pm, while Birmingham to London travellers could also make use of a shorter-distance service starting from Wolverhampton Low Level at 8.30 pm.

A broadly-similar pattern of operation persisted for many years, albeit with various small changes in the times of arrival and departure. In 1922, for instance, the principal daytime services via the GW&GC route left Paddington at 9.10, 10.15, 10.40 am, 12.50, 2.20, 4.00, 6.10 and 7.10 pm. All of these services ran through to Birmingham and Wolverhampton, from where most workings continued onwards to Birkenhead via Shrewsbury and Chester. Some services conveyed through coaches for Aberystwyth, while the 10.15 am down service ran through to Aberystwyth, Barmouth and Pwllheli.

By 1939, the main northbound services were leaving Paddington at 9.10, 11.05 am, 2.10, 4.05, 6.10 and 7.10 pm, and arriving in Birmingham Snow Hill at 11.10 am, 1.10, 4.10, 6.10, 8.10 and 9.10 pm respectively. There was, in addition, an overnight service that left Paddington at 1.30 am and reached Birmingham at 4.00 am. Most of these workings ran through to Birkenhead, which remained the principal destination for Great Western express services over the GW&GC Joint route.

Although, as we shall see, the line could boast four daily named trains in the post-Nationalisation era, the situation in pre-war days was slightly different. The GWR did not regard the fact that a train was 'named' as a major selling point; instead, the company aimed to attract customers by providing a good, all-round service of fast,

Robinson 'A5' 4-6-2T No. 9806 running bunker-first at Neasden on 14th August, 1947.

H.C. Casserley

Sister locomotive No. 5128 at Ruislip during the 1930s.   *John Alsop Collection*

convenient trains. Thus, there was nothing particularly special about the timings, or even the appearance of a 1930s named train - headboards and special liveries were not yet in vogue. Nevertheless, for a route which lasted as a main line for only 50 years, the GW&GC Joint route saw an unusually large number of named expresses, and for this reason, some details of the Great Western named services are called for.

The 'Belfast Boat Express' was possibly the prime named train on the Great Western & Great Central route in the 1930s; introduced in 1928, this appellation was applied to the 9.05 am from Birkenhead to Paddington and, in the down direction, to the 4.10 pm from Paddington.

The two most interesting named trains of the period were not, however, perennial named expresses at all; they were Summer-only specials, both of which had been introduced in 1927. The 'Shakespeare Express' - which ran until 1933 - left Paddington at 9.25 am every weekday in the Summer. Calling at High Wycombe at 9.57 am, the train then ran to Stratford-upon-Avon with a stop at Leamington Spa for an optional coach tour of the Kenilworth and Stratford areas. Better known, perhaps, was the 'Cambrian Coast Express', which ran on Summer Fridays and Saturdays only. The down working departed from Paddington at 10.10 am, while the balancing up service left Aberystwyth at 10.15 am.

Apart from these officially-named trains, there were one or two unofficial 'named' trains. The auto-train from Princes Risborough to Banbury for example, was known as 'The Risborough Dasher'! At the other end of the scale, the up express which left Birmingham at 3.00 pm (originally 2.45 pm) was dubbed 'The Zulu'. The 'Zulu' in fact, was one of the crack trains of the period; a descendant of the old Northern Zulu of the Victorian period, it covered the 67½ miles between Banbury and Paddington in only 70 minutes.

Freight traffic was shared more or less evenly between the two companies. There were perhaps 25 goods trains each way over the main section of the GW&GC route on weekdays. Both companies provided their own pick-up freights on their respective connecting lines, although the GWR was responsible for serving the intermediate stations and sidings *en route* from Northolt Junction to Princes Risborough.

Slip Coaches

Slip coach working was widely practised on the GW&GC Joint line. In the early days, it was considered that the two-hour schedules of the main Birmingham expresses could be maintained only if the trains ran non-stop. Hence, from the earliest days of the route, the main Great Western expresses would slip one, two, or even three specially-constructed vehicles at the main intermediate stations; the 4.00 pm down service from Paddington, for example, used to slip at Bicester, Leamington Spa and Knowle, while the 6.05 pm express conveyed slip portions for Banbury, Leamington and Lapworth.

These slip coaches would normally be detached at speed when approaching their respective stations, and the released vehicles would then coast down to the platforms under the control of a 'slip guard'. Alternatively, at some locations the slipped portion would be brought to a stand before entering the station, and taken into the platform by another locomotive. The vehicles themselves were normally 'double-ended', with a guard's compartment at each end, although there were also a limited number of single-ended slip coaches. The guards' compartments were fitted with windows in each end, and bells were fitted so that an audible warning could be given to persons on the line when necessary.

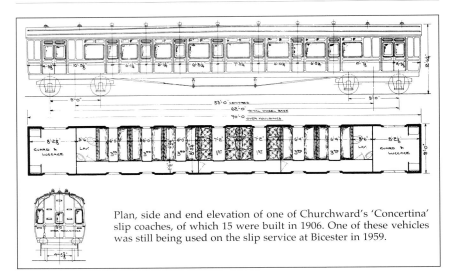

Plan, side and end elevation of one of Churchward's 'Concertina' slip coaches, of which 15 were built in 1906. One of these vehicles was still being used on the slip service at Bicester in 1959.

The slip guard controlled his vehicle by applying brake power once the coach had been detached. This was effected by the use of the 'slip lever', which released the couplings and then worked the vacuum braking system in such a way that several applications could be made without exhausting the vacuum.

With the introduction of powerful locomotives such as the 'King' class 4-6-0s, slip working declined; it was found that trains could stop *en route* and still maintain a fast overall schedule. Nevertheless, slipping was long a part of the GW&GC scene, and the trains of both companies included slip portions in the years between the wars. Multiple slipping was not by any means confined to the GWR; the 6.20 pm Marylebone to Bradford service, for example, conveyed two slip coaches, which were detached once the train had regained Great Central metals north of Grendon Underwood Junction, to serve Finmere, Woodford Halse, and other intermediate stations.

The LNER abandoned slipping in the 1930s, and World War II brought Great Western slip coach workings to an end for the duration; after the war the practice was resumed on a limited scale. Happily, slipping survived on the GW&GC route for many years thereafter, and to jump ahead to the British Railways era, it is worth recording that the very last slip coach workings in Britain were to be found on the Joint Line.

The last train to carry a slip portion was the 5.10 pm from Paddington to Wolverhampton Low Level, and in the final years it was the practice to slip when approaching Bicester North. The main portion of the train passed through the station on the centre track, while the slip coach rolled down the grade to a point just short of the down platform. It would then be picked up by the engine of a slow train, which waited in the platform loop, and brought it into the platform. The slip coach would be coupled to the local, and go forward to Banbury - thereby enabling Banbury travellers to travel on the 5.10 pm, even though it did not stop at their destination! The last slip in railway history was carried out at about 6.12 pm, at Bicester, on 9th September, 1960, when coach No. 7374 was detached from the 5.10 pm express service from Paddington.

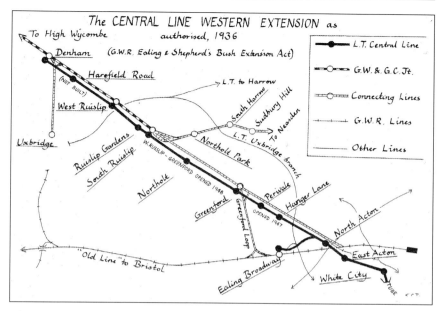

The Underground Extension Scheme

In 1933 - the year in which Hitler came to power - the Metropolitan and other London Underground lines were amalgamated into the London Passenger Transport Board (LPTB). The LPTB, together with the GWR and the LNER, were soon examining ways in which the suburban passenger services of the capital could be improved. The result was the 1935-40 New Works Programme (commonly called 'The £40,000,000 Plan'), which envisaged, among other things, an 11 mile western extension of the LPTB Central line from Acton to Denham.

The Great Western agreed to build new up and down electric tracks from a junction with the Ealing & Shepherd's Bush line at North Acton, running parallel to the 'New Line' as far as Denham. Powers were obtained on 14th July, 1936, and by 1939 the Ealing & Shepherd's Bush route had been quadrupled between Shepherd's Bush and North Acton, and the main running lines were down as far west as Greenford.

Unfortunately, the outbreak of World War II in September 1939 put a stop to this ambitious scheme, and the newly-laid track was lifted for emergency use elsewhere. When, in the post-war era, the work was resumed, the scheme was cut short by a little under three miles, the Central Line's western terminus being established at Ruislip & Ickenham rather than Denham.

It is interesting to speculate, however, on the proposed Underground terminus at Denham; the main line station here is perched precariously on top of a massive embankment, and one wonders where in fact the LT platforms would have been sited! One possibility might have been a two-level arrangement, with the electric trains on a lower level. Also of interest is the projected intermediate station at 'Harefield Road' - this would have been situated midway between Denham and Ruislip & Ickenham, roughly on the position of the closed Harefield Halt.

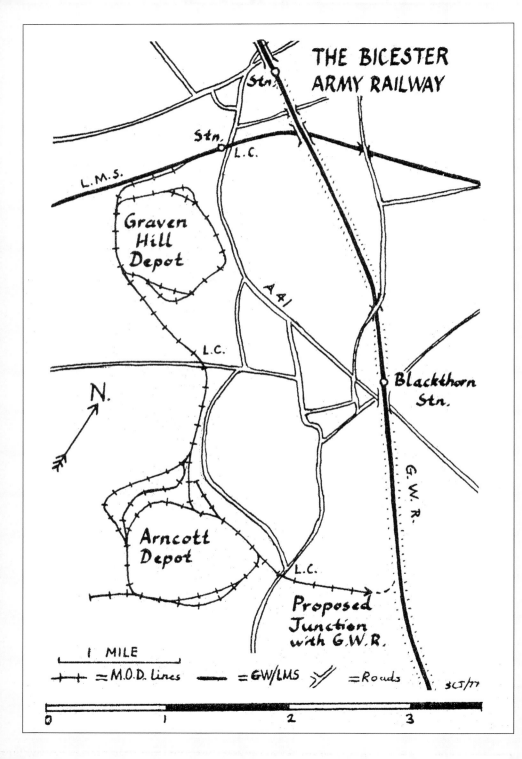

THE BICESTER
ARMY RAILWAY

Stn.

Stn.
L.C.

L.M.S.

Graven
Hill
Depot

A 41

L.C.

N.

Blackthorn
Stn.

G.W.R.

Arncott
Depot

L.C.

Proposed
Junction
with G.W.R.

1 MILE

┼┼ = M.O.D. lines   ━━ = GW/LMS   〉〉 = Roads

SCJ/77

0   1   2   3

World War II

On Sunday 3rd September, 1939, a deteriorating international situation culminated in the outbreak of World War II. With horrific memories of the 1914-18 Great War still fresh in many minds, it was expected that the United Kingdom would soon be devastated by fleets of massed Nazi bombers, but in reality the first months of the war were so uneventful that cynics began to speak derisively of a 'Phoney War'.

Trains were decelerated and curtailed all over the system at the very start of the conflict, while to make matters worse, harassed travellers and railwaymen had to contend with a nightly 'blackout', which was imposed as an 'Air Raid Precaution' measure. The 'blackout' was strictly enforced, platform lighting being severely restricted, while stations and other buildings were fitted with blackout curtains. Carriage lighting was dimmed, and trains ran through the night with their blinds drawn down. Great Western locomotive cabs were equipped with steel shutters, while many engines had their glazed cab windows plated-over.

Initially, surviving train on the Joint Line were packed with servicemen hurrying to joint their ships or units, and 'evacuees', fleeing from London in anticipation of large scale air raids on the City. The children, with their pathetic bundles of clothing, and enormous luggage labels round their necks, presented a touching spectacle in the early stages of the conflict.

It is interesting to note that one of these youthful evacuees was the comedy-actor Kenneth Williams, who recalled that he was billeted at the home of a retired-veterinary surgeon in Sheep Street, Bicester - a 'rambling old house ... lit by oil lamps and candles'. Later, as the war effort got into its stride, the railway conveyed large numbers of service personnel to and from the various RAF stations and army establishments that had been set up on or near the route of the line.

These aerodromes and depots included RAF Upper Heyford (near Ardley station), RAF Bicester, RAF Thame (which was actually at Haddenham), RAF Booker (near High Wycombe), RAF Denham, RAF Westcott (near Ashendon Junction), and the Battle of Britain fighter base at RAF Northolt. These airfields fulfilled a variety of roles during the war years, some being active front-line stations such as Northolt, while others were associated with flying training. Booker and Denham, for instance, were used by the Tiger Moth trainers of No. 21 Elementary Flying Training School, while RAF Bicester and RAF Westcott were the homes of Nos. 13 and 11 Operational Training Units respectively.

In addition to the aerodromes, there was also a rail-connected Air Ministry depot at Ruislip & Ickenham, and an immense Army Ordnance depot at Bicester - which is of particular interest on account of its extensive internal railway system. Bicester Depot was first set up in 1940, when the Royal Engineers laid in a railway line from the LMS route at Bicester to Langford Farm. The line branched out to serve a depot at Graven Hill, to the south of the town, and then continued southwards, parallel to the GWR main line, but a little over a mile away, until it reached a second depot at Upper Arncott, some four miles to the south of Bicester.

It was, at one stage, intended to link the Army Railway to the Great Western line near Brill & Ludgershall, and indeed the 'main line' of the military system was taken eastwards from Arncott to terminate at a point just a quarter of a mile short of the proposed junction. In the event, the junction was never made - although, should the need have arisen, the installation of a temporary connection would have been a comparatively simple operation.

There was always a considerable amount of passenger traffic between the depot and the Great Western, and off-duty servicemen frequently travelled to or from London via the GW&GC line from either Bicester or Blackthorn stations, using special road transport to and from the camp.

In 1940, following the Fall of France, it was thought that the Germans might attempt an invasion of the British Isles. A volunteer force known as the 'Local Defence Volunteers' was created to help repel the expected invaders, and in June 1940 these enthusiastic part-timers were re-named 'The Home Guard'. Their duties included guarding railway installations, and in some places railway stations became Home Guard headquarters or assembly points. At Greenford, for example, an old 'Iron Mink' van was adapted for use as a 'guard room' at an estimated cost of £24, this work being ordered in November 1940.

A similar vehicle was fitted-out for Home Guard use at High Wycombe - in this case the 'Home Guard Coach' was condemned four-wheeled composite No. 6615. At a later stage of the war, it was decided that a dismounted coach body (possibly the same vehicle) would be lifted onto the up platform as accommodation for the Home Guard, at an estimated cost of £59. Unfortunately, the final cost was £76 16s. 3d., because 'Sunday labour had to be worked', and the 'engine power and crane hire' was more costly than had been anticipated. In addition to the Home Guard, High Wycombe station also served as a base for a detachment of Air Raid Wardens, who were comfortably installed in the ladies' waiting room on platform one; cupboards and beds were specially provided, together with a gas ring in the nearby foremen's office.

Quite apart from the threat of invasion, their was an ever-present fear of air attack. The German dictator was, at first, unwilling to bomb British civilian targets, and the first raid on London was carried out against his orders. However, Churchill immediately ordered a reprisal attack on Berlin, and this led inevitably to the start of the 'Blitz' on 6th September, 1940. In general, the GW&GC line escaped serious damage, though Paddington was hit on at least one occasion. The worst incident took place on the night of 13th October, 1940, when a high-explosive bomb landed on the 'Underground' station at Praed Street, killing eight people and injuring many more; although the incident had not occurred on Great Western property, GWR personnel were immediately on the scene.

Towards the end of the war, the Germans deployed their newly-developed 'V1' and 'V2' rockets in a last, desperate attempt to stave off defeat. In 1944, one the 'V1' 'doodlebugs' landed on the Mono Containers Factory at Park Royal, causing damage to the adjacent GWR goods depot. A report, compiled shortly afterwards, described the incident as follows:

> At 6.45 am Saturday, July 1st, a Flying Bomb dropped on Messrs Mono's premises immediately adjoining Park Royal Yard on the North Side, and caused damage and some loss of life on that firm's premises. The blast swept over the yard and blew Shunter Payne some yards, causing shock, but he was able to continue with his duties and has not since felt any ill effects.
>
> Windows and frames of Inspector's and Shunter's cabins broken and damaged. Civil Defence and Police personnel were soon available and the Yard Inspector and Staff went over to see what assistance they could give. The Yard lighting was damaged and Electric Light Dept. advised.

Notes appended to the report showed that 14 wagons were damaged.

Air raids on London and Birmingham sometimes resulted in delays or disruption to train services on the Joint Line, but public morale remained at a high level throughout the war, and British travellers took most wartime 'incidents' in their stride. On one occasion, however, a very heavy overnight attack on Birmingham had resulted in single line working, long delays and (inevitably) no dining car facilities. Against this background of mounting frustration, an up train called as usual at Princes Risborough, and a passenger forced his way into an already-crowded coach and began complaining in a very loud voice of 'the very bad night' that they had just suffered in very rural Thame.

Thinking that there must have been some kind of saturation bombing raid on Oxfordshire, concerned passengers asked if many bombs had been dropped? On no, replied the 'victim' of Nazi aggression, but we had a 12 hour alert. (A witness to this wartime exchange recalled that he had never before experienced so much 'spontaneous indignation', and he reflected that the incident had almost resulted in a case of 'murder on the morning train to Paddington'!)

The exigencies of total war placed great demands on the line, but called for few physical alterations; the relatively modern stations on the 'New Line', with their long loops and straight parallel sidings, were able to handle the extra traffic with ease. Among the minor alterations which were carried out was the lengthening of the up running loop at High Wycombe, and the addition of two extra sidings known as the 'Chalk Sidings' near the North Yard.

At Beaconsfield, the goods yard run-round loop was extended, while at neighbouring Gerrards Cross, both running loops were lengthened by about 6 chains. Gerrards Cross, it is interesting to recall, also became the wartime home of the LNER Central Timing Office; the department established itself in temporary buildings about half a mile to the west of the station.

The end of the war in Europe was followed in 1945 by the election of Mr Attlee's Labour Government, pledged to nationalise the railways and other important industries, and at midnight on 31st December 1947, the independent life of the Great Western & Great Central Railways Joint Committee was brought to an end. Joint operation was to continue, however, for although the GW&GC Joint Line passed to the Western Region of British Railways, the Marylebone suburban services remained in Eastern Region hands until 1958, when operational responsibility was transferred to the London Midland Region.

Stanier class '8F' 2-8-0 No. 8414, on loan to the GWR, photographed between Aynho Junction and Kings Sutton on 6th May, 1946.   *H.C. Casserley*

SPECIAL NOTICE

CLOSING OF STATIONS

AND

Withdrawal of Steam Passenger Train Service

The undermentioned Halts WILL BE CLOSED for passenger traffic
ON AND FROM SUNDAY, JUNE 15th, 1947 :—

PARK ROYAL WEST PLATFORM
BRENTHAM PLATFORM
PERIVALE PLATFORM

During the period from Sunday, June 15th, to Sunday, June 29th, 1947 (both dates inclusive), a Rail Auto-Car Service will operate at times shewn in the Company's Time Tables between Westbourne Park, Greenford and Northolt, calling only at Old Oak Lane Halt and at North Acton.

For passengers travelling between Westbourne Park, Old Oak Lane Halt and Park Royal, Brentham and Perivale, an alternative service by road operated by the London Passenger Transport Board is available as under :—

ROUTE 105—From Gipsy Corner (which is a short walk from North Acton Station) for Park Royal, Brentham and Perivale and vice versa.

ROUTE 187—From North Acton Station for Park Royal and to Hanger Lane (for Brentham) and vice versa.

For passengers travelling between Northolt, Greenford and Perivale, Brentham and Park Royal, an alternative service by road from and to Greenford Station is available as under :—
(Northolt passengers travel by G.W. Steam Service between Northolt and Greenford.)

ROUTE 92—From Greenford Station to the Roundabout, Western Avenue.

ROUTE 105—From the Roundabout, Western Avenue, for Perivale, Brentham and Park Royal and vice versa.

Rail Tickets will NOT be available by the L.P.T.B. Road Services in either direction.

WITHDRAWAL OF RAIL AUTO-CAR SERVICE
between
WESTBOURNE PARK AND GREENFORD

Coincident with the extension of the Central Line (electric) from North Acton to Greenford serving new Stations at HANGER LANE, PERIVALE and GREENFORD on and from Monday, June 30th, 1947, THE RAIL AUTO-CAR SERVICE BETWEEN WESTBOURNE PARK AND GREENFORD WILL BE WITHDRAWN ON AND FROM MONDAY, JUNE 30th, 1947, and the undermentioned Stations WILL ON AND FROM THAT DATE ALSO BE CLOSED for passenger traffic :—

OLD OAK LANE HALT
NORTH ACTON (G.W. Steam Line Station)

An alternate service is available for passengers from Westbourne Park to North Acton, Hanger Lane, Perivale and Greenford by London Passenger Transport Board Road Service ROUTES No. 7 and No. 7A (Weekdays only) from Cornwall Road to EAST ACTON STATION and thence by Central Line, and vice versa.

Rail Tickets will NOT be available by the L.P.T.B. Road Services in either direction.

Passengers from Northolt to Perivale and Hanger Lane travel by G.W. Steam Service (as advertised in the Company's Time Tables) to Greenford and change on to the new Electric Service at the latter point, and vice versa.

Paddington Station, W.2.
May, 1947.

JAMES MILNE,
General Manager.

A special notice issued in May 1947 in connection with the Central Line extension scheme.

Gresley 'K3' class 2-6-0 No. 2455 joins the GW&GC main line with a southbound LNER freight working at Ashendon Junction on 20th July, 1946.   *H.C. Casserley*

Thompson 'B1' 4-6-0 No. 1109 enters Princes Risborough station with a southbound freight working on 26th July, 1947.   *H.C. Casserley*

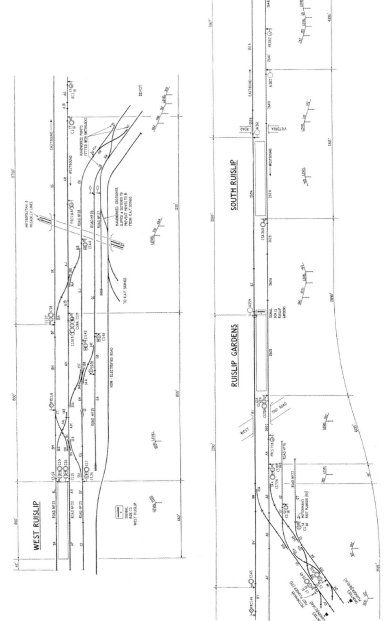

A diagrammatic plan showing the signalling arrangements at the western end of the Central Line extension between South Ruislip, Ruislip Gardens and West Ruislip.

Chapter Four

Nationalisation and Privatisation

The immediate results of Nationalisation were few - indeed, as in 1923, the only noticeable change was in the liveries of the locomotives and rolling stock. The chocolate and cream of the former GWR, and the teak brown of the ex-LNER stock was replaced by the striking red and cream coach livery of the new national system or, in the case of suburban stock, by all-over crimson. The 'King' class 4-6-0s used on the main Paddington to Birmingham services appeared briefly in a cheerful blue livery, while other main line locomotives remained painted in GWR style lined green livery.

Sadly, other ex-Great Western classes were repainted in black, but in the case of those types designated 'mixed traffic' engines, this sombre livery was relieved by red and grey lining. By the mid-1950s, however, several more classes were appearing in GWR green - including former LNER classes such as the 'V2' 2-6-2s and 'A3' class 4-6-2s!

Post-War Developments

The post-war years saw the completion of the Underground extension scheme that had been started in the 1930s. On 30th June, 1947, the GWR opened the electric lines between North Acton and Greenford, and Brentham - replaced by Hanger Lane - and Perivale became London Transport Central Line stations when the line was transferred to the LPTB on 1st January, 1948. Less than 12 months later, on Sunday 21st November, 1948, the final 4½ miles between Greenford and Ruislip & Ickenham were energised, and Ruislip & Ickenham (renamed West Ruislip) took on a new importance as the western terminus of the Central Line, and an interchange point between the British Railways and London Transport systems.

The stations at Northolt, South Ruislip & Northolt Junction, and Ruislip Gardens, became 'Underground' stations, but British Railways trains continued to call at South Ruislip and Ruislip Gardens. A steam-worked push-pull service between Greenford and Ealing continued to run - a bay platform being provided between the up and down LT tracks at Greenford. One by-product of the London Transport takeover was the up-grading of Hanger Lane, Perivale, Northolt, and Ruislip Gardens; whereas in GWR days, these stopping places had been merely halts, the rebuilt and re-sited 'Underground' stations were fully staffed.

The new Central Line stations were initially equipped with substantially-built platform buildings and canopies, although the main station buildings were left in an incomplete state. The buildings at West Ruislip had been virtually completed prior to the war, but elsewhere the booking halls and ticket offices were an untidy mixture of unfinished structures and temporary buildings; at South Ruislip, for instance, the skeletal concrete ribs of a circular booking hall presented a curious appearance. (The buildings remained in an unfinished state for 20 years, but in May 1961, *The Railway Magazine* was able to report that the work needed to complete the stations had finally been put in hand.)

The years immediately following World War II were a time of rigid austerity in which petrol and other commodities were strictly rationed, and this ensured that the

Thompson 'B1' class 4-6-0 No. 1185 hauls the 'Master Cutler' through Ruislip Gardens on 6th October, 1947.
C.R.L. Coles/Rail Archive Stephenson

Gresley 'A3' Pacific No. 60102 *Sir Frederick Banbury* hurries the prestigious 'Master Cutler' express through typical Chiltern countryside near Saunderton in July 1949.
H.K. Harman/Rail Archive Stephenson

railway system remained busy. Moreover, the post-war Labour government was openly pro-rail in its transport policies, and this factor seemed to guarantee that the railway system would have a secure future as part of a fully integrated transport system. In 1951, however, an incoming Conservative government initiated a reversal of policy, and the railways were soon being portrayed as obsolete relics of the industrial revolution that would have to be replaced by private road transport wherever possible.

The nationalised railways were, at this time, still showing a 'profit', but with operating costs rising inexorably, the future for unremunerative rural lines was becoming increasingly bleak. In these circumstances, BR withdrew passenger services from 2,114 route miles between 1948 and 1959, one of the victims being the branch line from Princes Risborough to Watlington, which was closed to passenger traffic with effect from Monday 1st July, 1957.

The British Railways era was also to see the rundown and eventual closure of the Great Central Railway as a through route. Planned as a result of Victorian competitive capitalism, there was no place for the Marylebone to Sheffield line in a unified transport system, and the GCR route was soon divided up between different British Railways regions. In April 1950, the Western Region (WR) assumed control of the extreme southern end of the line from Marylebone to Harrow-on-the-Hill, together with the connecting line to the Great Western & Great Central Joint Line at Northolt Junction. North of Rickmansworth, the former GCR route became London Midland Region (LMR) property. These transfers were for commercial and administrative purposes only and did not generally affect operating, train and traffic working which remained with the Eastern Region under the 'penetrating lines' arrangement. All trains from Marylebone were worked by the Eastern Region. The line between Harrow and Rickmansworth was owned by the London Transport Executive which continued to run trains to Aylesbury from Baker Street.

In an effort to lose 'penetrating lines', on 1st February, 1958 Marylebone to Harrow and Neasden South to Northolt Jn East passed to the LMR, together with train operation, and this, it could be said, heralded the final demise of the GCR line as a through route between London and the North of England. London Transport's interest in the route's services was cut-back to Amersham in 1961 following electrification between Rickmansworth and Amersham/Chesham.

Post-War Train Services

The rundown of the Great Central main line meant that, over the years, the number of GCR line trains using the GW&GC route was further reduced. One bright spot, however, was the routeing of the 'Master Cutler' via High Wycombe. The 'Master Cutler' was one of only two named trains to run on the Great Central route. Introduced on 6th October, 1947, this heavy, 11-coach express left Marylebone at 6.15 pm and arrived in Sheffield at 10.02 pm. By 1956, the departure time had been put back to 6.18 pm on weekdays, while the arrival time was put forward to 9.58 pm. In the southbound direction, the balancing up service left Sheffield Victoria at 7.50 am, and arrived in Marylebone at 11.24 am.

The 'Master Cutler' was the lineal descendant of the pre-war 6.20 pm service from Marylebone to Bradford which, as we have seen, had been worked for many years by a Robinson Atlantic. It was fitting, therefore, that in early British Railways days the 'Master Cutler' was normally headed by another famous LNER locomotive type

'Castle' class 4-6-0 No. 5012 *Berry Pomeroy Castle* enters West Ruislip with an Oxford to Paddington service on 24th July, 1958.   *H.C. Casserley*

'Hall' class 4-6-0 No. 4994 *Downton Hall* passes Beaconsfield with the 6.08 pm (Fridays only) Paddington-West Midlands relief on 24th July, 1959.   *Brian W. Leslie*

in the shape of the Gresley 'A3' Pacifics. Gresley 4-6-2s had first appeared on the Great Central line prior to World War II, but they returned to the Great Northern line around 1943, and did not reappear on the GCR section until 1949, when six 'A3s' were sent to Leicester and three more were allocated to Neasden for use on main line passenger services.

In retrospect, the 1950s saw the Great Western & Great Central Joint Line at its peak. Although, as a result of the war, timings were slower than they had been in the 1920s and 1930s, the BR policy of naming certain prestige expresses added a certain glamour to the route; while the Eastern Region could boast of its 'Master Cutler' service, the Great Western Flag was kept flying by not one but two named trains between Paddington and the Midlands.

The crack Western Region train of the period was the 'Inter-City', which left Paddington at 7.13 am, enabling businessmen to travel to the Midlands at a civilised time, and spend the whole day in Birmingham or Wolverhampton. In the reverse direction, the train left Wolverhampton Low Level at 4.35 pm and, stopping at Birmingham Snow Hill, Leamington Spa and High Wycombe, it reached Paddington at 7.13 pm. This restaurant car express service was introduced on 25th September, 1950, and it ran on Mondays to Fridays only.

The second Western Region named train of the 1950s and 1960s was the 'Cambrian Coast Express', which had been revived as a daily working in June 1951. The Cambrian Coast ran every weekday between Paddington, Birmingham Snow Hill, Wolverhampton Low Level, Shrewsbury, Aberdovey, Barmouth, Pwllheli and Aberystwyth. In June 1962, the up working departed from Aberystwyth at 9.45 am and arrived in Paddington at 4.15 pm, while the balancing down service was booked to leave Paddington at 11.10 am. The train ran non-stop over the 'New Line', the 67½ mile journey between Paddington and Banbury being accomplished in 80 minutes in each direction.

Like other Western Region named trains of the period, the 'Inter-City' and the 'Cambrian Coast Express' were both composed of British Railways Mk I stock in the re-introduced GWR chocolate and cream livery. The usual motive power on these prestigious services was a spotless 'King' or 'Castle' class 4-6-0, Nos. 6004 *King William III* and 6014 *King Henry VIII* being among the regular performers.

The local services provided in the early British Railways era were solidly Marylebone-based. There were, in general, 30 or so workings each way on weekdays; the 1956 timetable, for example, provided 34 up and 34 down workings. Twenty-two of these started or terminated at High Wycombe, but some trains worked through to Princes Risborough, or Aylesbury, and a few services continued northwards to such diverse destinations as Haddenham, Brackley and Woodford Halse.

Advertised Western Region outer suburban through trains were by this time confined to a handful of long distance workings. These included the 7.43 am up service from Aylesbury to Paddington via Maidenhead and the 11.30 am Oxford to Paddington working, together with a number of down services from Paddington to Bicester, Aylesbury or Princes Risborough.

There were, in addition, several shorter-distance Western Region local services covering the branches and sections of the main line. It was, in consequence still possible to travel from Paddington to Princes Risborough or Aylesbury by travelling outwards via the Old Line to Maidenhead, and then catching a High Wycombe branch train; with luck, this would continue northwards over the main line to one's destination! On the other hand, travellers hoping to reach Thame, Oxford, or other destinations beyond Princes Risborough, were normally faced with an intermediate change.

Table 13   MARYLEBONE, PADDINGTON, WEST RUISLIP, HIGH WYCOMBE, PRINCES RISBOROUGH and AYLESBURY

Week Days

Miles from Marylebone	Miles from Paddington	Station	am 2	am 2 S	am 2	am E	am 2	am 2 S	am 2	am B	am 2	am 2	am 2	am R	am 2	am 2	am E	am 2	am R	am 2	am E	am A	noon 2	pm 2 R	pm 2 S	pm 2 E	pm 2 E S
		Marylebone dep	3 45	5 20	5 50	6	6 30	7 07	7 30	7 47	8 15	8 39	9 10	9 20	10 0	10 20	10 28	11 20	11 55	12 0	12 15	12 20	12 20	12 24
4¾	6	Wembley Hill			5 55	6	6 307	07			8 6													
8½		**Paddington** dep																						
	8¼	Sudbury and Harrow Road	5 37		6	6 21				8 28													
9¾		Sudbury Hill, Harrow	5 40		6 5	6 26				8 35													
11¼	10¼	Northolt Park	5 44		6 16	6 30																	
12½	10¾	South Ruislip ¶	5 46		6 21	6 37																	
12¾	12¼	Ruislip Gardens ¶	5 50		6 296	6 296				8 46	9 17												
14		West Ruislip ¶	5 55		6 35	6 43																	
14¾		Denham	6		6 42	6 51		7 53								10 48							
15½		Denham Golf Club	6 4		6 46	6 58		8 0															
17		Gerrards Cross	6 9		6 52	7 4	7 20	8 6															
18¼		Seer Green and Jordans	6 13		6 57			8 11								11 6							
21¼		Beaconsfield	6 17		7	7 17		8 16															
23	20¼	**High Wycombe** arr	6 23		7 7	7 26		8 27															
		dep	6 27		7 20	7 30		8 28		9 22													
27¾	26¼	West Wycombe					7 31			9 35													
30	28¾	Saunderton						8 39															
32¼	31¾	**Princes Risborough** C arr			7 30																		
		dep	7 44 59											9 44 9 45									
34¼	34¾	Monks Risborough C									9 50 9 58											
37¼	37¾	Little Kimble									10 1 10 8											
38½	41¼	South Aylesbury Halt									10 10											
43¼	42	**Aylesbury (Town)** arr									10 18											

Via Woodford Halse (arr 6 3 am) — *Via Harrow on the Hill To Woodford Halse*

To Haddenham (arr 7 45 am) · *Via Harrow on the Hill To Leicester (arr 11 45 am)* · *To Oxford (arr 10 37 am)* · *To Birkenhead (arr 2 55 pm)* · *To Banbury General (arr 11E44, 11S31 am)* · *Via Harrow on the Hill To Oxford (arr 12E22, 12S25 pm)* · *Via Harrow on the Hill To Manchester (arr 3E8, 3S14 pm)* · *Via Harrow on the Hill To Brackley (arr 12 35 pm)* · *To Nottingham (arr 3 3 pm)* · *To Manchester (arr 5E39, 5S44 pm)* · *To Banbury (arr 3 3 pm)* · *Via Harrow on the Hill To Brackley (arr 2 25 pm)*

Week Days—continued

Station	pm 2 E S	pm 2	pm 2 E S	pm 2 S	pm 2 E	pm B	pm 2 2 2	pm S	pm E	pm 2 R	pm 2	pm 2 2 2	pm 2 2 S	pm 2	pm 2	pm R	pm 2	pm 2	pm 2 S	pm 2 S	pm 2 E	pm E	pm 2 S
Marylebone dep	1 228	12 30	1245	2	2 20	2 20	2 36	2 39	2 42	2 43	3 01	3 23 3 23 3 48	3625	4 10	4 34	4 504	4 55	5 05	5 135	5 24	5 30 5 34	6 44
Wembley Hill			1241																			
Paddington dep								2 55					3G25									
Sudbury and Harrow Road			1245				3 40													5 30		
Sudbury Hill, Harrow			1248				3 43													5 34		
Northolt Park			1251																			
South Ruislip ¶			1255																			
Ruislip Gardens ¶			1257																			
West Ruislip ¶			1 0																			
Denham																						
Denham Golf Club																						
Gerrards Cross																						
Seer Green and Jordans																						
Beaconsfield																						
High Wycombe arr																						
dep				2 26						2 543					5c12		6 17					
West Wycombe					2 29																	
Saunderton																						
Princes Risborough C arr																						
dep																						
Monks Risborough C																						
Little Kimble																						
South Aylesbury Halt																						
Aylesbury (Town) arr	2		1212	2	2 16											5 47		6	6 106	6 35		6 44

Via Harrow on the Hill · *Via Maidenhead* · *Via Harrow on the Hill To Woodford Halse (arr 4 13 pm)* · *Via Harrow on the Hill To Woodford Halse (arr 4 38 pm)* · *Via Harrow on the Hill To Sheffield (arr 6 47 pm)* · *Via Harrow on the Hill To Manchester (arr 8E22, 8S51 pm)* · *Via Harrow on the Hill To Quinton Road (arr 5 32 pm)* · *To Bicester (arr 6 1 pm)* · *To Brackley (arr 7 7 pm)* · *To Bradford (arr 10 17 pm)* · *Via Harrow on the Hill To Woodford Halse (arr 7 19 pm)* · *Via Harrow on the Hill* · *Via Harrow on the Hill To Quinton Road (arr 7 0 pm)*

Through Trains from Marylebone or Paddington except where otherwise shown
For Notes, see page 217

Passenger timetable, Marylebone to Aylesbury, 1956.

Table 13—continued MARYLEBONE, PADDINGTON, WEST RUISLIP, HIGH WYCOMBE, PRINCES RISBOROUGH and AYLESBURY

Week Days—continued

Station																							
Marylebone ... dep																							
Paddington ... "	5 29																						
Wembley Hill ... "																							
Sudbury and Harrow Road ... "																							
Sudbury Hill, Harrow ... "	5 46																						
Northolt Park ... "																							
South Ruislip ¶ ... "																							
Ruislip Gardens ¶ ... "	5 54																						
West Ruislip ¶ ... "	5 59																						
Denham ... "	6 5																						
Denham Golf Club ... "																							
Gerrards Cross ... "	6 13																						
Seer Green and Jordans ... "																							
Beaconsfield ... "	6 23																						
High Wycombe { arr	6 34																						
High Wycombe { dep																							
West Wycombe ... "																							
Saunderton ... "																							
Princes Risborough C { arr	6 50																						
Princes Risborough C { dep	6 54																						
Monks Risborough C ... "	6 58																						
Little Kimble ... "	7 5																						
South Aylesbury Halt ... "	7 8																						
Aylesbury (Town) ... arr																							

Sundays—continued

Station																			
Marylebone ... dep																			
Paddington ... "																			
Wembley Hill ... "																			
Sudbury and Harrow Road ... "																			
Sudbury Hill, Harrow ... "																			
Northolt Park ... "																			
South Ruislip ¶ ... "																			
Ruislip Gardens ¶ ... "																			
West Ruislip ¶ ... "																			
Denham ... "																			
Denham Golf Club ... "																			
Gerrards Cross ... "																			
Seer Green and Jordans ... "																			
Beaconsfield ... "																			
High Wycombe { arr																			
High Wycombe { dep																			
West Wycombe ... "																			
Saunderton ... "																			
Princes Risborough C ... "																			
Monks Risborough C ... "																			
Little Kimble ... "																			
South Aylesbury Halt ... "																			
Aylesbury (Town) ... arr																			

A Saturdays only. Not after 1st September
B Saturdays only. Commences 30th June
B Arr 4 minutes *earlier* (7 minutes *earlier* on Saturdays)
C Monks Risborough and Whiteleaf Halt
c Arr 3 minutes *earlier*
D Change at Maidenhead and High Wycombe
d Arr 4 minutes *earlier*
E or E Except Saturdays
F Arr 6 minutes *earlier*
G Change at Maidenhead
H 8 minutes *earlier*
K On 9th and 16th September, runs
N Arrives 3 minutes later on Saturdays
R Refreshment Car
S or S Saturdays only
U Saturday nights only
ᵈ Second class only
‡ Arrival by Slip Carriage
§ Second class only except on Saturdays

Through Trains from Marylebone or Paddington except where otherwise shown

¶ A frequent service of London Transport trains operates between the Central Line and Greenford (change from Paddington & Ealing (Broadway)) and these stations

Via Harrow on the Hill To Nottingham (arr 12 37 pm)
To Brackley (arr 7 26 am)
Via Harrow on the Hill To Sheffield (arr 5 18 am)
Via Harrow on the Hill To Manchester (arr 4 0 am)
Via Harrow on the Hill To Manchester (arr 3 53 am)
Via Harrow on the Hill To Brackley (arr 11 45 pm)
Via Harrow on the Hill
To Princes Risboro' (arr 8 14 pm)
From Marylebone (dep 6 50 pm)
To Brackley (arr 8 23 pm)
Via Harrow on the Hill To Woodford Halse (arr 8 31 pm)
Via Harrow on the Hill To Woodford Halse (arr 8 31 pm)
Via Harrow on the Hill To Nottingham (arr 12 56 pm)
Via Harrow on the Hill To Manchester (arr 3K39 pm)
To Woodford Halse (arr 1 31 pm)
To Brackley (arr 7 18 pm)
Via Harrow on the Hill To Manchester (arr 9 31 pm)
Via Harrow on the Hill To Woodford Halse (arr 8 59 pm)
Via Harrow on the Hill To Nottingham (arr 11 25 pm)
Via Harrow on the Hill To Nottingham (arr 2 25 am)

Passenger timetable, Marylebone to Aylesbury, 1956.

Table 13—*continued* AYLESBURY, PRINCES RISBOROUGH, HIGH WYCOMBE, WEST RUISLIP, PADDINGTON and MARYLEBONE

Week Days

Miles		am 2 E	am 2 S	am 2 E	am 2	am 2	am 2	am 2	am 2 E	am 2 S	am 2	am 2 E	am	am 2 E	am 2	am 2 E	am 2 S	am
—	**Aylesbury (Town)** dep	..	..	..	..	..	..	6 58	..	..	7 18	..	7 30	..	7 39	..	..	7 43
¾	South Aylesbury Halt	..	..	..	..	..	..	..	..	..	..	..	Via Harrow on the Hill From Woodford Halse (dep 6 23 am)	..	Via Harrow on the Hill	..	..	7 46
4½	Little Kimble	..	..	..	..	..	..	7 7	..	..	7 27	..		..		..	..	7 54
6	Monks Risborough C	..	..	..	..	..	..	7 11	..	..	7 31	..		..		..	..	7 58
7½	**Princes Risborough**	..	..	..	..	..	..	7c18	..	..	7 35	7 40		..		..	..	8c 5
10½	Saunderton	..	..	..	..	..	..	7 25	..	..	..	7 47		..		..	..	8 12
13¼	West Wycombe	..	..	..	..	..	..	7 30	..	..	..	..		..		..	..	8 17
15½	**High Wycombe** arr	..	..	..	..	..	..	7 34	..	..	..	7 54		..		..	..	8 22
	High Wycombe dep	5 55	6 15	6 25	6 48	7 15	7 23	7 36	7 44	7 44	..	7 58		8 8		8 16	8 16	8 24
20¼	Beaconsfield	6 3	6 23	6 33	6 56	7 23	7 31	7 44	7 52	7 52	..	..		8 16		8 24	8 24	Via Maidenhead
21¾	Seer Green and Jordans	6 7	6 27	6 37	7 0	..	7 35	..	7 56	7 56	..	8 8		..		8 28	8 28	
24½	Gerrards Cross	6 13	6 33	6 43	7 6	7 31	7 41	7 52	8 2	8 2	..	8 14		8 24		8 34	8 34	
26¼	Denham Golf Club	6 17	6 37	6 47	7 10	..	7 45	7 56	..	8 6	..	..		..		8 38	8 38	
27¼	Denham	6 20	6 40	6 50	7 13	7 36	7 48	7 59	..	8 9	..	8 19		..		..	..	
30	West Ruislip ¶	6 25	6 45	6 55	7 18	7 41	..	8 4	8 11	8 14	..	..		8 32		..	8 44	
31¼	Ruislip Gardens ¶	6 28	6 48	6 58	7 21	..	..	8 7	..	8 17	..	..		..		..	..	
31¾	South Ruislip ¶	6 31	6 51	7 1	7 24	..	7 56	..	8 15	8 20	..	..		..		..	..	
33½	Northolt Park	6 35	6 55	7 5	7 28	..	8 0	..	8 19	8 24	..	..		..		..	..	
34½	Sudbury Hill, Harrow	6 38	6 58	7 8	7 31	7 50	8 3	..	8 22	8 27	..	..		..		..	..	
35¼	Sudbury and Harrow Road	6 41	7 1	7 11	7 34	..	8 6	..	8 25	8 30	..	..		..		..	..	
36¾	Wembley Hill	6 45	7 5	7 15	7 38	..	8 10	8 17	..	8 34	..	..		..		..	..	
42	**Paddington** arr	..	..	..	..	..	..	..	..	..	..	..		..		..	..	9 34
43¼	**Marylebone** „	6 59	7 19	7 29	7 52	8 10	8 24	8 31	8 41	8 47	..	8 46	8 51	8 55	9 0	9 5	9 7	..

Miles		am 2	am 2 E	am 2	am 2 E	am	am 2	am 2	am 2	am	am S	am E	am	am 2	am 2	am 2	am 2
—	**Aylesbury (Town)** dep	7A56	..	..	..	8 44	..	..	8 55	..	9 38	9 44	..	..	..	1045	1050
¾	South Aylesbury Halt	Via Harrow on the Hill	..	..	..	Via Harrow on the Hill From Woodford Halse (dep 7 40 am)	..	..	8 57	..	Via Harrow on the Hill From Nottingham (dep 6 0 am)	Via Harrow on the Hill From Nottingham (dep 6 20 am)	..	..	..	Via Harrow on the Hill	1052
4½	Little Kimble		..	..	..		..	..	9 5	..			..	..	..		11 0
6	Monks Risborough C		..	..	..		..	..	9 9	..			..	..	..		11 4
7½	**Princes Risborough**		8 16	..	..		8 50	9 4	9 13	9 16			9D39	..	..		11 8
10½	Saunderton		8 23	..	..		8 57	From Banbury (dep 7 45 am)	..	From Wolverhampton (dep 6 45 am)			9D46	..	..		..
13¼	West Wycombe		..	..	..		9 2		..				9D51	..	..		..
15½	**High Wycombe** arr		8 30	..	..		9 6	9 18	..				9D55	..	..		..
	High Wycombe dep		8 33	8 40	8 55		9 10	..	..				..	10 5	11 10		..
20¼	Beaconsfield		8 41	8 48	9 3		9 18	..	..				..	1013	11 18		..
21¾	Seer Green and Jordans		..	8 52	9 7		9 22	..	..				..	1017	11 22		..
24½	Gerrards Cross		8 49	8 58	9 13		9 28	..	..				..	1023	11 28		..
26¼	Denham Golf Club		..	9 2	9 17		9 32	..	..				..	1027	11 32		..
27¼	Denham		..	9 5	9 20		9 35	..	..				..	1030	11 35		..
30	West Ruislip ¶		..	9 10	9 25		9 40	..	..				..	1035	11 40		..
31¼	Ruislip Gardens ¶		..	..	..		From Haddenham (dep 8 35 am)	..	..				..	..	..		..
31¾	South Ruislip ¶		..	9 14	..		..	..	..				..	..	..		..
33½	Northolt Park		..	9 18	..		..	..	..				..	..	..		..
34½	Sudbury Hill, Harrow		..	9 21	..		..	..	..				..	..	..		..
35¼	Sudbury and Harrow Road		..	9 24	..		..	..	..				..	..	..		..
36¾	Wembley Hill		..	..	..		..	..	..				..	..	..		..
42	**Paddington** arr		..	..	..		..	..	..	10 5			..	..	..		..
43¼	**Marylebone** „	9A13	9 17	9 40	9 48	9 52	10 2	..	..	..	1046	1050	..	1057	12 3	12 9	..

Week Days—*continued*

	pm 2	pm 2 S	am 2 E	pm 2 S	pm 2 S	pm	pm R E	pm R S	pm 2 E	pm 2 E	pm 2 S	pm 2 S	pm 2 S	pm 2 E	pm 2 E	pm 2 S	pm 2 S	pm 2 E
Aylesbury (Town) dep	..	..	1155	..	12 5	..	1249	1 2	..	..	..	..	..	1 25	..	1 25	..	1 41
South Aylesbury Halt	..	..	..	..	..	..	Via Harrow on the Hill From Manchester (dep 8 30 am)	Via Harrow on the Hill From Manchester (dep 8 30 am)	..	..	..	..	..	1 27	..	1 27	..	Via Harrow on the Hill From Brackley (dep 1 0 pm)
Little Kimble	..	..	12 4	..	1214	..			..	..	..	..	..	1 35	..	1 35	..	
Monks Risborough C	..	..	12 8	..	1218	..			..	..	..	..	..	1 39	..	1 39	..	
Princes Risborough	..	..	1213	..	1222	1230			1245	..	1255	..	..	1 45	..	1 43	2 0	
Saunderton	..	..	..	..	..	From Oxford (dep 11·30 am Calls at Greenford 1 17 pm)			1252	..	1 2	..	..	1 52	..	..	..	
West Wycombe	..	..	..	..	..				1257	..	1 7	..	..	1 57	..	..	..	
High Wycombe arr	..	..	1227	..	..	1243			1 1	..	1 11	..	..	2 1	..	..	2 13	
High Wycombe dep	1210	..	..	1230	..	1246			..	1 10	1 15	..	..	..	2 10	..	2 15	
Beaconsfield	1218	..	..	1238	..	..			..	1 18	1 23	..	..	..	2 18	..	2 23	
Seer Green and Jordans	1222	..	..	1242	..	..			..	1 22	1 27	..	..	..	2 22	..	2 27	
Gerrards Cross	1228	..	..	1248	..	..			..	1 28	1 33	..	..	..	2 28	..	2 33	
Denham Golf Club	1232	..	..	1252	..	..			..	1 32	1 37	..	..	..	2 32	..	2 37	
Denham	1235	..	..	1255	..	..			..	1 35	1 40	..	..	..	2 35	..	2 40	
West Ruislip ¶	1240	1250	..	1 0	..	1 7			..	1 40	1 45	1 50	2 20	..	2 40	..	2 45	
Ruislip Gardens ¶	..	1253	..	1 3	..	..			..	..	..	1 53	2 23	..	..	..	..	
South Ruislip ¶	..	1256	..	1 6	..	..			..	..	..	1 56	2 26	..	..	..	..	
Northolt Park	..	1 0	..	1 10	..	..			..	..	..	2 0	2 30	..	..	..	..	
Sudbury Hill, Harrow	..	1 3	..	1 13	..	..	..	..	..	..	..	2 3	2 33	..	..	..	..	..
Sudbury and Harrow Road	..	1 6	..	1 16	..	..	..	..	..	..	..	2 6	2 36	..	..	..	..	..
Wembley Hill	..	1 10	..	1 20	..	..	..	..	..	..	..	2 10	2 40	..	..	..	..	..
Paddington arr	..	..	..	..	..	1 32	..	..	..	..	..	..	..	..	..	..	..	..
Marylebone „	1 2	1 24	..	1 34	..	..	1 40	1 54	..	2 2	2 7	2 25	2 55	..	3 3	..	3 8	3 8

	pm 2 S	pm 2 S	pm R	pm 2 E	pm 2 E	pm 2 S	pm 2 E	pm E	pm S	pm 2 S	pm 2	pm	pm 2 E	pm 2	pm	pm E	pm
Aylesbury (Town) dep	2 3	2 22	2 37	..	2 45	..	3 15	..	3 20	3 37	..	..	..	..	4 42	4 46	..
South Aylesbury Halt	Via Harrow on the Hill From Brackley (dep 1 15 pm)	..	Via Harrow on the Hill From Bradford (dep 10 0 am)	..	Via Harrow on the Hill	..	3 17	..	3 22	Via Harrow on the Hill From Brackley (dep 2 52 pm)	..	..	..	..	4 45	Via Harrow on the Hill From Nottingham (dep 1 15 pm)	..
Little Kimble		2 31		..		..	3 25	..	3 30		..	..	..	..	4 52		..
Monks Risborough C		2 35		..		..	3 29	..	3 34		..	..	..	..	4 56		..
Princes Risborough		2 39		..		2 55	3 33	3 48	3e48		..	..	..	..	5 2		..
Saunderton		..		..		3 2	..	3 55	3 55		..	..	..	..	5 9		..
West Wycombe		..		..		3 7	..	4 0	4 0		..	..	..	..	5 14		..
High Wycombe arr		..		..		3 11	..	4 4	4 4		..	..	..	..	5 18		..
High Wycombe dep		..		3 10		3 15	..	..	..		4 10	4 15	4 30	5 10	..		5 33
Beaconsfield		..		3 18		3 23	..	..	..		4 18	..	4 38	5 18	..		..
Seer Green and Jordans		..		3 22		3 27	..	..	..		4 22	..	4 42	5 22	..		..
Gerrards Cross		..		3 28		3 33	..	..	..		4 28	..	4 48	5 28	..		..
Denham Golf Club		..		3 32		3 37	..	..	..		4 32	..	4 52	5 32	..		..
Denham		..		3 35		3 40	..	..	..		4 35	..	5 5	5 35	..		..
West Ruislip ¶		..		3 40		3 45	..	..	..		4 40	..	5 10	5 40	..		..
Ruislip Gardens ¶		..		..		..	..	..	..		..	..	5 13	..	..		..
South Ruislip ¶		..		..		..	..	..	..		..	..	5 16	..	..		..
Northolt Park		..		..		..	..	..	..		..	..	5 20	..	..		..
Sudbury Hill, Harrow		..		..		..	..	..	..		..	..	5 23	..	..		..
Sudbury and Harrow Road		..		..		..	..	..	..		..	..	5 26	..	..		..
Wembley Hill		..		..		..	..	..	..		..	..	5 31	..	..		..
Paddington arr		..		..		..	..	..	..		..	5B30	..	..	..		7B 3
Marylebone „	3 24	..	3 29	4 3	4 7	4 10	..	..	..	4 59	5 3	..	5 46	6 3	..	6 25	..

Through Trains to Paddington or Marylebone except where otherwise shown

For Notes, see page 219

Passenger timetable, Aylesbury to Marylebone, 1956.

Table 13—continued AYLESBURY, PRINCES RISBOROUGH, HIGH WYCOMBE, WEST RUISLIP, PADDINGTON and MARYLEBONE

Week Days—continued

Sundays

Station list (left column):

Aylesbury (Town) — — — dep
South Aylesbury Halt ....
Little Kimble ....
Monks Risborough C. ....
Princes Risborough ....
Saunderton ....
West Wycombe ....
High Wycombe — — — { arr
{ dep
Beaconsfield ....
Seer Green and Jordans ....
Gerrards Cross ....
Denham Golf Club ....
Denham ....
West Ruislip ¶ ....
Ruislip Gardens ¶ ....
South Ruislip ¶ ....
Northolt Park ....
Sudbury Hill, Harrow ....
Sudbury and Harrow Road ....
Wembley Hill ....
Paddington — — — arr
Marylebone — — — " "

Notes / legend:

A On Saturdays runs 9 minutes later
B Change at Maidenhead
C Monks Risborough and Whiteleaf Halt
c Arr 3 minutes earlier
D On Saturdays runs 4 minutes earlier
E or E Except Saturdays
e Arr 10 minutes earlier
F Fridays and Saturdays only
F On Saturdays arrives Marylebone 9 24 pm
K Arr 6 43 pm
k Arrive 8 minutes earlier
R Refreshment Car
S or S Saturdays only
Z Except Fridays and Saturdays
Ⓠ Second class only
¶ A frequent service of London Transport trains operates between these stations and Greenford (change for Ealing (Broadway) and Paddington) and the Central Line

Through Trains to Paddington or Marylebone except where otherwise shown

Passenger timetable, Aylesbury to Marylebone, 1956.

'B1' class 4-6-0 No. 61187 leaves Seer Green with the 11.20 am Marylebone-Woodford Halse train on 18th March, 1956.   *Brian W. Leslie*

'L1' class 2-6-4T No. 67747 leaves Beaconsfield with the 12.20 pm High Wycombe to Marylebone service on 18th May, 1958.   *Brian W. Leslie*

Motive Power in the British Railways Era

Youthful 'spotters' could always be sure of seeing plenty of engines on the Joint Line. Besides the usual ex-Great Western 4-6-0, 2-6-2T and 0-6-0PT classes, the Eastern Region locals and through workings yielded considerable variety in the shape of 'A3' class 4-6-2s, 'A5' class 4-6-2Ts, 'B1' class 4-6-0s, and 'L1' class 2-6-4Ts. The highlight of the day, however, would come at approximately 6.45 pm, when, somewhere in the quiet Buckinghamshire countryside, the 'King'-hauled 'Inter-City' express and its long train of chocolate and cream coaches would thunder past the maroon and cream-liveried 'A3'-headed 'Master Cutler' at a combined speed of around 150 miles per hour!

In 1950, Neasden's allocation of 'A3' Pacifics comprised Nos. 60050 *Persimmon*, 60051 *Blink Bonney* and 60111 *Enterprise*, while Nos. 60048 *Doncaster*, 60049 *Galtee More*, 60052 *Prince Palatine*, 60054 *Prince of Wales*, 60102 *Sir Frederick Banbury*, 60103 *Flying Scotsman*, 60104 *Solario* and 60107 *Royal Lancer* were shedded at Leicester for use on the GCR main line. These locomotives were among those seen on the GW&GC route during the 1950s, while other large engines employed on Great Central main line services at that time included 'V2' class 2-6-2s such as Nos. 60831, 60842, 60862, 60863, 60879 and 60911.

Although many Great Central main line engines had survived long enough to become British Railways locomotives, most of these were withdrawn from service in the next few months. The last 'Lord Faringdon' 4-6-0, for example, was withdrawn in April 1949, while the last 'Immingham' class mixed traffic 4-6-0 was taken out of service in November 1950; that same year saw the demise of the Robinson Atlantics, which had spent their final years on undemanding duties in Lincolnshire. There was consolation for locomotive enthusiasts, however, in the form of new locomotives such as the Thompson 'B1' class 4-6-0s and the 'L1' class 2-6-4Ts.

The numerically-strong 'B1' class had been developed during World War II as an efficient, standard design for general purpose work all over the LNER system. They soon appeared on the GW&GC route, sometimes replacing 'A3' Pacifics on important services such as the 'Master Cutler', and eventually taking over most long distance passenger workings on the former Great Central system. Numerous examples turned up on the GW&GC route at various times, including Nos. 61088, 61092, 61136, 61154, 61185, 61187, 61188 and 61299.

The Western Region services that ran between Paddington and Oxford via High Wycombe and Princes Risborough were sometimes worked by 'Hall' class 4-6-0s, but in general the familiar '61XX' class 2-6-2Ts remained the predominant locomotive type on secondary services to and from Paddington. The Marylebone services, in contrast, were hauled by the remaining 'A5' class 4-6-2Ts such as Nos. 69805, 69822, 69827, 69828 and 69829 - all of which were shedded at Neasden in 1950 - or by more modern 'L1' class 2-6-4Ts.

The latter engines, designed by Edward Thompson and introduced in 1945, soon became virtually the standard form of motive power on the Marylebone suburban routes, Neasden having a large allocation of around 38 engines by the early 1950s.

From the locomotive enthusiast's point of view, the transfer of control to the London Midland Region was significant, insofar as it brought new types of motive power onto the GW&GC line. Whereas, before 1958, LNER motive power had been the rule, after 1958 LMS types appeared. Marylebone locals passed into the hands of Fowler, Fairburn, Stanier or BR 2-6-4Ts, while, on the few main line trains left, one could see Stanier class '5MT' 4-6-0s, which had taken over many Great Central main

Right: 'Manor' class 4-6-0 No. 7821 *Ditcheat Manor* with a down freight near Beaconsfield on 12th March, 1955.
Brian W. Leslie

Below: BR Standard class '4MT' 2-6-4T No. 80142 arrives at High Wycombe with the 1.03 pm Princes Risborough-Marylebone service on 4th August, 1957.
Brian W. Leslie

Fairburn class '4MT' 2-6-4T No. 42291 stands in Platform Two at High Wycombe on 19th April, 1960 while working the 7.10 pm up service to Marylebone.   *H.B. Priestley*

line services by the early 1960s. Few GCR main line trains now used the GW&GC Joint Line, and those that did tended to be car sleepers, summer Saturday through trains to the South Coast, or other specialised workings - none of which called to pick up or set down *en route*.

A summary of some of the locomotive classes known to have worked over the Great Western & Great Central Joint Line is given in an Appendix. It should be stressed that the list is by no means exhaustive, and numerous other types worked over the line on various occasions.

Dieselisation of the GW&GC Joint Line

The early 1960s saw the appearance of the first diesels on the route, led by the Western Region's de-luxe 'Blue Pullman' diesel-electric multiple units. Built by Metropolitan-Cammell, and introduced in 1960, these streamlined Pullman trains can be seen, perhaps, as forerunners of today's High Speed Train (HST) sets. The Western Region was allocated two eight-car Pullman formations, and used one set between Paddington and Birmingham Snow Hill and the other on the Bristol main line.

The power cars at each end of the trains contained 1,000 horse power, 12-cylinder diesel engines, giving a total power output of 2,000 bhp. The diesels drove GEC generators, designed to supply traction current at between 1,250 and 1,700 amperes, and there were also auxiliary generators for lighting, heating, refrigeration and air conditioning purposes. Each eight-car set could accommodate 108 first class and 120 second class passengers, who were expected to book their seats in advance on these all-Pullman formations. Externally, the new trains sported an unusual 'Nanking blue' livery, with grey roofs and a broad white band at window level.

A down Blue Pullman service speeds northwards along the GW&GC route near West Ruislip in June 1966.   *C.R.L. Coles/Rail Archive Stephenson*

A Derby four-car (later class '115') unit emerges from Whitehouse Farm tunnel while working the 12.20 pm Marylebone to Princes Risborough service on 30th December, 1963.

Brian Stephenson

Brush type '2' (later class '31') A1A-A1A No. D5692 approaches West Ruislip with a passenger service during the early 1960s.   *C.R.L. Coles/Rail Archive Stephenson*

Unlike the later HST sets, the 'Blue Pullmans' had limited seating accommodation in the power cars, and travellers at the extreme end of the trains were therefore subjected to a certain amount of oscillation and engine noise. This was, however, a minor point, and did nothing to detract from the general luxury and superb hill-climbing capabilities of these distinctive units. The top speed was nominally 90 miles per hour.

The Birmingham Pullman formed two daily workings; leaving Wolverhampton Low Level at 7.00 am, the first up train arrived at Paddington at 9.35 am (later 9.30 am). At 10.10 am (originally 12.10 pm) it made an out and back run to Birmingham Snow Hill, returning at 2.55 pm. Finally, at 4.50 pm, it set off back to Wolverhampton. The Pullman ran non-stop between Paddington and Leamington for the first few years, but the mid-morning service later called at High Wycombe. High speed running was the norm; 80 mph was common up Denham bank, and then, after High Wycombe, the train would streak down off the Chilterns at speeds of up to 100 miles an hour.

With the mighty 'Kings' still handling the heaviest trains to Birmingham, and the 'Blue Pullmans' adding a new prestige to the route, the early 1960s were one of the most exciting periods in the GW&GC Joint Line's history. Local services were still steam-hauled, but the diesel invasion was soon to start with a vengeance. The first British Railways diesel multiple unit (dmu) train appeared on the line in January 1961, and thereafter more were delivered, until in June 1962, with the start of the new timetables, local services to and from the Joint Line out of Marylebone were fully dieselised.

The opportunity was taken to recast the entire local service on the route, and the new timetable provided a basic hourly service, with numerous additional trains

'Warship' class diesel-hydraulic Bo-Bo No. D817 *Foxhound* heads southwards through High Wycombe with the 7.30 am Shrewsbury to Paddington service on 31st August, 1962.

H.K. Harman/Rail Archive Stephenson

'Western' class (later class '52') Co-Co diesel-hydraulic No. D1064 *Western Regent* passes West Wycombe with a southbound train of oil empties from Thame. West Wycombe church, with its famous 'golden ball' can be discerned in the distance.   *Brian Stephenson*

during peak hours. As before, some trains terminated at High Wycombe, others at Princes Risborough or Aylesbury. Basic journey time was: to High Wycombe (27¾ miles) 50 minutes; Princes Risborough (36 miles) 70 minutes; and Aylesbury via the GW&GC Joint Line (43¼ miles) 90 minutes.

The new multiple units, which were based at Marylebone and operated on the Metropolitan & Great Central Joint Line as well as the GW&GC Joint route, were all four-car sets, built by BR at Derby works. These sets were of a type associated with the London Midland Region (thereby underlining the continued 'joint' nature of the service!), and they were destined to remain in use on the GW&GC route for over 40 years. Each train was composed of a driving motor brake second seating 78, a trailer second seating 106, a trailer composite seating 30 first class and 70 second class passengers, and another driving trailer seating 78.

The total seating capacity of each four-car set was thus 30 first class and 302 second class travellers (or 664 passengers when coupled together to form an eight-car multiple unit). The initial allocation for the combined Marylebone services was 35 trains. Externally, the new vehicles were of traditional appearance, each seating bay having a separate door with traditional grab handles, while the elliptical roofs of the 64 ft vehicles were lined with 'shell' ventilators. Four British United Traction 230 hp diesel engines produced a total of 920 hp, while the maximum speed was 70 miles per hour. The interior decor of the coaches was replete with 1960s plastics and veneers.

When first delivered, the new units were painted in an overall green livery, with yellow lining and yellow 'speed whiskers' at each end; roofs were painted grey with white ends, and underframes and bogies were black. Later, this attractive livery was replaced by overall blue livery with chocolate underframes, though after a few years this somewhat unattractive colour scheme was itself replaced by a blue and off-white livery with black underframes. These Marylebone-based units had, by that time, been designated BR class '115'.

If necessary, the class '115's were permitted to haul 'tail traffic' when working between Marylebone, High Wycombe and Aylesbury, the maximum load being 35 tons for loaded trains and 60 tons for unloaded workings.

Meanwhile, while the London Midland authorities were busy replacing steam on their local services from Marylebone, the Western Region was considering further dieselisation of the Joint line's express passenger trains. The 'Kings', now over 30 years old, were in any case nearing their retirement, and from the September 1962 timetable, they were replaced by newly-built 2,700 horse power 'Western' diesel-hydraulic Co-Cos. The 'Westerns' - later designated class '52' - were designed by BR at Swindon, weighed 108 tons, and had a theoretical tractive effort of 72,600 lb.

The engines were numbered in the D1000-D1073 series, and all 74 locomotives carried the class name 'Western' plus an individual name which, in many cases, harked back to the earliest days of the Great Western broad gauge – examples being *Western Thunderer* and *Western Star*.

The new form of motive power enabled the fastest ever service between Paddington and Birmingham to be put into operation. History was made on the very first day, when the 9.00 am express from Paddington, headed by No. D1038 *Western Sovereign*, arrived at Snow Hill by 10.44 am, having taken only 1¾ hours for the whole trip! In the reverse direction, the first up train, the 8.20 am service from Birmingham, headed by No. D1039 *Western King*, arrived at Paddington two minutes early.

To mark the historic nature of the occasion, the Lord Mayor of Birmingham and the Lady Mayoress travelled on board the train, and were welcomed at Paddington

WD 2-8-0 No. 90448 leaves Whitehouse Farm tunnel with a down empty wagon train on 13th April, 1959. The heavy earthworks and rolling chalk hills are characteristic of this central part of the GW&GC route.   *Brian W. Leslie*

Brush type '4' (later class '47') Co-Co No. D1689 passes through Princes Risborough with a Wembley Cup Final special bound for Wembley Hill on 1st May, 1965. The passengers on board witnessed Liverpool's 2-1 victory over Leeds United.   *Brian Stephenson*

by the General Manager, Mr Stanley Raymond. The press were invited to travel on the inaugural trains, and both the BBC and independent television covered the event.

The new service provided 14 trains each way daily, with eight down and nine up workings booked to perform the journey in two hours or less, with intermediate stops. Two trains, booked to maintain speeds of over 80 miles an hour on fast stretches, were scheduled to reach their destinations in 1 hour and 50 minutes - the fastest timings ever; these were the 2.10 pm from Paddington, and a Mondays-only businessman's train, which left London at 9.00 am. With the Blue Pullmans still running on the line, the advent of the 'Westerns' heralded a glorious 'Indian Summer' on the Great Western & Great Central Joint Line.

The Rundown Begins

Unfortunately, the new form of traction was introduced onto the GW&GC route at a time when government policies and road competition were poised to do irreparable harm to the entire railway industry. In 1962, most people still assumed that the nationalised railway system would be maintained in perpetuity as part of the vital infrastructure of a modern industrial state. Sadly, the ruling political party appeared to view the railways as an expensive anachronism and, from the later 1950s onwards, more and more tax payers' money was directed into massive road building programmes, and away from the cash-starved railway system.

The pace of closure and rationalisation increased after the October 1959 general election, when Ernest Marples was appointed Minister of Transport by Prime Minister Harold Macmillan. Ominously, the new Transport Minister was the founder of a road-building firm known as Marples, Ridegway & Partners, and he was known to be in favour of a programme of grandiose motorway construction schemes as the answer to Britain's transport problems.

Meanwhile, the local railway system was beginning to suffer progressive 'rationalision', Blackthorn station having been closed in June 1953, while West Wycombe was deleted from the BR passenger network in November 1958. Five years later, in January 1963, passenger services were withdrawn from the Oxford to Princes Risborough line, and from most of the intermediate stations between Princes Risborough and Banbury. The closures were with effect from Monday 7th January, 1963, on which date Ilmer and Dorton halts, and Haddenham, Brill & Ludgershall, Ardley and Aynho Park lost their passenger services.

It was, by this time, abundantly clear that the government of the day was simply no longer interested in maintaining the national railway system in anything like its entirety, and in 1963 the publication of a report by Dr Richard Beeching entitled 'The Reshaping of British Railways' sounded the death knell for vast swathes of the railway network. The report recommended the withdrawal of passenger services from around 5,000 miles of line and the closure of 2,363 stations out of a total of 4,709. Local goods yards would be swept away, while competing routes would be eliminated in as many cases as possible so that limited resources could be concentrated on a much-smaller core system.

Railway enthusiasts and local travellers hoped that the election of a Labour government in October 1964 would bring an end to the Beeching closures. It was assumed that the new administration would adopt a more sympathetic attitude towards the problems of transport in rural areas, and to some extent, this was indeed the case, though in retrospect it must be said that Tom Fraser, the new Minister of Transport, made little attempt to halt the closure programme. To the dismay of the railway trade unions, the Labour Minister (a former Scottish miner) consented to the closure of over 800 route miles during his short and decidedly lacklustre term of office.

Matters finally started to improve after Barbara Castle became Minister of Transport on 23rd December, 1965. Although Mrs Castle agreed to the closure of 606 route miles, she claimed that she would concentrate on the 'improvement rather than the reduction of the system', and in 1967 the new Transport Minister presented what appeared to be a blueprint for future railway development. A so-called 'basic railway network' of about 11,000 route miles was envisaged and, notwithstanding the fact that some closures were still contemplated, the Castle Plan was much better than the final Beeching proposals which (if fully implemented) would have reduced the railway system to a pitiful 3,000 route miles.

Ironically, having done much to halt the Beeching closure programme, Mrs Castle implemented the largest closure of all when she agreed to the withdrawal of through passenger services from the Great Central main line between London Marylebone, Leicester Central and Nottingham Victoria. A local service would be retained between Nottingham and Rugby, but a major section of the London Extension would be closed to all traffic between Aylesbury and Rugby Central.

As we have seen the Great Central main line had been deliberately run-down and neglected for several years, and the closure - carried out on Saturday 3rd September, 1966 - was, to many enthusiasts, a thankful release. The Metropolitan & Great Central Joint Line, which, like the GW&GC route, carried a heavy commuter traffic, was excluded from the closure proposals, but the end of the Great Central proper meant the final demise of the Ashendon Junction to Grendon Underwood line.

Once an important link between the Great Western and Great Central systems, the Ashendon Junction to Grendon Underwood route was little-used after 1958, and, by 1966, it carried only one passenger train a week. This working ceased with the closure of the Great Central main line though, amusingly, the Ashendon Junction to Grendon Underwood line remained officially 'open' after September 1966. Its intermediate stations at Akeman Street and Wotton had been closed in 1931 and 1953 respectively but, although the line ran nowhere and carried no passengers, BR still had to implement the formal closure procedures. Notices were, accordingly, posted in the area, saying that the line was about to be closed, and inviting objectors to contact the East Midlands Area of the Transport Users' Consultative Committee. In the event, there were no serious objections, and the Grendon Underwood 'Ghost Line' was formally closed in 1967.

The electrification of the former London & North Western main line from Euston to Birmingham and the North heralded the decline of the GWR route to Birmingham. Built, like the now-closed Great Central, to challenge the London & North Western's hold on the Birmingham route, the Nationalisation of Britain's railway system carried out in 1948 rendered the Great Western line superfluous. Once BR had taken the decision to concentrate investment on the main West Coast main line from Euston, there could be no place in the system for a competing line from London to Birmingham, Wolverhampton, Shrewsbury, Chester and Birkenhead.

The end did not come immediately - in fact the electrification of the Euston main line meant, in the short term, that more traffic was routed from Birmingham to London via the Western Region. By April 1966 however, the full electric service was in operation, and a few months later, on Sunday 5th March, 1967, the GW&GC Joint Line and its extension through Bicester ceased to be worked as part of a major long-distance through route between London and the North of England.

The end was celebrated on Saturday 4th March, when a special train, called (appropriately) 'The Zulu', ran from Paddington to Banbury, from where preserved 'Castle' class 4-6-0 No. 7029 *Clun Castle* took over for a run to Birkenhead, the steam locomotive coming off at Chester. The 'Birmingham Pullman' and the 'Cambrian Coast Express' ran for the last time on that same day.

The new timetable, which came into effect on Monday 6th March, provided the GW&GC Joint Line with a simplified service of local and semi-fast trains. The route was still worked as a 'joint' line, in that the local dmus were concentrated on Marylebone, whereas the locomotive-hauled Birmingham trains ran to and from Paddington. With stops at High Wycombe, Bicester, Banbury, Leamington Spa, and Solihull, the overall journey time was around 2½ hours between Paddington to Birmingham. On the other hand, the revised train service was convenient for people living in many of the places served *en route*, and High Wycombe, Bicester and Banbury travellers were pleased with their extra trains.

One by-product of the rundown of the Great Western northern lines was that the terminus of the Birmingham service was now New Street - ironically, on the rival London & North Western line! The number of trains varied over the next few years, but there were usually six or seven workings each way. In May 1968, for instance, there were six up and seven down main line services, with southbound services from Birmingham New Street at 7.20, 8.40, 11.40 am, 2.40, 4.40 and 6.40 pm, and corresponding down workings from Paddington at 8.25, 10.25 am, 1.25, 3.50, 4.15, 5.38 and 7.35 pm.

There had, meanwhile, been a considerable rationalisation of facilities on the GW&GC Joint Line and the Bicester Cut-Off. Freight services, in particular, were virtually eliminated during the 1960s, when most of the stations on the 'New Line' lost their goods yards. A concomitant of this reduction in services was the singling of 26 miles of line between Princes Risborough and Aynho Junction, which was carried out in the Autumn of 1968. The singling involved the closure of Princes Risborough South, Bicester North, Ardley and King's Sutton signal boxes, together with a simplification of the trackwork at Princes Risborough.

An emergency passing place and siding was retained at Bicester, but it was intended that all services would use the former down platform. Otherwise, there were no longer any loops, sidings or other connections on the singled section between Princes Risborough and Aynho Junction, apart from some little-used quarry sidings in the vicinity of Ardley.

The singling evoked a storm of protest in Banbury and Bicester, and many people living at the Oxfordshire end of the line feared that further run-downs were about to begin. Sure enough, in the Spring of 1974, BR announced that they intended to divert five up and five down main line trains from the GW&GC route to the Old Line via Oxford, leaving the 8.18 am up service from Birmingham New Street and the 5.40 pm down working from Paddington to Birmingham as the only remaining locomotive-hauled services on the shorter route via High Wycombe.

Oxford was delighted by the news; in effect, the University City had got back the trains it lost when the 'New Line' was opened back in 1910! Banbury and Bicester, on the other hand, were shocked to find that, apart from the two remaining locomotive hauled semi-fasts, they would have only a local dmu service to London. Banbury commuters, it was true, could opt to travel via Oxford, but the journey time

Looking along Platform Four at West Ruislip on 11th March, 1989, as a Derby class '115' unit enters the station with the 3.10 pm up service from Aylesbury to Marylebone.   *P.G. Barnes*

A hybrid multiple unit formation photographed near Princes Risborough while working the 10.15 am service from Marylebone to Banbury on 11th November, 1989; the ensemble includes Derby class '115' and Metro-Cammell class '101' vehicles.   *P.G. Barnes*

was lengthened by 25 minutes, and of course the longer distance would be reflected in higher fares.

The new timetable, effective from May 1974, provided Banbury with 10 trains to and from London and Bicester with 12. Apart from the 8.18 am up and the 5.40 pm down workings, all trains ran to or from Marylebone. The new service remained unpopular locally, but in spite of protests from local MPs, the GW&GC did not get its locomotive-hauled trains back; as a Department of the Environment spokesman put it, the Paddington-Bicester-Birmingham route 'competed with Euston to Birmingham services'. Here, in a nutshell, was the reason why the Great Western & Great Central Joint Line was built, and why it was run down.

On 24th March, 1974 the services from Marylebone to Banbury and Aylesbury were transferred from the Western Region to the London Midland Region. At the same time the former WR stations at South Ruislip, West Ruislip, Denham, Denham Golf Club, Gerrards Cross, Seer Green & Jordans, Beaconsfield, High Wycombe, Saunderton, Princes Risborough and Bicester became LMR stations, together with Monks Risborough and Little Kimble on the Aylesbury branch. These changes left the London Midland Region with total responsibility for all passenger services operating out of Marylebone.

Local travellers continued to hope that their line would remain in being as a through route, but there were widespread fears that passenger services would be cut short at either Princes Risborough or Bicester if government policy turned once more to thoughts of closures. In such circumstances, curtailment of services at the northern end of the line seemed to be a distinct possibility, though in view of the heavy traffic that was still being carried at the southern end of the route, the line between Marylebone and High Wycombe seemed secure.

The Network SouthEast Era

Although the 1974 down-grading seemed, at the time, to have heralded the ultimate demise of the Great Western & Great Central Joint Line, external developments such as vastly-increased oil prices and rising house prices in the south-east did much to secure the route's long term future. In fact, the post-1974 period was a time of remarkable stability in which little further rationalisation took place - there were, indeed, some welcome improvements, such as the opening of a new station known as 'Haddenham & Thame Parkway' in 1987, near the site of the long-defunct Haddenham station.

Long-distance commuting became increasingly popular during the 1980s and early 1990s, and in this context the speed, comfort and efficiency of rail transport ensured that just about every line radiating from London experienced an upsurge in passenger traffic. Lines serving fashionable areas such as the Cotswolds became especially popular among middle class commuters, particularly when, as in the case of the Great Western main line, the majority of train services were formed of fast and comfortable High Speed Train sets. In this respect, the GW&GC route was placed at something of a disadvantage, insofar as its trains were no longer particularly fast or comfortable.

The two remaining Paddington to Birmingham semi-fast workings were virtually the only locomotive-hauled workings on the GW&GC route. The usual motive power on these residual main line services were the familiar class '47' Co-Cos, while Derby class '115' four-car suburban units continued to work the rest of the passenger

Gresley 'A4'class 4-6-2 No. 4498 *Sir Nigel Gresley* passes Seer Green & Jordans while working a steam special during the 1980s.   *Mike Marr*

A typical view of Marylebone station during the later years of the BR era on 8th August, 1985. Class '115' multiple units occupy the platforms, but the terminus seems strangely deserted - Marylebone having been demoted to suburban status.   *Mike Marr*

services. In May 1982 there were 16 up and 18 down workings between London and Princes Risborough, including the Paddington to Birmingham services. Banbury was served by 11 up and 9 down trains, while High Wycombe travellers were offered a choice of 37 up and 37 down workings to and from London.

Like other British railways, the Great Western & Great Central line has served the public in perfect safety for many years, but this proud record was marred on the morning of 11th December, 1981 when, after an unexpected snowfall, a tree fell into one of the deep cuttings near Seer Green. The obstruction was spotted by the driver of a northbound empty stock working, who brought his class '115' multiple unit to a stand, and immediately telephoned a warning. Unfortunately, the following 7.31 am Marylebone to Banbury passenger train ran into the rear of the empty dmu with such force that the driver and three young travellers were killed.

On a happier note, the GW&GC Joint Line found considerable favour as a weekend 'steam' route, and a variety of large main line steam locomotives worked over the line during the 1980s at the head of 'William Shakespeare' and other specials. These special workings recalled those far-off days when prestige expresses such as the 'Master Cutler' had linked Marylebone and the North, and ensured that this down-graded route retained a few vestigial traces of its former main line status.

The first steam working ran on 12th January, 1985, when Gresley 'A4' Pacific No. 4498 *Sir Nigel Gresley* worked over the GW&GC route at the head of 'The Thames Avon Express'. The same engine was steamed in connection with the launch of a new series of Post Office stamps on 21st January, and in the next few years *Sir Nigel Gresley* and other locomotives including 'Castle' class 4-6-0 No. 7029 *Clun Castle*, 'Princess Royal' class 4-6-2 No. 6201 *Princess Elizabeth*, 'West Country' class 4-6-2 No. 34027 *Taw Valley* and 'Black Five' 4-6-0 No. 44932 were used to haul regular steam specials to Stratford-upon-Avon and other destinations.

By the mid-1980s, the steam specials were running on a weekly basis during the summer months. There were, for instance, 'Shakespeare Ltd' workings from Marylebone to Stratford-upon-Avon on Sundays 1st, 8th, 15th, 22nd and 29th June, 1986. The trains normally left Marylebone at about 10.25 am, picking-up at High Wycombe and Banbury, and setting down at Warwick. The return fare was £35, inclusive of morning coffee, a three-course lunch and afternoon tea.

A less welcome development concerned Marylebone station which - claimed the National Bus Company - could be transformed into an ideal coach terminal with road vehicles using the approach tunnels. British Rail, in apparent agreement with this curious scheme, posted closure notices for the Marylebone to Northolt Junction line, the idea being that all GW&GC train services would be diverted into Paddington, while Aylesbury line travellers could transfer into London Transport trains at Amersham. If implemented, these proposals would have resulted in the elimination of Marylebone, Wembley Hill, Sudbury & Harrow Road, Sudbury Hill and Northolt Park stations.

In March 1984, BR formally announced that Marylebone station would be closed. The immediate result was hostility from organisations such as the Marylebone Travellers' Association, the Aylesbury Society and the Railway Development Society. Protest meetings were held throughout the Chiltern area, and no less than 600 formal objections were received before the official deadline for objections on 8th October. Faced with this level of opposition, BR withdrew the closure notices in April 1986.

In retrospect, the Marylebone 'busway' scheme was deeply flawed for a number of reasons - among them the obvious fact that tunnels designed for rail traffic would not have been wide enough to allow speeding motor vehicles to pass safely in subterranean conditions. Moreover, London Transport claimed that increasing rail traffic on the busy Metropolitan Line made it unlikely that additional travellers could have been accommodated at Baker Street - while the travellers themselves would clearly have resented the delays and discomfort resulting from an intermediate change from British Railways to London Transport services at Amersham.

An important organisational change took place in the early 1980s, when BR was sub-divided into a number of separate business sectors. Main line passenger services, for example, became the Inter-City sector, while the Scottish system became known as ScotRail. A similar situation pertained in the case of railways in south-eastern England, which became the BR London & South Eastern sector. On 10th June, 1986, the sector was relaunched as Network SouthEast - a striking red, white, grey and blue livery being introduced as a means of promoting a stronger brand image for the new organisational and trading sector.

The ensuing months were a time of tangible progress in which stations and trains were repainted and refurbished throughout the extensive Network SouthEast area. Railcards and other marketing initiatives were developed to attract off-peak customers, and orders were placed for new rolling stock. In 1988, for example, it was announced that the existing fleet of ageing class '115' multiple units used on the Chiltern lines would be replaced by 89 newly-built class '165 Network Turbo' vehicles by May 1990. The contract for construction of these new units was awarded to British Rail Engineering Ltd at York Works.

In the summer of 1988 it was reported that the NSE 'Chiltern lines' from Marylebone to Aylesbury and High Wycombe had been selected for what was described as a 'total route modernisation'. This process would include a package of improvements including the renewal of signalling systems, new passenger information systems, a new diesel maintenance depot at Aylesbury, and station modernisation. The scheme would cost £50,000,000 inclusive of the new fleet of class '165' two- and three-car multiple units that had already been announced.

The promised improvements were welcomed by regular travellers, but there were, nevertheless, fears that station 'modernisation' would entail the demolition of original facilities - though the introduction of a new signalling system (based upon a single operating centre at Marylebone) would obviously necessitate the removal of semaphore signals and mechanical signal boxes. The route modernisation scheme was completed in 1991, and the lines from Marylebone to Banbury and Aylesbury thereby became one of Network SouthEast's most attractive and modern routes. Unfortunately, the spectre of privatisation was already casting its long shadow over both the GW&GC and the Metropolitan & Great Central lines.

The completion of the route modernisation scheme brought further traffic to the line, and in the summer of 1995 it was reported that passenger numbers on the Chiltern Lines had grown by a staggering 60 per cent over a period of three years. An interesting development took place in that same year, when 'station masters' were reintroduced at Marylebone, Gerrards Cross, High Wycombe, Aylesbury and Banbury. The new appointments were focused specifically on customer relations and customer care, as well as the efficient operation of train services on the routes from Marylebone.

Motive Power in the later BR period

Although the 'Westerns' had put up some spectacular performances over the GW&GC route, they were unpopular with the London Midland Region which, after 1963, assumed responsibility for the old Great Western Birmingham line north of Banbury and in 1974 took over the Joint Line itself. The Paddington to Birmingham expresses therefore went over to diesel-electric haulage, using 2,700 hp Brush-Sulzer type '4' Co-Cos (later class '47s').

In October 1967 the Western Region tried once again to use its diesel hydraulics on the Birmingham run. This time Warship class '43' Bo-Bos Nos. 833-53 were allocated to the route but, as before, London Midland Region enginemen objected, and after a series of failures and delays the class '47's returned, and they worked most main line services over the Great Western & Great Central route for the next 20 years.

Other types have occasionally appeared on express passenger workings; on 26th November, 1965, for example, the up 'Cambrian Coast Express' arrived at Paddington behind Stanier class '5MT' 4-6-0s Nos. 45349 and 45493! More usual replacements for failed class '47s' included 'Westerns', 'Warships', and 'Hymek' class '35s', while, on occasions, LMR class '40s' were commandeered at short notice. On 23rd December, 1966, for example, No. D294 worked the 12.35 pm Wolverhampton to Paddington service, whilst just three weeks later, on 17th January, 1967, class '40' No. 330 headed the up 'Cambrian Coast Express' following a class '47' failure at Banbury.

Freight workings saw greater variety; steam locomotives - which should have been banished from the Western Region at the end of 1965 - appeared throughout the early months of 1966. The 9.00 am freight working from Banbury to High Wycombe, for example, brought LMR-based Standard class '9F' 2-10-0s onto the route, together with occasional Stanier class '5MT' 4-6-0s. Local Western Region freight workings passed into the hands of North British Locomotive Company class '22' Bo-Bos, following the demise of Great Western steam power.

By the early 1970s, the class '22s' had themselves been scrapped, and what little local freight traffic then remained was usually handled by former Eastern Region class '31' A1A-A1As. Inter-regional workings yielded more variety, and the Thame branch oil traffic (*see Chapter Eight*) was a particularly fruitful source of locomotive interest. Engines seen on these workings - apart from the usual 'Hymek' Bo-Bos, class '47' Co-Cos and class '31' A1A-A1As - included Eastern Region class '37s' that normally worked through from Thames Haven (presumably as a result of class '47' failures), class '40' 1Co-Co1s, and Southern Region class '33' Bo-Bos.

Meanwhile, the class '115' multiple units that had worked on the line since the 1960s were continuing to carry large numbers of daily commuters. By the late-1980s several of the class '115' intermediate trailers had been sent to Tyseley depot in exchange for a number of class '108' driving trailers, the idea being that some of the four-car sets could be replaced by two-car formations for use on off-peak services. There were, as a result, several hybrid sets, although the minor external differences between class '115' and '108' stock were disguised by the application of colourful 'Network SouthEast' livery.

Unfortunately, the multiple units employed on the GW&GC and Metropolitan & Great Central lines were nearing the end of their working lives by the 1980s, and in these circumstances breakdowns and maintenance problems were perhaps inevitable. Some of the longer distance services between Marylebone and Banbury therefore

A 'Peak' class '45' 1Co-Co1 glides through High Wycombe with an empty 'bin liner' working between Calvert and Northolt on 3rd January, 1987.   *P.G. Barnes*

Class '56' Co-Co No. 56062 passes Princes Risborough with an Aylesbury to Cricklewood Redland hopper working on 11th November, 1989.   *P.G. Barnes*

reverted to locomotive haulage, the 7.23 am down service and the 9.30 am return working being regularly composed of a class '47' Co-Co and five Mk I coaches.

Long distance services between Paddington and Birmingham continued to run until 1986 when, following the creation of Network SouthEast, the remaining main line workings were cut short at Banbury. These services continued to be worked by class '47's, although English Electric class '50' Co-Cos also appeared during the 1980s. These locomotives, which had worked on the West Coast Main Line prior to their transfer to the Western Region, became quite popular among locomotive enthusiasts, and their withdrawal from service in 1990 was regretted by many. The last scheduled class '50'-hauled service ran on 11th May, 1990, when No. 50026 *Indomitable* worked the 6.12 pm Paddington to Banbury service.

The Paddington to Banbury workings returned to class '47' haulage following the run-down of the class '50' fleet although, surprisingly, No. 50044 *Exeter* reappeared on 31st July, 1990 when it hauled the 5.37 pm down service to Banbury. The Paddington to Banbury trains were finally withdrawn on Friday 17th January, 1992, the last up service being hauled by class '47' Co-Co No. 47441 while the final down working was headed by sister locomotive No. 47364. Both trains carried commemorative 'Chiltern Loco-Hauled Farewell' headboards, and special announcements were made at both Paddington and High Wycombe.

The first class '165' units, Nos. 165001 and 165002, were delivered in 1991, and the new trains were progressively introduced into regular service as further sets were delivered. The first class '165' sets to be placed in service were two-car units, formed of one driving motor composite and one driving motor standard. Later, as further trains were delivered from the manufacturers, a number of three-car formations were placed in service. These were identical to the two-car units, but they incorporated an intermediate motor standard, this additional powered coach being marshalled between the two driving vehicles.

The two and three-car 'Turbo' sets were designated class '165/0' to distinguish them from the otherwise similar class '165/1' units that had been ordered for service on the neighbouring 'Thames' services from Paddington. There was, at first, some interchange of units between the Thames and Chiltern lines, but as the class '165/1' sets were placed into service in increasing numbers the original class '165/0' units were returned to their own line. When the final deliveries had been completed, the full allocation of class '165/0' sets was 27 two-car units (Nos. 165001 to 165028) and 11 three-car sets (Nos. 165029 to 165039).

The introduction of the class '165/0' units heralded the demise of the veteran class '115' diesel multiple units that had worked the Marylebone suburban services for the previous 32 years. The official 'last train' ran on the evening of 29th July, 1992 when an eight-car formation departed from Marylebone amid a barrage of exploding detonators. The leading vehicle carried a special headboard bearing the legend 'Farewell Class 115 on the Chiltern Line 1960 1992', and enthusiasts had travelled from as far away as Scotland to ride on this last 'classic' dmu from Marylebone to Aylesbury (via Great Missenden).

Technically, the class '165's were more advanced than the class '115s' that they had replaced. They featured sliding plug doors, and each vehicle was powered by a 350 hp Perkins 2006-TWH diesel - producing 1,050 hp for a three-car unit. Their powers of acceleration were impressive, and internal noise levels were minimal. On the other hand, the high-density '2 + 3' seating was disliked by many regular travellers, who also complained of insufficient leg room; moreover, when their crude hopper windows were opened to provide ventilation, passengers experienced drafts of unimaginable ferocity.

Class '165' unit No. 165020 at Princes Risborough *circa* 1994. The line on the right veers off towards Chinnor (on the former GWR branch to Watlington). *Mike Marr*

Despite these minor problems, it was recognised that the 'Turbo' units were an asset to the Marylebone suburban routes. There was, nevertheless, a feeling of regret among some travellers in that the GW&GC route was no longer regarded as part of the long-distance main line network. This situation was, however, about to be transformed by a series of external developments.

The Privatised Railway

The British Railways era lasted for half a century, its 50 year life span between 1948 and the completion of the controversial privatisation process in 1997 being comparable to the life span of the preceding GW&GC Joint Committee. Unfortunately, the Nationalisation of Britain's railways opened the way for continual political interference, much of which was hostile if not downright vindictive. In the 1990s the Conservative party, having successfully privatised many other nationalised industries, decided to return the railways to private ownership.

As a first step towards this goal, the Government created a number of distinct train operating units, one of which was known as 'Thames & Chiltern'. The Thames and Chiltern lines were subsequently split into two units, Thames Trains being responsible for local services on the former GWR lines from Paddington to Reading, Oxford and Newbury, while Chiltern Railways assumed responsibility for the routes from Marylebone to Aylesbury via High Wycombe and Great Missenden. In the meantime, the locomotives and rolling stock that would be used by these and other companies on the privatised railways were allocated to three rolling stock leasing companies.

The rolling stock companies were sold to private owners in November 1995 while, in the next few weeks, the American-based Wisconsin Central Transportation Corporation successfully bid for BR's three freight operating companies. On 21st July, 1996, Chiltern Trains was transferred to a 'management buy-out' team known as 'M40 Trains', while in the previous May Railtrack had been floated on the Stock Exchange. The initial Chiltern Trains franchise was for a period of seven years, and the successful buy-out team were a joint venture with Laing; unsuccessful bids had been received from Stagecoach and French-based Connex Rail.

The most important result of these developments was the creation of Railtrack as an infrastructure company, and the consequent fragmentation of the railway system. The method of denationalisation adopted was extraordinary, in that it entailed a complete divorce between the railway network and the trains that were to run upon it. Moreover, the Tory theorists who concocted this unusual scheme envisaged that myriad train operators would compete with each other to run commercial services over the same stretches of line, the 'commercial' nature of these operations being heavily-subsidised by enormous amounts of taxpayers' money.

In effect, this system harked back, not to the highly successful Victorian era, but to the Georgian period, when canal companies and tramways had allowed a diversity of different operators access to their systems in return for the payment of tolls. The 'last great privatisation' therefore turned the clock back 200 years, and destroyed the essential unity of a system that had been carefully built-up successively by the Wycombe Railway, the Great Western Railway, the Great Central Railway, the London & North Eastern Railway, and finally BR.

It had at first been announced that Railtrack would remain within the public domain - a course of action that would have allowed the government to introduce an element of competition in the day-to-day operation of the railways, while retaining firm control of rail safety, overall planning and other vital functions. Sadly, following an abrupt change of policy, it was decided that the entire railway industry would be sold off before an impending general election. Many commentators wondered if the Tories were trying to privatise BR in such a way that the next Labour government would be unable to unravel the resulting mess.

In the event, the private owners of Railtrack failed to provide sufficient investment - although the increasingly unpopular company continued to pay dividends to its shareholders. 'It was clear', opined *The Railway Magazine,* 'that this discredited and debt-ridden firm - which was unique among floated companies in that it depended on the Government for two-thirds of its revenue - had degenerated into an enormous black hole which had sucked-in billions and billions of pounds of taxpayers' money since being formed in 1994 and floated in 1996'.

After a series of high profile rail crashes at Southall, Ladbroke Grove and Hatfield, and the deaths of 52 people, the situation finally became intolerable to the Labour government which had inherited the situation from its predecessors, and in 2001 the failed company was placed in receivership. The six-year history of Railtrack was finally brought to an end at an extraordinary general meeting held on 23rd July, 2002, when a majority of the shareholders voted to sell the undertaking to a government-created 'not for dividend' organization to be known as 'Network Rail'.

The infrastructure of Britain's railways was thereby returned to public ownership, but the Labour government had no desire to pursue renationalisation of the train operating companies, some of which were operating successfully. In this context, it must be recorded that Chiltern Railways had achieved some very encouraging results in its new guise as a private company. It is true that the virtually self-contained Chiltern routes had recently benefited from state investment, but Chiltern's private operators promised to inject a further £371,000,000, with the aim of increasing line capacity and achieving an increase in passenger numbers of 50 per cent by the year 2007.

In April 2002, it was reported that the Strategic Rail Authority had awarded a 20-year franchise to Chiltern Railways - this unprecedented extension being widely seen as a reward for success at a time in which many other train operators were in danger of losing their franchises. In that same year, Chiltern Railways was named 'Train Operator

Bicester North, looking towards London from the footbridge on 31st August, 2001, with class '168' unit No. 168108 in the down platform, which is now signalled for bi-directional working. *Bob Sweet*

of the Year' in recognition of the company's commitment to customer service and its outstanding performance during a period of great difficulty for the railway industry.

Meanwhile, the Chiltern Line had gone from strength to strength, an important development being the re-introduction of through services between London and Birmingham in 1992. By May 1993 there were seven up and seven down workings between Marylebone and Birmingham Snow Hill, the average journey time being around 2 hours 30 minutes in the down direction. These leisurely timings could not stand comparison with the two hour schedules of the steam era, but the extension of services to England's 'second city' was seen as a step in the right direction - the 'New Line' was again fulfilling its historic role as a link between major cities that offered a viable alternative to the former LNWR route from Euston.

The fact that the 'Bicester Cut-Off' had been reduced to single track inevitably detracted from the route's ability to function as a main line, but in 1998 a double

Princes Risborough station after refurbishment, showing the new footbridge and platform layout on 12th May, 2002. *P.G. Barnes*

track had been reinstated between Princes Risborough and Bicester. This partial re-doubling produced an immediate effect on route profitability, and it was, in consequence, decided that the double track section would be continued north-westwards to Aynho Junction. Details of a £60,000,000 doubling scheme, to be undertaken on a partnership basis between Chiltern Railways, Railtrack, GTRM, Westinghouse and Birse, were announced in February 2002, and the project was complete by the following August.

As the class '165' Turbo units were not entirely suitable for use on the extended route between London and Birmingham, orders had been placed in September 1996 with Adtranz of Derby for a fleet of five 3-car diesel trains. Additional centre vehicles were subsequently ordered from the same manufacturers, so that these new 'Turbostar' units could be placed into service on the Marylebone to Birmingham route as more capacious 4-car sets. A further order for five 2-car 'Turbostars' was placed in April 1999, followed by an order for three more 3-car units in February 2000.

Aylesbury received its first class '168' Turbostar unit, No. 168002, on 7th May, 1998, and when the remaining trains were delivered they were placed in service on the Birmingham route, allowing the class '165s' to be used more effectively on the shorter-distance services to Aylesbury. An order was placed for five additional powered intermediate vehicles in December 2001, and in March 2002 another four 3-car sets were ordered. When the various class '168' vehicles were completed, they formed 16 sets, which were numbered in sequence from 168001 to 168017.

The class '168' units are powered by one 400 hp engine in each car, a 3-car set having a total output of 1,200 hp. Each vehicle is 75 ft 5 in. long, with a weight of approximately 90 tons; the top speed is 100 mph. Externally, the class '168' units are painted in an attractive two-tone blue and white livery relieved by a narrow red band along the lower body panels. From an operational viewpoint the new units have enabled Chiltern Trains to run to and from Birmingham in two hours or less on the reinstated double-track route between London, Princes Risborough, Bicester and Aynho.

Bicester North on 31st August, 2001, showing class '168' unit No. 168004 alongside the up platform.   *Bob Sweet*

Diesel power at Denham as class a class '33' Bo-Bo heads through the widely-spaced platforms with a southbound block oil train from Thame during the mid-1970s.   *Author*

This artificial tunnel, being constructed at Gerrards Cross to allow a Tesco store to be built overhead, collapsed in June 2005 bringing thousands of tons of material onto the tracks. During the obstruction Birmingham services were diverted via Harrow to Aylesbury (reverse) and Princes Risborough (reverse) before gaining their correct route.   *Bob Sweet*

The Decline of Freight Traffic

The decline of rail freight traffic in recent years can only be described as catastrophic. At the time of Nationalisation, the railways were still common carriers with a legal obligation to accept any form of freight traffic. This placed them at a disadvantage in relation to the road hauliers, who were free to pick and choose the most profitable forms of traffic. In an attempt to introduce competition between road and rail, the railways lost their common carrier status, and for a period of several years BR was encouraged to concentrate on profitable bulk train load traffic. At the same time, goods yards and sidings were removed to reduce overheads, and large numbers of wagons were scrapped.

In retrospect, these measures resulted in a serious loss of capacity, which meant that the severely rationalised freight network was no longer able to cope with any form of goods other than specialised bulk traffic flows. As late as 1983, there were still around 400 private sidings and 130 public freight depots on the BR system, but by the start of the privatised era, many of these facilities had ceased to exist. Park Royal goods depot, which had become a Freightliner depot in the late 1960s, had closed in 1982, thereby reducing the likelihood that traffic could be regained from the road hauliers.

At the start of the 1980s the GW&GC line had carried block oil trains to a terminal at Thame, on the Princes Risborough to Oxford route, but this traffic flow came to an end in April 1991, following the construction of an oil pipeline. Coal traffic to Chinnor Cement Works on the former Watlington branch ceased in December 1989, while the closure of Aylesbury goods depot and High Wycombe North Yard resulted in a further loss of transhipment facilities.

In the short term, it appeared that the food and drink industry would become an important customer. The Guinness Brewery at Park Royal, for instance, was served by five block trains a week during the 1980s, traffic being conveyed in 'Cargowaggons' to the Otis Distribution Terminal at Ordsall Lane, Salford for distribution by road throughout the North of England and North Wales. Regrettably, this high-profile traffic flow came to an end in July 1995, when Guinness changed from rail to road transport.

The end of the Guinness trains meant that little freight traffic was carried over any part of the GW&GC system or its connections. The only significant forms of traffic then remaining were regular train loads of household waste from Northolt to an infill site at Calvert, on the former GCR route north of Aylesbury, and consignments of sea-dredged sand and gravel from Angerstein Wharf to the Marcon private siding at Park Royal.

Much interest surrounded the activities of the Wisconsin Central Transportation Corporation following its acquisition of a large part of the former British Railways freight operation. In its native North America, Wisconsin had successfully won back a significant proportion of freight traffic from rival road transport operators, much of this traffic being in the form of wagon load consignments. It was suggested that similar business strategies would be adopted in Britain by Wisconsin's 'English Welsh & Scottish' (EWS) subsidiary, but in the event the overall volume of freight traffic carried by EWS and other freight operators has continued to decline.

In September 1997, EWS delivered a small amount of coal to the Guinness sidings at Park Royal, and there were hopes that this modest revival would lead to a return of the 'Guinness trains'. At the time of writing, however, freight traffic is no longer a significant feature of operations on the Great Western & Great Central Joint route.

Moveable diamond crossing, Old Oak Common West Junction.   *C.R. Potts Collection*

The interior of Old Oak Common East signal box, opened on 26th April, 1927 and closed on 8th October, 1962.   *British Rail*

Chapter Five

The Route from London to Ruislip

Having recounted the history of the Great Western & Great Central Joint Railway from its inception until the present day, it would now be appropriate to examine the stations and other infrastructure of the line in greater detail. The following chapters will therefore take readers on an imaginary journey along the route from London to Banbury. The journey will begin at Old Oak Common, but as trains now run to and from the former Great Central terminus at Marylebone, the Marylebone to Northolt Junction section will also be described. The datum point for the calculation of distances will be Paddington station, some 3¼ miles to the east of the junction at Old Oak Common.

As the line is still part of the national railway system, the present tense can be used when describing the actual route, though a problem arises in the case of closed stations or other infrastructure that no longer exists. In such cases, the past tense must inevitably be employed, notwithstanding the stylistic blemishes that may thereby occur. Moreover, the pace of rationalisation in recent years has also been so rapid that descriptions of signalling or other equipment can quickly become anachronistic. The following sections may therefore contain one or two incorrect tenses, though it is hoped that readers will understand how these minor problems cannot always be avoided.

Old Oak Common

On departure from Paddington, westbound trains pass beneath a series of massive girder bridges which carry busy thoroughfares such as Bishop's Bridge Road and Westbourne Road over the multiple-tracked Great Western main line. These impressive structures are named after the roads that they carry, the first half dozen being known as Bishops bridge, Westbourne bridge, Ranelagh bridge, Lord Hill's bridge, Green Lane bridge and Golborne Road bridge.

Although many goods lines and sidings have been lifted in recent years, the approaches to the station are still filled with a complex web of trackwork. The platform lines used by main line and suburban services merge into six parallel tracks, while the eastbound and westbound Hammersmith & City 'Underground' lines, which initially run on the north side, descend to a lower level before passing beneath the main lines and re-appearing on the south side. Gaining speed, main line services approach Ladbroke Grove Junction, at which point the six main running lines merge into down and up main and down and up relief lines respectively.

With carriage reception lines running parallel to the right, and with North Pole International Depot visible to the left of the former GWR route, trains soon reach Old Oak Common. The sheer scale of the infrastructure here is impressive, the multiple running lines being flanked by the 'North Pole International Depot' to the left and Old Oak Common sidings and depot to the right - the view being one of railway lines as far as the eye can see!

Opened on 11th November, 1993, North Pole Depot is a comparatively recent addition to the railway infrastructure at Old Oak Common. Extending alongside the Great Western main line for a distance of 1¾ miles, it is the main servicing and repair centre for the class '372' multiple units and class '92' electric locomotives employed on the Channel Tunnel route to France and Belgium. The depot contains stabling sidings, a 6-road servicing shed and a 4-road repair shop. Access to the rest of the railway system is by means of a connection to the West London line, which passes over the site at right angles.

Old Oak Common, the largest motive power depot on the Great Western system, is still one of the largest maintenance depots in the country. It was opened in 1906 to replace an earlier shed at Westbourne Park, a large carriage shed and storage sidings being laid out alongside on a contiguous site. The new depot incorporated a massive 'enclosed roundhouse' measuring no less than 360 ft by 444 ft, and containing four turntables, each of 65 ft diameter. There were also extensive repair shops and maintenance facilities, together with a large coaling stage with a 290,000 gallon water tank above.

From its inception, Old Oak Common had a huge allocation of locomotives, many of which would have appeared on the GW&GC Joint Line on a regular basis. In 1921, for example, the allocation consisted of 157 locomotives, including 'top link' motive power such as 'Star' class 4-6-0s Nos. 4003 *Lode Star*, 4013 *Knight of St Patrick*, 4021 *King Edward*, 4034 *Queen Adelaide*, 4036 *Queen Elizabeth*, 4041 *Prince of Wales*, 4042 *Prince Albert*, 4048 *Princes Victoria* and 4056 *Princess Margaret*. The allocation also included a number of 'Saint' class 4-6-0s including Nos. 2904 *Lady Godiva*, 2906 *Lady of Lynn*, 2939 *Croome Court*, 2942 *Fawley Court*, 2952 *Twineham Court*, 2979 *Quentin Durwood* and 2989 *Talisman*.

In December 1947, at the very end of the GWR period, Old Oak's allocation had increased to 232 locomotives of all types. There were 88 'King', 'Castle', 'Star', 'County', 'Hall' or 'Grange' class 4-6-0s, 21 '28XX' class 2-8-0s, 19 large prairie tanks, 97 assorted pannier tanks, and a number of other types, including the pioneer Great Western 0-6-0 diesel shunter No. 2 (later 15100). In GWR days, Old Oak was coded 'PDN', while under British Railways auspices the shed code was changed to '81A'.

The facilities at Old Oak Common included a large railwaymen's hostel. Staff hostels of this type originated during World War II, but they remained in use during the British Railways period, by which time the Old Oak Common Hostel had become the largest in Western Region. It was situated between Old Oak Common Lane and the motive power depot, and contained a main block with 276 single rooms, a separate building with accommodation for a further 288 men in single or shared rooms, and domestic quarters for a Manager, Matron and 23 staff. There was also a dining room, games room, concert hall, a television room and various other amenities. The Manager and Matron in 1960 were Mr and Mrs S.R. Lewis.

Old Oak Common shed was officially closed to steam on 22nd March, 1965, but this large depot remained in use for diesel locomotives. The shed was officially re-opened as a diesel servicing and maintenance depot on 20th October, 1966, although in practice the facilities had remained in use throughout a lengthy period of rebuilding. In its new guise, the depot comprised a new, 3-road servicing shed and new office and staff accommodation, together with one of the former steam repair shops, which was adapted for use as a diesel maintenance shed. One of the 65 ft turntables was retained, while an existing 175,000 gallon fuel tank, which had once served oil-fuelled steam locomotives, became the main fuel store.

The rejuvenated shed provided full maintenance facilities for 95 diesel locomotives, and daily servicing for 65 locomotives. Its initial diesel allocation included an interesting range of Western Region motive power, including 'Western' Co-Cos, class '47' Co-Cos, 'Hymek' Bo-Bos, class '22' Bo-Bos and class '08' 0-6-0 shunting locomotives. Old Oak Common depot and sidings are now used by several rail operators, including First Great Western, Mendip Rail, Heathrow Express and EWS.

A view of Old Oak Lane Halt in 1931.   *John Alsop Collection*

Old Oak Lane Halt

The 'New Line' leaves the Bristol route at Old Oak Common West Junction (3 miles 22 chains), and immediately takes up a north-westerly heading. There was, at one time, a halt at Old Oak Lane (3 miles 44 chains), which was opened on 1st October, 1906. The halt was equipped with up and down platforms, and typical Great Western 'pagoda' shelters on each side, the platforms being longer than those normally provided at railmotor halts. In June 1932, a terminal bay was constructed on the down side in order that a more intensive auto-train service could be run to and from Old Oak Lane without adding to congestion on the busy GWR main line.

In September 1932, *The Railway Magazine* suggested that the extra push-pull services that would be provided as a result of the new platform would enable the GWR to arrange more frequent connections with the Central London line (presumably at nearby North Acton). It was also pointed out that Old Oak Lane Halt must have been one of the few halts to have 'a bay line as well as through platforms, making a total of three platform faces'. The halt was illuminated by electric lights, and equipped with watering facilities - the latter being used by the auto-trains that worked most of the services calling at this West London stopping place until its closure with effect from 30th June, 1947.

A '517' class 0-4-2T pauses at Old Oak Lane Halt while working a Great Western local passenger service during the 1930s.   *Lens of Sutton Collection*

A general view of North Acton station in 1945, looking east towards London, with the Ealing & Shepherds Bush platforms visible to the right while the up and down GWR platforms can be seen to the left; the independent lines to Wood Lane pass between the passenger platforms and the high level booking office is on the extreme right of the picture.   *Lens of Sutton Collection*

A closer look at the Great Western platforms at North Acton, showing '54XX' class 0-6-0PT No. 5417 and auto-trailer No. 90, forming the 5.58 pm local service from Old Oak to Northolt.
H.C. Casserley

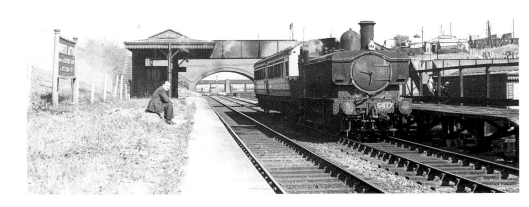

North Acton

Curving away from the Paddington to Bristol route beyond Old Oak Common, the 'New Line' passes beneath a bridge carrying the North London route overhead, and is immediately joined by the Central Line, which converges from the south-east as the main line passes beneath the North London Line. The Central Line was constructed and opened by an independent company known as 'The Central London' Railway, which had obtained its Act on 5th August, 1891, and was opened between The Bank and Shepherd's Bush on 30th July, 1900.

In 1905, the GWR obtained Parliamentary consent for a four mile branch from Ealing Broadway to Shepherd's Bush, where a new terminus was planned. In the event, the latter station was never built, the suggested terminal station being replaced by a link to the Central London Railway at Wood Lane. When opened for passenger traffic on 3rd August, 1920, the Ealing & Shepherd's Bush branch became in effect an extension of the Central London line, with a service of through electric trains between Ealing and Liverpool Street. Links to the 'New Line' at North Acton, and the West London route at Wood Lane, had enabled the Shepherd's Bush line to be opened for freight traffic from 16th April, 1917.

Although a halt had been provided at North Acton when the 'New Line' was opened on 1st May, 1904, this simple railmotor halt had a very short life, and it was closed in 1913. The opening of the Ealing & Shepherd's Bush route led to a revival, and on 5th November, 1923 a new station was opened on a fresh site, about half a mile to the east of the earlier halt, and 3 miles 65 chains from Paddington. The revived station consisted of four platforms, those on the north side being used by Great Western services, while the two southernmost platforms were used by Central Line electric trains running to and from Ealing Broadway.

The station was situated in a cutting, with a triple-span brick bridge to the east and a girder bridge to the west. The facilities available here were somewhat Spartan, and having obtained their tickets at a high level booking office, travellers had to await their trains on bare platforms equipped with simple waiting shelters. The two sides of the station were linked by a plate girder footbridge. On 19th June, 1938, independent up and down tracks were opened for steam-worked services proceeding to and from the West London line, the new lines being laid in a cutting between the Great Western and London Transport platforms.

The Great Western platforms were closed with effect from Monday 30th June, 1947, while the independent lines were closed in 1964. The adjacent Central Line platforms have nevertheless remained in use, and in its present-day configuration, North Acton is a purely 'Underground' station, served by Central Line services running to and from Ealing Broadway and West Ruislip.

Park Royal

Leaving the 'Underground' station at North Acton, the route passes beneath two road overbridges, the first of which carries Chase Road, while the second carries Park Royal Road over the line. A signal box known as North Acton Junction was sited on the down side of the line at 4 miles 15 chains to control the junction between the main line and the Ealing & Shepherd's Bush route. The box was opened in 1940 to replace an earlier one that had been sited on the up side; like many other GWR boxes erected at that time, it was a wartime 'ARP' structure, designed to give at least some protection from blast and shrapnel damage in the event of enemy air attack.

Early days at Park Royal, showing a GWR steam railmotor car in this short-lived, but generously-equipped station.   *John Alsop Collection*

The Central Line is perhaps the most interesting feature on this first section of the GWR 'New Line' to Birmingham. The Extension to West Ruislip leaves the earlier Ealing & Shepherd's Bush line about a quarter of a mile beyond North Acton station, and, for the next few miles, the main line and LT tracks continue north-westwards on parallel alignments. Although, at the time of writing, there are hardly any regular passenger services on this section of the former GWR line, present day travellers are able to view the route from the adjacent Central Line, which provides a frequent and convenient service between North Acton, Northolt and West Ruislip.

Passing under Park Royal Road, trains reach the site of the short-lived Park Royal station (4 miles 46 chains), which had been built in connection with the Royal Agricultural Society's permanent showground at Twyford Abbey. The station was ceremonially opened by the Prince of Wales, the Society's President, on 25th May, 1903, though exhibitors and members of the public were not carried until the following June.

The passenger station at Park Royal was equipped with commodious passenger facilities, while a short branch line on the up side of the running lines ran directly into the show ground. This split into two terminal sidings on either side of a 700 ft loading bank, a 'steam travelling crane' being available to expedite the loading and unloading of agricultural machinery or other equipment. There was also a spacious carriage loading dock 'so arranged that four carriages may be loaded or unloaded from four sidings at the same time, while the side of the landing is available for dealing with horses'.

In 1904, the Queen's Park Rangers Football Club transferred its headquarters from Kensal Rise to Park Royal, and began using the show ground for their match fixtures. It was hoped that the site would become a Mecca for Association Football supporters, and in anticipation of heavy passenger traffic in the years to come, the Great Western laid out a new football ground on the company's own land and rented it to the club. At one stage, Park Royal station building was used as a changing room, but World War I intervened before the football club could become fully established at its new site.

In 1906, the Great Western opened a new, rail-connected power station on the up side of the main line. This was intended mainly to supply power for the electrified Hammersmith & City branch, though it also generated current for electric lighting at Paddington station, which had hitherto obtained its power from a generating station at Westbourne Park. In the meantime, the 'permanent show ground' had failed to prosper, and in 1905 the venture was abandoned after three successive failures; the 100-acre site was then sold off as separate building plots.

Industries at Park Royal

Much of the infrastructure at Park Royal became redundant after the closure of the show ground, though in the next few years the site was used for industrial development, and Park Royal became increasingly important as a goods station. This process was accelerated during World War I, when much of the site was occupied by an ammunition factory. At the same time, an aircraft factory was set up on the south side of the line, all of these wartime facilities being served by siding connections from the main line. Park Royal station had, meanwhile, been closed for the duration of the war, and, having been re-opened in 1920, its passenger services were withdrawn for good in September 1937.

Although the 1920s and 1930s have become associated with the catastrophic decline of many traditional British industries, that same period also was also a time of expansion for 'new' industries such as car making, food processing and the manufacture of consumer goods. Large numbers of new factories were built in areas such as Slough and West London, and the GWR actively encouraged the development of new industries in places such as Park Royal, Perivale and Greenford. The Park Royal area, with its rail links and other infrastructure already in place, became particularly popular as an industrial location, and by the late 1930s numerous factories had been established in the immediate vicinity.

The 1938 Railway Clearing House *Handbook of Stations* gives an interesting glimpse of the range of industrial premises at Park Royal in the years before World War II. The firms with their own private siding connections included: J. Lyons & Sons; Mono Service Containers Ltd; W. Scot & Middleton Ltd; R.H. Neal & Co.; Norman Garages Ltd; Renault Ltd; Fiat (England) Ltd; H. Yager Investments Ltd; Thomas Baines & Woodhatch Ltd; Peter Keevil & Sons; W. Kayley; and A. Guinness & Sons. Most of the sidings were on the north side of the main line, but the Renault Works and some of the other rail-linked industrial concerns were sited on the south side of the running lines.

The factories at Park Royal varied in size and importance, some being relatively small concerns while others were major national or international undertakings. The best-known firm at Park Royal was perhaps A. Guinness & Son, the makers of a famous brand of dark stout. The company already had a well-established brewery at St James' Gate in Dublin, but it was decided that a second brewery would be set up in London to cater for the English market, and the necessary rail link was in place by the mid-1930s. The new brewery was laid-out on a lavish scale, its various departments being dispersed around an attractively-landscaped site. Production started in 1936, the first brew being on 21st February.

Rail transport played an important part in the operations at Park Royal Brewery, the malt house, boiler house and other departments being served by a network of

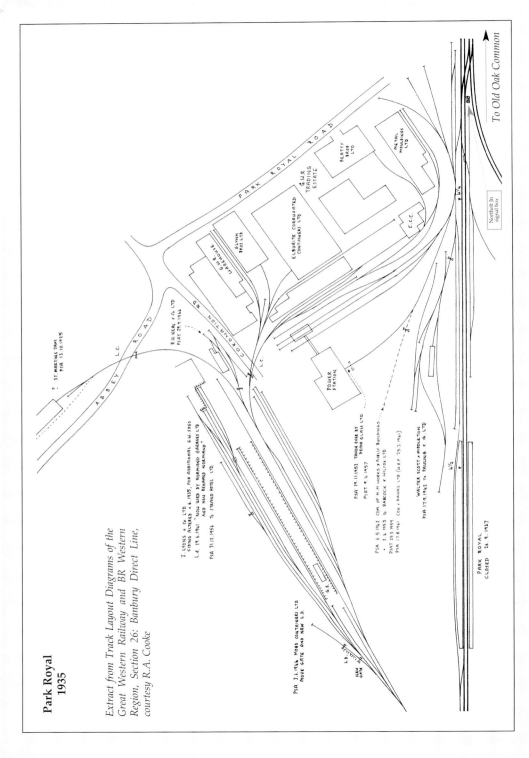

Park Royal
1935

Extract from Track Layout Diagrams of the
Great Western Railway and BR Western
Region, Section 26: Banbury Direct Line,
courtesy R.A. Cooke

To Old Oak Common

Northolt Jn
signal box

PARK ROYAL
CLOSED 26.9.1937

PARK ROYAL ROAD

CORONATION RD

ABBEY ROAD

St MARTINS TRAM
PSA 13.10.1935

G.W.R. WAREHOUSE

GLYNN BROS LTD

ELBURITE CORRUGATED
CONTAINERS LTD

G.W.R.
TRADING
ESTATE

BEATTY
BROS
LTD

METAL
MOULDINGS
LTD

E.C.C.

POWER
STATION

R.H. NEAL & Co LTD
PSAT 25.9.1966

J. LYONS & Co LTD
SIDING ALTERED c 6.1935, FOR ADDITIONAL G.W.1955
L.d. 19.6.1941 NOW USED BY NORMAND GARAGES LTD
AND NOW RENAMED NORLMAND
PSA 31.12.1956 TO STRAND HOTEL LTD

PSA 14.11.1951 TAKEN OVER BY
PSAT 4.6.1957 DENNIS GLASS LTD

PSA 6.5.1942 COM. OF H M WORKS & PUBLIC BUILDINGS
· 2.6.1953 TO BABCOCK & WILCOX LTD
PSAT 15.1.1954
PSA 17.6.1961 COX & BANKS LTD (W.E.F. 25.3.1961)

WALTER SCOTT & MIDDLETON
PSA 17.9.1942 TO PAULING & Co LTD

PSA 2.6.1966 MONO CONTAINERS LTD
MOVE GATE AND NEW L.B.

sidings. These were linked to the GWR main line by a single track branch that diverged northwards from Park Royal goods yard and passed through a cutting before crossing Cumberland Road on the level. A gate marked the boundary between Great Western and Guinness property, and having entered the brewery premises the line reached an array of six parallel sidings. One of the sidings was served by a travelling gantry crane, which was used for loading and unloading large casks, while a short spur ran into a single road engine shed.

Various sidings ran westwards to reach the malt house, brew house, boiler house and loading docks, and a headshunt extended for a short distance beyond the loop sidings. The firm employed its own shunting locomotives for internal work, two Hibberd Planet 4-wheeled diesel-mechanical engines being delivered in December 1948 and February 1949. These were named *Carpenter* (Works No. 3270) and *Walrus* (Works No. 3271) respectively, after two Lewis Carroll characters featured on Guinness posters at that time. In July 1985, these two engines were replaced by former BR class '08' 0-6-0 locomotives Nos. 08022 and 08060, which were named *Lion* and *Unicorn* respectively and painted in Guinness black livery.

The public and private goods sidings at Park Royal were important enough to justify the provision of two shunting engines during the early 1960s. In June 1962, an 0-6-0 diesel shunting locomotive ran light from Old Oak Common on Monday mornings, and returned to the depot at 6.00 am on Sundays, having worked for a total of 144 hours. The working timetable stipulates that this engine would work in Park Royal Yard and, after 9.00 am, would 'berth traffic to Trading Estate and Messrs Guinness Sidings'. A second engine worked as required at North Acton and performed trip workings between North Acton and Park Royal; at night, it was berthed in the Mono Containers Siding at Park Royal.

The sidings and connections in and around Park Royal were worked from three signal boxes. These included North Acton Junction, to the east of the station, Park Royal East (4 miles 38 chains) and Park Royal West (4 miles 64 chains). Park Royal East was closed in 1931, but North Acton Junction and Park Royal West signal boxes remained in use until 1966 and 1979 respectively. Many of the industrial sidings had, by that time, been abandoned, while in August 1982 *The Railway Magazine* reported that BR had given notice that freight facilities would be withdrawn from Park Royal goods depot in July.

There was slightly better news in the following October, when that same magazine announced that a government grant of £568,000 had been awarded to Marcon (RMC) Ltd towards the cost of an entirely new siding for sand and gravel traffic at a ready-mix concrete plant at Park Royal. The siding was situated on the up side of the line near the site of the abandoned North Acton Junction Box, and it was anticipated that when brought into use the new terminal would bring about a reduction of 30,000 lorry movements each year. In connection with this scheme, a train of 102 tonne hopper wagons was brought into use, though in 1998 Marcon sold all of its wagon fleet to EWS.

The arrival of the '08' shunters seemed to guarantee the long-term future of the Guinness rail system. However, as mentioned in Chapter Four, this traffic was transferred to road transport in the mid-1990s, and the last Guinness train was hauled out of the Park Royal Brewery by class '56' Co-Co No. 56054 *British Steel Llanwern* on 6th July, 1995. In 1997, the two Guinness class '08' shunters were taken by road to the Cholsey & Wallingford Railway, where they have continued to operate in their distinctive Guinness 'stout black' livery.

The double track section between Old Oak Common West and Park Royal was singled as part of the Paddington resignalling during the period 21st June to 5th July, 1993.

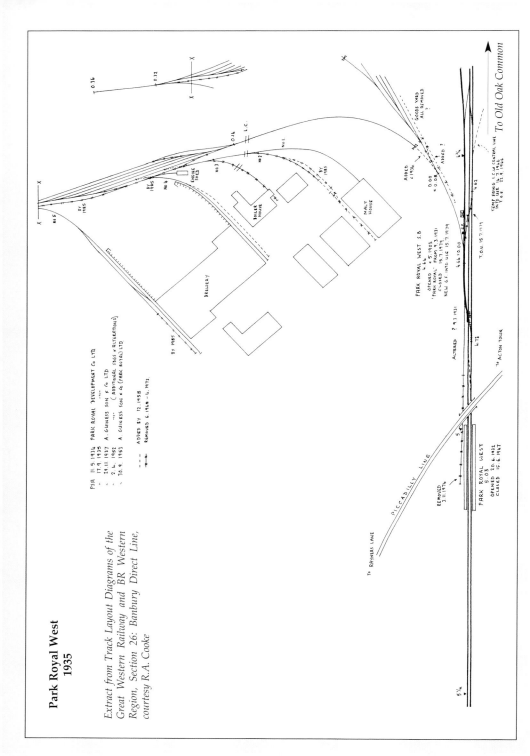

Park Royal West
1935

Extract from Track Layout Diagrams of the Great Western Railway and BR Western Region, Section 26: Banbury Direct Line, courtesy R.A. Cooke

To Old Oak Common

Park Royal West Halt

Passing beneath the Uxbridge branch of the Piccadilly Line, westbound trains reach the site of a closed stopping place known as Park Royal West (5 miles 3 chains). This was not one of the original railmotor halts, having been opened on 20th June, 1932 at a time when industrial development was starting to have a major impact on the surrounding area. The halt was positioned immediately to the west of the Piccadilly Line girder bridge - which had originally carried District Railway services - and it was conveniently sited in relation to the new factories along the Western Avenue. Park Royal West was closed with effect from 15th June, 1947, following the opening of the new Central Line station at Hanger Lane.

Brentham/Hanger Lane

Hanger Lane, the next stop, is barely a quarter of a mile further on. Situated in a cutting, with the Hanger Lane road bridge immediately to the east, Hanger Lane is typical of the stations on the Central Line western extension. It consists of an island platform, with street level station buildings on a corner site between Hanger Lane and the Western Avenue. Completed on 2nd January, 1949, this brick-and-concrete structure incorporates a circular booking hall with a raised cupola, the design being in many ways reminiscent of pre-war Underground architectural practice - although the building had been erected during the post-war 'austerity' period.

No trace remains of Brentham closed from 15th June, 1947, the forerunner of Hanger Lane (5 miles 41 chains) but its name is commemorated by 'Brentham Halt Road', to the west of the present Central Line station. Interestingly, Hanger Lane is the third station to occupy more or less the same site, the first stopping place

'King' class 4-6-0 No. 6008 *King James II* passes Brentham with the 9.00 am up service from Birkenhead to Paddington on 5th June, 1937.   *Ken Nunn/LCGB Collection*

provided here having been opened on 1st May, 1904. This simple, railmotor 'halte' was known as Twyford Abbey, and it was sited a short distance to the east of Brentham at 5 miles 30 chains). Twyford Abbey was closed on 30th April, 1911, following a landslip, the replacement stopping place at Brentham being opened to public traffic on the following day, 1st May, 1911.

Emerging from the cutting, the lines are carried north-westwards on embankments, with the Central Line at a slightly lower level than the Great Western route. Two parallel brick viaducts span the River Brent, and it comes as a surprise to find that the Underground bridge - opened as recently as 1947 - is, like its main line neighbour, built on the traditional arched pattern. At the time of its construction, the original bridge was described by *The Engineer* as 'a brick viaduct, 320 ft in length, and with the rail level at an altitude of 38 ft'.

Perivale

Perivale, the next stop for Central Line services, was opened on 30th June, 1947. It replaced the nearby Great Western stopping place at Perivale Halt (6 miles 65 chains), which had been in use since the opening of the 'New Line' on 1st May, 1904. The original Perivale Halt had been equipped with up and down platforms and corrugated iron 'pagoda' shelters of the usual prefabricated type. When the Central Line extension was being planned during the 1930s, it was decided that the halt would be replaced by a new island platform on an adjacent site, with a low-level station building on the down side.

A general view of Perivale, *circa* 1912, showing the timber platforms and characteristic GWR 'pagoda' buildings. This simple halt was closed a wartime economy measure in 1915 but, having re-opened in 1920, the platforms remained in use until the opening of the adjacent Central line station in 1947.   *Lens of Sutton Collection*

By the time that the new station was finally opened after World War II, the pre-war plans had been modified in the light of prevailing economic conditions, the canopies and ticket office being more modest than originally intended. The nearby GWR platforms were closed, although various private sidings on the up side of the main line remained in use for many years thereafter.

A private siding had been installed at Perivale in 1930 to serve a nearby wallpaper factory, authorization for 'the construction of new sidings at Perivale Halt for Messrs A. Sanderson & Sons' having been given by the GWR Directors on 14th February, 1929. The estimated cost of the siding was £3,859, including a contribution of £2,000 from Sanderson & Sons. In the event, a further £644 was deemed necessary for the provision of a temporary siding and additional drainage, the total cost to the Great Western company being £2,503.

By 1938, the original siding was being used as a means of access to the Electric Metallic Recovery Company's nearby premises, while a third private siding appeared during the 1940s, under a private siding agreement made between the GWR and H.P. Bulmer & Co. All of these sidings were sited on the up side of the line, and entered by means of connections from Sandersons' Siding. The latter siding was in effect a short, single track goods branch, the connection with the main line being by means of a single turnout that was trailing to the direction of up trains. The siding was closed in 1955, and subsequently removed.

Greenford

Continuing north-westwards, trains soon reach Greenford, where the loop line from West Ealing converges from the left. The now-closed GWR station at Greenford (7 miles 64 chains) had been opened on 1st October, 1904. Like most stations on the 'New Line', it incorporated a spacious, quadruple track layout, the platforms being served by loop lines on each side of the up and down main lines, so that freight trains or local passenger workings could be overtaken by faster main line services. The station was sited immediately to the west of the Greenford triangle, by means of which the loop line from West Ealing joined the 'New Line'.

The station buildings were utterly typical of Great Western practice during the early 20th century, being single-storey, brick-built structures with low-pitched hipped roofs and projecting platform canopies. Buildings of this standardised type had first appeared during the 1870s, one of the earliest examples being erected at Moreton-in-Marsh in 1874. Distinguishing features included tall chimney stacks with 'oversailing' brick work and prominent stone or concrete lintels that accentuated the door and window apertures. As Greenford station was sited on an embankment its station building was a two-storey design, with its rear entrance at ground level.

The goods yard was opened on 1st October, 1904, with provision for 'general goods, grain, timber, bricks, stone, coal and coke, hay and straw, and all descriptions of merchandise and mineral traffic'. The yard, which was sited to the west of the platforms on the up side, was extended during World War I, when the GWR Directors authorised the construction of 'two loop sidings on the up side, between Greenford Station and Greenford East Loop, 2,299 ft and 2,130 ft respectively'. These new sidings would have a 'direct connection with the up platform line', while the land upon which the sidings would be laid would be 'levelled by tipping spoil from the Ealing & Shepherd's Bush Railway'.

An early view of the up side station buildings at Greenford, probably taken shortly after opening in 1904. Note the approach ramp to the goods yard and Messrs Paulings construction depot to the right of the picture.   *Lens of Sutton Collection*

A detailed view of the split-level station buildings on the up side at Greenford, photographed from the station forecourt, *circa* 1912.   *Lens of Sutton Collection*

The up and down main line platforms at Greenford, looking west towards Princes Risborough, while a push-pull auto-train occupies the up platform. *Stations UK*

Looking northwards from the Central Line platform at Greenford towards the main line platforms on 14th June, 1958, as 'Castle' class 4-6-0 No. 5012 *Berry Pomeroy Castle* runs through the station with an Oxford to Paddington service. *H.C. Casserley*

A detailed view of the high level Central Line platform at Greenford *circa* 1960, showing Collett
'14XX' class 0-4-2T No. 1438 in the Ealing branch bay.   *Lens of Sutton Collection*

The present Greenford station is served by London Transport Central Line trains, and by main
line dmus from Paddington via Ealing Broadway, which arrive and depart from a bay platform
between the eastbound and westbound LT tracks. The abandoned main line station was situated
at a lower level, on the right-hand side of the photograph.   *Lens of Sutton Collection*

Greenford goods yard was altered and extended during the 1930s, when the GWR Directors authorised the construction of a new, and much larger goods shed on a new site, in lieu of the existing shed. The existing sidings were extended, and three new sidings were provided, one of these being the new 'Goods Shed Road' while the others were for mileage traffic. The estimated cost of these new works, inclusive of new roadways, lighting, and all other works, amounted to £6,025. The rebuilding scheme was put into effect in 1931, and when completed, the up side yard contained five goods sidings, together with a short spur to the end-loading dock, and the private siding to Joe Lyons' factory.

The new goods shed was semi-prefabricated structure with a 100 ft loading platform and a full length verandah over the loading bay. The goods yard also contained coal wharves, a goods office, cattle pens, an end-loading dock, a 6-ton yard crane and a 20-ton cart weigh-bridge. The goods facilities were expanded still further by the addition of a down side 'Mileage Yard' with two dead-end sidings. The provision of this additional infrastructure was authorized in 1936 at an estimated cost of £9,101. Meanwhile, even greater upheavals were being put into effect at Greenford in connection with the building of a lengthy concrete viaduct for the proposed Central Line extension to Denham.

Work on the Central Line extension was well advanced by the start of World War II, the viaduct having been completed before the start of the conflict, while the new LT station was also well advanced. When belatedly opened to public traffic on Monday 30th June, 1947, Greenford's new station featured an island platform layout, with a terminal bay at its east end to accommodate the steam worked auto-trains from Ealing. The low level station buildings, of brick and concrete construction, were on the south side of the line, with a subway connection to the London Transport and main line platforms.

Greenford's GWR station was, for all intents and purposes, rendered superfluous by the opening of the Central Line station, although its increasingly shabby platforms were not officially closed until 17th June, 1963. In its final years of operation, the former GWR station was used mainly by parcels and empty stock workings.

In steam days, the area around Greenford station was signalled from four signal boxes, which were, from east to west, Greenford East Loop (7 miles 15 chains), Greenford Station East (7 miles 44 chains) and Greenford Station West (7 miles 74 chains); the fourth box, known as Greenford South Loop, was sited at the southern extremity of the Greenford Triangle. Greenford East Loop and South Loop boxes were closed on Saturday 8th December, 1956, and Greenford Station West box was closed in August 1971. The 2½ miles from Greenford to Northolt Junction was reduced to single line between 26th and 29th May, 1990.

Industrial Activities at Greenford: The Up Side

There were a number of private sidings at Greenford, some of these being sited alongside the up main line, while others branched out from a short goods branch known as 'Watson's Siding' that diverged south-westwards from the goods yard, and passed beneath the Central Line viaduct. As in the case of Park Royal, these industrial sidings were probably at their peak during the later 1930s, and for this reason the 1938 Railway Clearing House *Handbook of Stations* can be used as a convenient source of information.

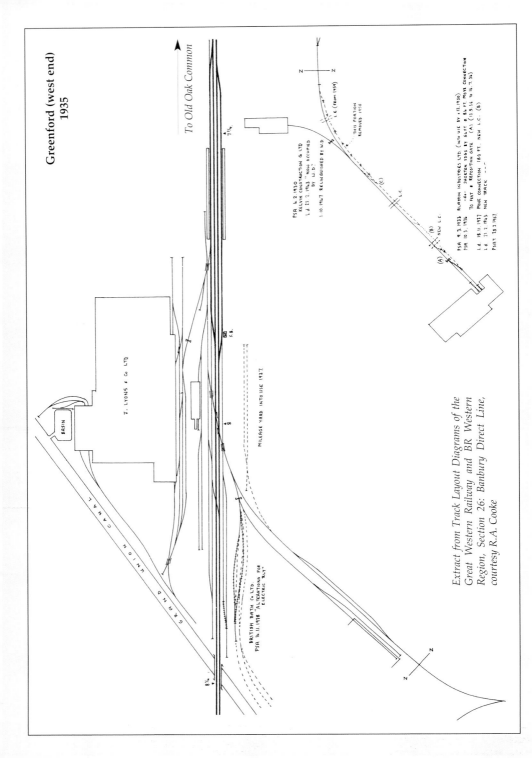

Greenford (west end)
1935

To Old Oak Common

Extract from Track Layout Diagrams of the
Great Western Railway and BR Western
Region, Section 26: Banbury Direct Line,
courtesy R.A. Cooke

Sidings on the north, or up side of the line included the Rockware Glass Syndicate and the British Hartford-Fairmont Syndicate sidings at the east end of the station, and Messrs J. Lyons & Company's private sidings to the west. Industrial sidings on the down side of the line included those serving the British Bath Company Ltd, the Kelvin Construction Company, and Aladdin Industries Ltd. Additional sidings were installed at Greenford for War Department and use during World War II, while some of the civilian factories were requisitioned for War Department use.

As in the case of Park Royal, the rail-served firms at Greenford varied in terms of size and importance, as well as the range of their products. The most famous undertaking here was perhaps Messrs J. Lyons & Co, a food company that could trace its origins back to the 1880s, when Montague and Isidore Gluckstein, the sons of a German immigrant, had started a catering business in association with their brother-in-law Barnett Salmon, and their cousin Joseph Lyons.

The Lyons Greenford factory was opened in 1923, the 70-acre site being immediately to the north of the station, and in convenient proximity to the Grand Union Canal. Lyons Siding left the up loop at the west end of the platform, and having entered the factory it branched out into several subsidiary sidings, some of which ran alongside the canal basin.

The other important firm on the north side of the line (and east of the station) was the Rockware Glass Syndicate Ltd. This was a somewhat older concern than Messrs Lyons, and could trace its history back to 1819, when the Bailey family commenced glass manufacturing at Portobello, near Edinburgh. The Rockware Syndicate was established in 1919 by Mr W.A. Bailey, and in that same year a private siding agreement was made with the GWR in respect of a new siding on the up side of the line between Greenford East and Greenford West junctions. The name, 'Rockware', commemorated the famous Rockingham teapots that had once been produced at Alloa in Scotland.

The Greenford factory initially employed just 110 people, who were able to manufacture 1,250 containers per week. From this modest beginning, the plant grew into a large factory covering 40 acres, with around 1,200 employees producing 750,000 bottles and jam jars every 24 hours. The internal railway system grew accordingly, the original siding being augmented by a further group of sidings about a quarter of a mile to the east that had once been used for War Department purposes during World War I. By the 1950s, these two sidings formed, in effect, two divergent branch lines, both of which formed connections with an array of parallel loops and sidings on the up side of the main line.

Industrial Activities at Greenford: The Down Side

With industrial development in full swing along the Western Avenue, there was a requirement for new sidings on the down side of the line, and on 27th June, 1927 the GWR Directors authorised the provision of a 'Trunk Siding' or goods branch. This was defined as a 'line from Greenford station to Western Avenue', which would enable 'Mr Watson's land on the south side of the railway and adjoining the Grand Union Canal' to be used for factory sites. Interestingly, it was agreed that the freehold of 'Watson's Siding' would be given to the Great Western Railway, while Mr Watson would be liable for a rent of £150 per annum for a period of two years. The estimated cost of the siding was £2,770.

The first part of the siding was brought into use around 1928 in connection with the newly-built British Bath Factory, which was one of the first factories to appear on the down side of the line. The relevant private siding agreement was signed between the British Bath Company and the GWR on 21st December, 1928.

The British Bath Works was opened by Allied Ironfounders in 1927. It specialised in the manufacture of enamelled baths, many of which were transported out of the factory in specially-fitted containers. The British Bath Works sidings were extended south-westwards during World War II in order to reach an array of new sidings provided for War Department use to the west of the Bath Works.

The siding link to the British Bath Works formed a convenient starting point for the 'Trunk Siding' (or 'Watson's Siding') proper, which was opened around two years later under the provisions of a private siding agreement with the Kelvin Construction Company that had been signed on 4th February, 1930. The new siding extended southwards towards new factory sites along the Western Avenue. When first built, the siding traversed a largely undeveloped area, but in the next few years further roads and factories were laid out, together with houses and bungalows for the workers.

The Aladdin oil lamp factory, at the very end of the 'Trunk Siding', was opened in October 1931, but Great Western timetables suggest that the firm had used rail transport from about 1930 - presumably during the construction of the new factory. A private siding agreement was made between the GWR and Aladdin Industries Ltd on 9th March, 1933, and this enabled the siding to be continued southwards for a short distance into the lamp factory. Further agreements dated 10th March, 1936 and 18th November, 1937 dealt with alterations needed in connection with extensions to the firm's warehouse, which involved 'a slight variation in respect of maintenance and renewal' as provided for under the original agreement.

The 'Trunk Siding' left the GWR main line on the down side by means of a connection from the down platform loop. There was also a link from the goods yard, and this crossed the running lines via a system of slips, so that the siding could be entered from the up side of the station, as well as the down. The siding passed beneath the eastbound and westbound Central Line tracks and immediately bifurcated, a facing connection providing access to the premises of the British Bath Company, while the 'main line' proceeded south-westwards on a parallel alignment to a road known as 'Long Drive'. A loop siding was provided at the north end of the main 'Trunk Siding'.

Passing over a gated level crossing that gave access to a Home Office depot, the 'Trunk Siding' curved southwards and threw off a spur to the Kelvin Construction Company; another level crossing was sited just before the junction so that road traffic could reach the Kelvin Iron Works from the Long Drive. Now heading due south, the siding doubled to form two parallel lines, and after passing over two more level crossings, it entered the aptly-named Aladdin lamp factory. The layout of the siding was altered slightly during World War II, when the double track section was extended north towards the Home Office storage depot.

Most of these private sidings remained in use during the 1950s and 1960s, an 0-6-0 diesel shunter being sent from Southall each week to work in Greenford yard and the 'Ordnance Sidings' as required. The engine concerned started work at 6.30 am on Monday mornings, and when not in use it was stabled in the loading dock. British Railways engines were prohibited from entering Lyons Siding, although the British Bath Co.'s sidings could be shunted by 0-6-0Ts (and presumably also by the 0-6-0 diesel shunter from Southall).

The private sidings in and around Greenford were important enough to avoid closure during the Beeching period, but they were progressively run-down during the next few years. The Aladdin and Kelvin Construction Company sidings were both taken out of use in 1967, while Lyons Siding was closed three years later. The Allied Ironfounders's (British Bath Works) Siding agreement was terminated on 30th June, 1976, though it was decided that the connection beneath the Central Line would be retained in case of 'possible developments'.

Northolt

From Greenford, the route continues north-westwards, the Grand Union Canal being crossed near the 8½ milepost. The original Great Western bridge consists of a 'bowstring' lattice girder bridge on brick abutments, with a single span of 98 ft, while the adjacent Central Line bridge has a truss girder span of 158 ft.

Continuing north-westwards on a gently-rising 1 in 264 gradient, down trains soon reach Northolt (8 miles 66 chains). The station here, like all others on this first section of the route apart from Greenford, is now served only by London Transport services. When first opened on 1st May, 1907, it was a simple railmotor halt with short, sleeper-built platforms, and corrugated iron 'pagoda' sheds on both sides. The original halt was much-improved in 1929, when the platforms were lengthened, and a single goods siding was installed on the up side. On 15th February, 1934, the GWR Directors authorised the expenditure of £770 for an extension of the 'cart roadway' alongside the goods siding.

An additional siding was laid on the down side of the line in 1932, together with a crossover, so that terminating auto-trains could, if necessary, be held at Northolt prior to returning towards London as up workings. To facilitate this mode of operation, Northolt had been made into a block post in 1929, a signal box having been erected on the up side of the line between the passenger platforms and the newly-installed sidings. The signal box was an all-timber, hip-roofed structure, with a 30-lever frame.

Despite the many improvements carried out in the 1930s, Northolt remained little more than a staffed halt, and its promotion to full 'station' status did not really occur until the opening of the Central Line station on 21st November, 1948. The last steam-worked service had called at the former GWR platforms on the previous day, although the goods siding and signal box remained in use until 1952.

The Central Line station is situated about seven chains to the west of the original GWR halt, its single, 440 ft island platform being positioned on the west side of the Mandeville Road overbridge. The platform is covered, for much of its length, by a concrete canopy supported by centre columns, while the flat-roofed brick and concrete station building is sited on the adjacent road overbridge. This structure was not completed until November 1961, a temporary ticket office and toilets having been in use until that date.

When building work resumed in 1961, these buildings were enlarged to form a large, rectangular booking hall with provision for bookstalls and tobacconist's kiosks. The permanent station frontage was faced with light-coloured brickwork, with two glazed shop fronts for the kiosks. The track layout at Northolt includes a reversing siding, which is conveniently-sited between the eastbound and westbound tracks at the 'country' end of the island platform.

The scenery along this stretch of line is entirely suburban in character, but the transport enthusiast may find some consolation at nearby Northolt aerodrome, where a Spitfire is preserved as a gate guardian. Northolt was used for a variety of

A detailed view of the down platform at Northolt, showing the iron 'pagoda' shed and road overbridge, probably taken shortly after opening in 1907. The apparent absence of an up platform suggests that, when first opened, the 'halte' may have been equipped with very short, staggered platforms. *Lens of Sutton Collection*

An Edwardian view of the typical GWR railmotor halt at Northolt, which was similar to the other halts provided by the Great Western at the London end of the New Line. The left-hand platform was used by up services, and the view is looking towards London.

Lens of Sutton Collection

purposes during World War II, though it is perhaps chiefly remembered as one of the protective ring of Fighter Command airfields that were used in the defence of London during the Battle of Britain. In the post-war period, RAF Northolt fulfilled a number of roles, though in recent years it has been particularly associated with VIP transport and related activities.

Northolt Junction, just over 10 miles from Paddington, marks the end of the first section of the route, and it would now be convenient to describe the Great Central line from Marylebone before venturing into South Ruislip station along the Great Western & Great Central Joint Line proper.

Marylebone

Marylebone, which is now the main London terminus of the present-day 'Chiltern Line', was formally opened by the Rt Hon. Charles T. Ritchie, the President of the Board of Trade, on 9th March, 1899. Public services began just six days later, on Monday 15th March. The new terminus had just four platform faces, although it was intended that others would have been added if traffic had increased to a sufficient extent. The platforms were covered by a triple-bay overall roof which, like the platforms beneath, could easily have been extended if required. There was also a large hotel that, in later years, became the headquarters of the British Railways Board.

The architecture at Marylebone was less pretentious that one might have expected at a major London station. The main block was a red brick structure finished in a sober 'Jacobean' style. Its most attractive feature was perhaps the elegant porte cochère that covered the station approach and formed a visual link with the nearby Great Central Hotel. The station's curious name was derived from the parish of Marylebone, which was itself a contraction of 'St Mary-le-Bourne'.

Marylebone was always the quietest of the London termini, the feeling of tranquillity being accentuated by the general absence of short-distance local travellers - who were encouraged to travel on the Metropolitan Line to neighbouring Baker Street. Metropolitan interests had been safeguarded from the very start by an agreement made between the Great Central and Metropolitan companies whereby the GCR would open no inner suburban stations on the east, or London side of the River Brent. The first suburban station out of Marylebone was therefore established at Wembley Hill, on the west side of the river, some 6½ miles from the terminus.

There were no engine sheds at Marylebone, but a locomotive yard was conveniently-sited beyond the platforms on the down (or west) side, and in pre-Grouping days this was equipped with a coaling plant and a 55 ft diameter turntable. In October 1937 *The Railway Magazine* reported that the LNER had decided to install 'modern 70 ft diameter turntables at Marylebone and Leicester' in order to 'facilitate the use of locomotives of the Pacific and Green Arrow classes on the Great Central section'. In the 1960s, a diesel servicing depot was established at Marylebone in connection with the introduction of the class '115' multiple units.

In the heyday of steam operation, Marylebone had also boasted a large goods yard - the various goods facilities being laid-out to the north of the passenger station on the down side of the running lines, while facilities on the up side included a spacious milk depot and carriage dock, and an array of carriage sidings. The exit from the terminus was multiple-tracked, the sequence being (from west to east): down slow, up slow, down fast, up fast, loop line, and a line known as 'The Short Coal Road'.

Great Central Railway Station, Marylebone.

A panoramic view of Marylebone during the early years of the 20th century, looking northwards across the concourse towards Platform Two.   *Lens of Sutton Collection*

A postcard view of Marylebone station, *circa* 1912, with a Robinson '1020' class 4-4-0 at the south end of Platform Two.   *Lens of Sutton Collection*

Great Central Railway, Marylebone Station, N. W.

Marylebone station, looking towards the terminal buffer stops during the Edwardian period.
John Alsop Collection

The platform ends at Marylebone on 24th February, 1957. 'N5' class 0-6-2T No. 69257 was fitted with a vacuum control regulator during World War II so that it could be used as 'spare' locomotive on the Chesham branch. *R.M. Casserley*

A platform end view taken at Marylebone on 8th August, 1985, showing a Derby class '115' unit in BR blue and grey livery.   *Mike Marr*

A general view of Neasden Junction, showing Neasden South signal box, which was of typical Great Central design.   *John Alsop Collection*

The terminus was reconstructed in connection with the 'total route modernisation' of the Chiltern Line, the principal alterations being the removal of one of the three roof spans, and the installation of two additional platforms. The station now has six terminal platforms, the present platforms 1 to 4 being fully covered, whereas Nos. 5 and 6 are situated beyond the confines of the train shed. The buildings have been fully modernised, while the attractive porte cochère received a £250,000 refurbishment.

Departing from Marylebone station, present-day trains follow the Great Central main line as far as Neasden South Junction, and then turn west along the Neasden-Northolt line. The exit from Marylebone is notable in that trains pass beneath Marylebone Cricket Ground and the surrounding area by means of three closely-spaced tunnels. Lords tunnel, has a length of 237 yards, while St John's Wood tunnel, a short distance further on, is 1,279 yards in length; Hampstead tunnel, the third and final tunnel on this section, is 673 yards in length.

The Metropolitan and Jubilee lines are, at this point, running alongside in parallel tunnels; the Metropolitan tunnel from Baker Street to Finchley Road having been opened by the Metropolitan & St John's Wood Railway on 13th April, 1868, whereas the twin Jubilee Line tube tunnels were opened on 20th November, 1939 to enable Bakerloo trains to reach the Metropolitan branch to Stanmore.

Emerging from its tunnel at Finchley Road, the Great Central route turns westwards, and with the 'Underground' lines now visible to the right, trains run past the London Transport stations at West Hampstead, Kilburn, Willesden Green, Dollis Hill and Neasden. These busy stopping places were originally served by Metropolitan Railway services, but they became part of the Bakerloo Line on 20th November, 1939, and are now served by Jubilee Line services between Stanmore and Charing Cross. Shortly after passing Dollis Hill, the GCR route passes beneath the former Midland line from Cricklewood to Acton Wells, after which trains pass the site of Neasden motive power depot.

Having reached Neasden, present-day Chiltern Line trains diverge westwards onto the Neasden to Northolt Junction line, while the Metropolitan and Jubilee routes run north-westwards to Wembley Park, where Jubilee services finally part company with the Metropolitan main line. For locomotive enthusiasts, Neasden was a particularly interesting place, as its motive power depot (34E, later 14D) was the most important depot on the GCR London Extension. Here, in and around a six-road 'northlight' pattern shed building, one could always be sure of seeing a wide range of LNER motive power.

In 1950, Neasden housed 82 locomotives. including three Gresley 'A3' class 4-6-2s, six Thompson 'B1' class 4-6-0s, eleven 'N5' class 0-6-2Ts, five 'N7' class 0-6-2Ts and no less than 43 'L1' or 'L3' class 2-6-4Ts. Other locomotives allocated to the depot at that time included a number of 'J11' 0-6-0s, 'A5' 4-6-2Ts, 'C13' 4-4-2Ts, two '61XX' class 2-6-2Ts, one '14XX' class 0-4-2T and a Sentinel shunter.

As today's diesel multiple units clatter across the pointwork at the junction, observant travellers can catch a glimpse of the London Transport Neasden works, visible to the right across the main line and LT tracks. Neasden was the home of the last steam locomotives to operate revenue earning services in the London area, and until 1971, red London Transport '57XX' class 0-6-0 panniers could sometimes be seen in or near the works. The first Western Region pannier tank was transferred to London Transport in 1956, and over the next few years a further 12 were acquired for use on engineering trains on the Metropolitan, Circle and District lines.

An early view of Wembley Hill station, showing the low-level platforms and platform building, with the high-level ticket office and station master's house in the right background.

Lens of Sutton Collection

The high-level station buildings at Wembley Hill, photographed in the early 1900s with the station master's house to the left. The posters advertise forthcoming GCR excursions to Doncaster and the North.

Lens of Sutton Collection

Wembley Hill

Now heading due westwards, Banbury-bound trains pass the site of Neasden North Junction, where the single track Wembley Stadium loop formerly diverged from the main line. The loop followed a circuitous course back to Neasden Junction, the Stadium station being situated at the approximate half way point. Trains ran around the loop in a clockwise direction, and having called at the Stadium, they returned to Marylebone to collect further passengers. These frequent, short-distance services were worked by 'A5' 4-6-2Ts, 'L1' 2-6-4Ts, 'N7' 0-6-2Ts or other tank locomotives. The loop line was signalled with colour light signals, and the platform at the Stadium station was 600 ft long and 22 ft 6 in. wide.

The Stadium station was last used on 18th May, 1968, on the occasion of a Rugby League Cup Final at Wembley, but it did not close officially until 1st September, 1969. In its last months, the old exhibition station was no longer situated on a loop, and the track was severed a few yards to the north of the platform. For this reason, the last trains to use the station were composed of multiple unit stock. The track was recovered in 1971, and much of the area was subsequently used for industrial purposes.

The line through Wembley Hill was originally quadruple-tracked, the up and down platforms being positioned on either side of the outer slow lines. Wembley Hill Road was carried across the railway on a substantial 4-span girder bridge at the west end of the station, the booking office and station master's house being sited at street level. Having purchased their tickets in the high level station buildings, travellers were able to reach the platforms by means of gently-sloping pathways. The platforms were 450 ft long, and both were equipped with waiting rooms and other accommodation.

The goods yard was sited to the east of the platforms on the up side of the running lines. It was linked to the up slow line by a trailing connection, and to the down slow and down main lines by means of a system of single slips. This relatively complex arrangement was necessary in order that the yard could be shunted by up or down trains - a similar layout being necessary at all of the quadruple-tracked stations on the Great Western & Great Central Joint Line and its connections. The station was signalled from a gable-roofed signal box, of typical Great Central design, sited on the down side of the line.

In 1906, when the railway was opened, Wembley was described as 'a village on the Harrow Road, midway between Harlesden and Harrow'. The village contained 'one or two good residential houses of the old-fashioned type', while the parish church of St John, built in 1846, was 'a gothic building of flint and stone, near the station'. The Wembley Park estate, on the north side of the GCR line, had been purchased by the Metropolitan Railway when the latter company was building its extension to Harrow-on-the-Hill, and portions of the estate were subsequently leased to a development company which hoped to create spacious pleasure grounds, complete with a 1,200 ft high tower.

The idea of building a tower formed in Sir Edward Watkin's mind after a visit to Paris, where, having seen the Eiffel Tower, he decided that 'The Watkin Tower' would be over 165 ft taller. A company was formed to construct the proposed structure, and the first stage was completed by 1895, the engineer being Sir Benjamin Baker - the designer of the Forth Railway Bridge. In the event, this gargantuan structure grew no higher than the first stage, over 2,700 tons of steel being consumed before the promoters reluctantly decided that 'The Metropolitan Tower Construction Company' was a financially-risky undertaking.

A view of Wembley Hill during the Edwardian period, showing the station's quadruple-track layout to full advantage.   *John Alsop Collection*

Wembley Stadium station during its final years of operation. As the station was situated on a loop line, only one platform was provided – the Stadium being served by trains which proceeded around the loop in a clockwise direction.   *R.M. Casserley Collection*

Despite the failure of the Tower Company, the construction of Wembley Stadium and the Empire Pool ensured that, in the longer term, the Wembley area would become inextricably linked with sporting and leisure activities. Its greatest moment, arguably, came in 1948, when London staged the first post-war Olympic Games. Wembley became a major venue, although other sites, including the Guinness Sports Ground at Park Royal and the Lyons Sports Ground near Sudbury Hill station were also pressed into use.

In the past, the annual FA Cup Finals gave rise to numerous 'Football Specials', which often brought unusual motive power to the GW&GC route, including 'Royal Scots', 'Jubilees', and 'Britannia' Pacifics. At the time of writing, Wembley Stadium, with its famous twin towers, is being demolished, but other parts of the Wembley complex continue to be used for major sporting events such as the Horse of the Year Show, and the former Wembley Hill station - now known as 'Wembley Stadium' - still handles extra traffic on these occasions.

In its present-day guise, Wembley Stadium has widely-spaced up and down platforms, both of which have been given new surfaces, modern shelters and improved lighting. A reversing line or 'turn-back siding' has been installed immediately beyond the Wembley Hill Road bridge, so that additional services can be run to and from the station in connection with events at the Stadium or Arena.

Sudbury & Harrow Road

Passing under Wembley Hill Road, the line continues westwards through an extensive cutting, which required the removal of approximately 641,000 cubic yards of spoil, and the provision of extensive brick and concrete retaining walls. Emerging from the Wembley cutting, trains cross the West Coast Main Line on an impressive girder bridge with a single skew span of 107 ft. Beyond, the railway is carried on embankments towards Sudbury & Harrow Road station (7 miles 73 chains), where the original quadruple-track layout has been abandoned in favour of a simple island platform arrangement.

In its heyday, this station had two 450 ft timber platforms, with commodious buildings on both sides, and a low level booking office beside Harrow Road. The two platforms were linked by a subway, which featured 'buff coloured bricks with a brown glazed dado', while the nearby goods yard incorporated an array of parallel sidings and a large, brick-built goods shed, measuring 78 ft by 35 ft at ground level. Other goods-handling facilities included cattle loading pens, a weigh-house, a carriage dock, a 1 ton 10 cwt hand crane within the goods shed, and a 7 ton yard crane.

The booking office was of brick construction, but the high-level platform buildings were timber-framed structures clad in horizontal weather boarding, and supported on concrete piers buried within the embankment upon which the station was constructed. The station was signalled from a gable-roofed GCR type signal box, which was sited on the down platform beside the down side waiting room. The box was a single-storey structure, of all-timber construction, and at the time of its opening it contained 39 working levers and seven spares.

Sudbury & Harrow Road seen here was situated on an embankment, whereas neighbouring Sudbury Hill Harrow was in a cutting. This Edwardian view shows the four-track station shortly after opening.   *Lens of Sutton Collection*

Sudbury & Harrow Road, looking east towards Marylebone before the removal of the centre 'fast' roads.   *Lens of Sutton Collection*

Sudbury Hill Harrow

After Sudbury & Harrow Road, down trains enter a cutting, which is spanned by two road overbridges, one of which carries a minor road known as 'The Avenue' over the railway, while the other carries Greenfield Road across the line; Sudbury Hill Harrow (8 miles 73 chains) is immediately beyond. Opened as 'South Harrow' on 1st March, 1906, Sudbury Hill had been a near-twin of Sudbury & Harrow Road, with a four-track layout and a spacious goods yard on the down side of the line. Today, in contrast, the station has been reduced to a mere shadow of its former self, and present-day travellers must find it hard to believe that their station was ever more than a rationalised halt.

In its prime, the station had featured a high-level booking office facing Greenford Road, and platform level waiting rooms. The goods yard was sited to the west of the platforms on the down side, while the GCR type signal box was sited on the up platform. The last-mentioned structure was of brick and timber construction, with a gable roof. It remained in operation until 1990, when the line through Sudbury Hill came under the control of the Marylebone Integrated Electronic Control Centre (IECC).

From Sudbury Hill, the line passes beneath the former Ealing & South Harrow Railway in a 203 yds-long 'cut-and-cover' tunnel or 'covered way'. The South Harrow company was sanctioned on 25th August, 1894, and with the help of the Metropolitan District Railway, the line was opened throughout by 28th June, 1903. It was worked as part of the District Railway for the first few years, but on 4th July, 1932 the route became an integral part of the Piccadilly Line. The tunnel or 'covered way' was built to placate the District Railway, which owned a wide swathe of land on either side of the Ealing & South Harrow route.

A high-level booking office was provided at Sudbury Hill Harrow, with pedestrian access down to the platform; the building to the right of the booking office was the station master's house.   *Lens of Sutton Collection*

Sudbury Hill Harrow (then known as 'South Harrow'), *circa* 1910, showing the quadruple track layout, which as similar to that at Wembley Hill and indeed at most of the intermediate stations on the GW&GC Joint line and its connections.   *Lens of Sutton Collection*

Robinson 'A5' class 4-6-2T No. 5024 pauses at Sudbury Hill Harrow while working an LNER suburban service during the 1930s.   *Lens of Sutton Collection*

This view of Northolt Park, taken on 5th July, 1960, underlines the somewhat basic nature of the facilities provided at this location.   *H.C. Casserley*

Northolt Park

Northolt Park, the penultimate stopping place on the purely Great Central section between Marylebone and South Ruislip & Northolt Junction, is a little under 10 miles from Marylebone. As mentioned in Chapter Four, it was opened under LNER auspices on 19th July, 1926, and was originally called 'South Harrow & Roxeth'. The station was able to deal with goods traffic and horse boxes, in addition to passengers and parcels. The station buildings were of starkly-simple design, and the platforms were linked by a plate girder footbridge. Beyond, trains continue westwards to Northolt Junction, where they join the Great Western line from Paddington.

South Ruislip

The junction with the Great Western at Northolt is spectacular, and involves a change of levels; the down GCR line burrows under the Great Western route and then turns north-westward and climbs a half mile incline to reach South Ruislip, 10 miles 22 chains from Paddington, and the first station on the Great Western & Great Central Joint Line proper. Opened on 1st May, 1908 as 'Northolt Junction', the name was changed to 'South Ruislip & Northolt Junction' on 12th September, 1932, and on 6th October, 1947 it became simply 'South Ruislip'.

The station is orientated on an approximate south-east to north-west alignment, the junction between the down Great Central line and the down Paddington to Birmingham lines being sited immediately to the east of the platforms. A similar junction on the up side provides a connection between the up Paddington line and the up GCR line. Prior to rationalisation, the station had featured a quadruple-tracked layout, but the up relief line was taken out of use in December 1973, and all up trains then used the up main line. Although South Ruislip was primarily a passenger station, there was a small goods yard to the west of the platforms on the up side, with private siding links to a factory and a dairy.

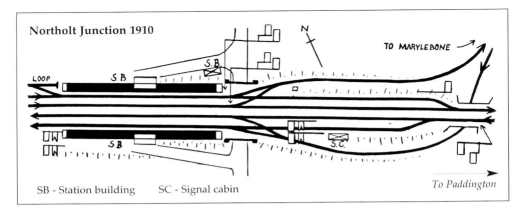

Northolt Junction 1910

LOOP
S.B.
S.B.
TO MARYLEBONE
N
SB
W
SC
W
W

SB - Station building   SC - Signal cabin

To Paddington

A general view of South Ruislip & Northolt Junction station in 1945, looking east towards London and showing the up and down platforms and up side station buildings.

Lens of Sutton Collection

Another view of South Ruislip in the post-war period, showing the up and down main line platforms and looking westwards in the direction of Princes Risborough.

Lens of Sutton Collection

As originally constructed, Northolt Junction had been equipped with a low-level booking office and high level waiting rooms, the booking office being a brick structure, whereas the platform buildings were built of timber. The down side building was subsequently replaced by a small waiting shelter, while the up side platform building was demolished in the 1970s. The station was signalled from two standard GWR hipped-roof signal boxes, both of which were situated on the down side. They were designated Northolt Junction East and Northolt Junction West. The West box closed on 17th July, 1966 while the East box lasted until the 26th-29th May, 1990 when control passed to Marylebone IECC.

The station is served by Central Line services, as well as Chiltern Line trains, the eastbound and westbound LT tracks being sited to the south of the main line station. The London Transport station was opened on 21st November, 1948, when the Central Line was extended to West Ruislip. It consists of an island platform, 440 ft in length, with a substantial concrete canopy, together with a low level station building, which was not completed until November 1961. The latter structure boasts an attractive circular booking hall, or 'rotunda', of vaguely 1930s appearance.

As mentioned in Chapter Four, this building was left unfinished for 20 years, but work resumed in 1961, when the domed booking hall became the central feature of a new structure, featuring a ticket office, staff quarters, toilets and a bookstall. A shop was incorporated into the street frontage, and a subway linked the London Transport and Western Region platforms. Externally, the station building was faced with dark blue-grey brickwork, while the interior of the booking hall included a frieze of pre-cast concrete panels which, as *The Railway Magazine* explained, were 'sculpted in relief to express the flow of passenger movement through the station'!

Ruislip Gardens

For the next two miles, the diminutive Tube trains run parallel to the Joint Line along the tracks laid for them by BR. The section of line between Northolt Jn and West Ruislip was originally quadruple, and with the two London Transport tracks to the south, this part of the line was an impressive sight - particularly when British Railways and London Transport trains were running neck and neck on the parallel lines. The down relief line between Northolt Jn and West Ruislip was taken out of use in May 1990, while the up relief line had closed much earlier in December 1973.

Heading north-westwards through a suburban landscape of houses, schools and playing fields, trains rush past Ruislip Gardens, only half a mile away from South Ruislip. Although for a time both London Transport and main line trains called here the station is now served by Central Line services only. Opened on 9th July, 1934, the original Ruislip Gardens was little more than a staffed halt, its timber trestle platforms being perched somewhat precariously on either side of a lofty embankment. The usual corrugated iron 'pagoda' sheds afforded rudimentary shelter for waiting passengers, but there was, in addition, a small hip-roofed ticket office at road level on the up side.

Although the facilities provided at Ruislip Gardens were somewhat primitive, this small station was, by the end of the 1930s, one of the busiest on the entire line. Suburban development in the immediate vicinity produced an upsurge in commuter traffic, and passenger bookings rose from 51,904 ordinary tickets and 501 seasons in 1935, to 97,952 tickets and 836 seasons by 1937. At that time, the station had a staff of two, the paybill expenses in the later 1930s being only 0.3 per cent of the total receipts - an excellent ratio.

A glimpse of Ruislip Gardens station during the 1930s, showing the timber-built platforms and standard GWR 'pagoda' buildings.   *Lens of Sutton Collection*

An ex-GCR 'A5' class 4-6-2T and LNER suburban train approaching Ruislip Gardens on a dismal winter's day; note the dual LNER and GWR notice boards on the classic Great Western pagoda shelter.   *Lens of Sutton Collection*

The later history of Ruislip Gardens echoes that of Hanger Lane and the other intermediate stopping places between Paddington, Greenford and West Ruislip. Plans for a new station on the Central Line extension were prepared in the 1930s, but the station was not opened until 21st November, 1948 - by which time the original scheme had been modified. The usual island platform layout was employed, its 440 ft length being dictated by the length of a standard London Transport 8-car formation. The platform was covered by a concrete canopy, and the high level platform buildings were of brick and concrete construction.

A subsidiary signal box was installed at Ruislip Gardens (Central Line) to control the eastern entrance to Ruislip depot, which was situated a short distance to the west of the station. The box contained a 22-lever power frame with miniature levers of the 'full stroke' type. Under normal circumstances, the box was remotely-controlled from nearby West Ruislip, but it could also be worked manually if required.

As the main line and LT tracks at Ruislip Gardens are situated on an embankment, the main station buildings are conveniently sited at a lower level, beside West End Road. The permanent buildings were not built until 1961, when the Western Region's Architect's Office designed a new, single-storey structure containing a ticket office, booking hall, staff accommodation, public toilets and a bookstall. The building was faced with brickwork and grey-green Broughton Moor slate panels, its flat roof and austere appearance being typical of 1960s architecture - albeit a considerable improvement on the accretion of temporary structures that had been in use for the previous 11 years!

The main line platforms remained in use until 21st July, 1958, and for a few years Ruislip Gardens was served by both British Railways and London Transport services. Like other stations on the Central Line extension, Ruislip Gardens was manned by a mixture of British Railways and London Transport employees, the station staff being BR personnel, whereas the signal box (when in use) was operated by LT staff. On 13th November, 1967, most of the staff at Ruislip Gardens, South Ruislip and West Ruislip were transferred to the London Transport payroll.

West Ruislip

Climbing gently at 1 in 430, trains cross the Uxbridge branch of the Metropolitan Line before entering West Ruislip station, 12 miles 7 chains from Paddington, and formerly known as Ruislip & Ickenham.

West Ruislip was a typical Great Western & Great Central Joint Line station, with a quadruple-tracked layout, and up and down platforms on each side. There was a small goods yard at the London end of the platforms, while the usual GWR hip-roofed station buildings were sited on the up side. In the words of the *Great Western Railway Magazine*, this single-storey, red brick structure was 'of the Great Western standard type, the buildings consisting of booking clerks' and station master's offices, waiting rooms and cloak rooms, and the usual offices'.

The station was signalled from a hip-roofed signal box sited to the east of the platforms on the down side, while the up and down sides of the station were linked by a fully-roofed GWR plate girder footbridge. The platforms were 400 ft in length, while the nearby goods yard contained 'a goods lock-up with cattle pens, horse landings, van shoot, cart weighbridge, etc.'. The yard crane was originally of 5 tons lifting capacity, but in May 1953 British Railways replaced the old crane with a more powerful 6 ton hand crane that had been transferred from Tipton.

An early view of West Ruislip station (then known as 'Ruislip & Ickenham'), looking east towards London from the road overbridge, and showing the up and down platforms, station master's house, staff cottages and standard GWR plate girder footbridge.

Lens of Sutton Collection

West Ruislip, looking towards London. The Central Line depot can be glimpsed in the right background.   *Lens of Sutton Collection*

The goods yard contained three sidings, one of which was arranged as a reception loop, while a second, parallel loop line served a covered loading bank. A dead-end spur extended westwards from the loop siding to reach a loading dock behind the up platform, while the rear, or 'back' siding was available for coal or other forms of 'mileage' traffic. It should perhaps be explained that, on the Great Western system, full wagon load traffic of this type was referred to as mileage traffic because it was paid-for on a mileage basis, whereas smaller consignments were normally charged by weight.

The goods yard was linked to the up relief line by trailing connections, while another trailing connection diverged from the down relief line and, having crossed the down main, up main and down relief lines by means of single slips, it converged with the goods reception loop in order to provide a link between the goods yard and the down lines. This was a standard arrangement found at all of the four-track stations on the GW&GC route and its connecting lines.

Passenger numbers at West Ruislip increased from 18,103 in 1913 to 46,492 in 1929 and 58,164 by 1933. By the end of the decade, sales of ordinary tickets amounted to about 68,000 per annum - a modest enough figure, although there were also around 2,000 season ticket holders, the majority of whom would have used the station on a daily basis. Goods traffic increased from 4,111 tons in 1913 to 31,008 tons in 1938. Domestic coal amounted to about 8,500 tons per year, while 'carted traffic' contributed another 4,000 tons of freight per annum; otherwise, West Ruislip's main traffic was mainly 'general merchandise' much of which was probably in the form of construction material for the Central Line.

The layout at West Ruislip has been altered considerably at different times, the first changes being implemented during World War I, when extra sidings were installed on the down side to deal with government traffic. These were subsequently used by the Air Ministry in connection with a neighbouring RAF depot. The station is of course the western terminus of the Central Line, and there is a large Underground depot here, together with extensive LT stabling sidings. A siding links the main line and London Transport systems, and all new Underground stock reaches LT metals over this connection.

When the Central Line extension was first planned during the 1930s it was envisaged that West Ruislip would be a through station with an additional platform for terminating services, but when finally opened on Sunday 21st November, 1948 it had just one island platform. A 'scissors' crossover at the London end of the passenger station enabled the two platform faces to be used by arriving or departing trains, while two sidings by-passed the platform on its south side. One of these was a non-electrified line that gave access to the BR system via a headshunt connection from the down BR main line.

The presence of the Air Ministry depot to the south of the GW&GC station meant that the Central Line Depot had to be built somewhat further to the east than would otherwise have been necessary. The requirement for rail access to the Air Ministry sidings also meant that the final track plan was more complicated than would otherwise have been the case - traffic for the Air Ministry being shunted along the above-mentioned non-electrified siding towards the LT Depot, and then reversed into the RAF sidings via another headshunt.

The new station buildings had reached an advanced state prior to World War II. The buildings were sited on the road overbridge at the west end of the station, with their main frontage facing towards the road. When work resumed in 1961, a projecting canopy was added, together with a glazed clerestory above the booking

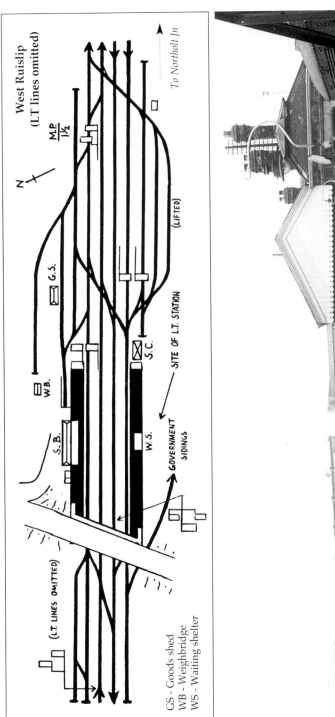

West Ruislip
(LT lines omitted)

To Northolt Jn

M.P. 1½

N

G.S.

(LIFTED)

SITE OF L.T. STATION

S.C.

W.B.

S.B.

W.S.

GOVERNMENT SIDINGS

(L.T. LINES OMITTED)

GS - Goods shed
WB - Weighbridge
WS - Waiting shelter

H.C. Casserley

West Ruislip, looking westwards along the up platform on 14th June, 1958.

West Ruislip (originally Ruislip & Ickenham) signal box is typical of those on the New Line, although some GW&GC boxes were of wooden construction.   *Brian W. Leslie*

View of the Central Line platforms at West Ruislip, in the early 1950s, with a train of pre-1938 clerestoried stock departing for Debden.   *Lens of Sutton Collection*

hall. The resulting structure appeared, at first glance, to be a typical 1960s 'glass box'- its general appearance being less substantial than the '1930s' style structure that would undoubtedly have been erected if World War II had not intervened.

The facilities at West Ruislip LT station included a large signal box with a 59-lever power frame, comprising 44 full-stroke levers and 15 'push-pull' levers - the latter being needed to work the subsidiary signal box at Ruislip Gardens by remote control.

The Central Line depot, covering 50 acres, had virtually been completed by the start of World War II, and during the years of conflict its spacious car sheds were pressed into use by the Royal Navy. When passenger services began running to and from West Ruislip on 21st November, 1948, the huge LT depot came into full use. The main car sheds were 941 ft in length, and contained no less than 16 parallel tracks. There was also a large cleaning shed, a permanent way depot, a machine shop, offices, mess rooms and a canteen; the complex contained about nine miles of trackwork, and there was sufficient siding space for 472 vehicles - in other words up to 59 full length Underground trains.

There was, at one time, considerable debate regarding the loading gauge of the London Underground system. Although the bitter arguments concerning the desirability of a standardised track gauge were settled as long ago as the 1840s, there was no attempt to impose a national loading gauge. In 1892, however, a Parliamentary committee recommended that tube tunnels should have a minimum internal diameter of 11 ft 6 in. In practice, much of the 'Underground' system utilises former main line routes, while the sub-surface Metropolitan and District Lines were built to full-size dimensions from their inception.

When the Central Line western extension was first planned, the GWR seems to have decided that the new line from Acton to Denham would in effect be a widened version of the existing line, and perhaps for this reason the bridges and stations conformed to a main line loading gauge. In the longer term, this has had particular ramifications in terms of West Ruislip depot, which is able to accommodate 'full size' locomotives and rolling stock, as well as the diminutive tube trains. On 8th July, 1980, for instance, class '47' Co-Co No. 47008 hauled a six-car BR 'Advanced Passenger Train' into the depot in connection with an engineering exhibition held there the following day.

When necessary, West Ruislip is able to carry out work on full size stock, such as the eight former Southern Region class '431' and '438' vehicles that were refurbished by London Transport in 1992 for use on steam-hauled specials. In its present form, West Ruislip station remains in use as an important interchange point between London Transport Railways and the main line system. On 24th July, 1974, a new connection was brought into use between Ruislip depot and the nearby Uxbridge branch of the Metropolitan Line, so that rails could be transferred from the welding plant to then-new Fleet Line (later renamed the Jubilee Line); this new link has also been used for stock transfer movements.

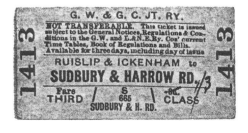

Chapter Six

The Route from Ruislip to Princes Risborough

As far as railway travellers are concerned, West Ruislip marks the end of the London suburban area. Here, the endless vistas of houses, shops, factories and playing fields finally come to an end, and the next section of the GW&GC Joint Line is entirely rural in character.

South Harefield Halt

Passing beneath the road bridge at the north end of West Ruislip station, down trains run along a dead-level section of track which, in steam days, was equipped with water troughs. Soon, the abandoned trackbed of the Uxbridge High Street branch can be seen to the left of the main line. The Uxbridge branch joined the GW&GC route by means of a triangular junction, the East Curve being controlled from a signal box known as Denham East Junction at 13 miles 60 chains, while the West Curve was controlled from another box, known originally as Denham West Junction, at 14 miles 22 chains. The East Junction box was closed in 1917, but the former West Junction box lasted, as 'Denham East Box', until December 1965.

The Uxbridge High Street branch will be considered in greater detail in Chapter Eight, but it is necessary to mention here that the little-used Denham East Curve ended its days as an Esso oil siding, and whatever traffic then remained on the Uxbridge line used the Denham West Curve, which joined the GW&GC Joint Line a short distance beyond.

On 24th September, 1928, the Great Western opened a small stopping place near the site of Denham East Junction, some 13 miles 52 chains from Paddington. This new station was known as 'Harefield Halt', and it was built in anticipation of large scale suburban development in the immediate vicinity. Up and down platforms were provided, with waiting shelters on each side and a small booking office. As the halt was situated in a cutting, public access was arranged by means of sloping pathways from an adjacent road overbridge. The halt was initially a passenger-only stopping place, but a goods siding was installed on Thursday 7th March, 1929, and brought into use on 27th June.

The siding was situated to the west of the platforms on the down side, and worked from a ground frame which also controlled down home and distant signals. The down main home signal was sited 48 yards to the east of the ground frame, and carried on the same post as the down main inner distant for Denham East box. As there was no connection with the up main line, there were no signals in the up direction, and Harefield Siding could be served only by down trains proceeding west towards Denham. When not in use, the siding was locked by a key that was normally kept in neighbouring West Ruislip signal box.

The key was collected by the guards of down trains having work to do at the siding, and on arrival at Harefield the guards concerned were required to unlock the ground frame and place the home and distant signals at danger. When any necessary shunting work had been carried out, the ground frame was re-locked and the signals were returned to the all-clear position, and trains were then able to continue to Denham. On arrival at that station, guards handed the key to the signalman on duty,

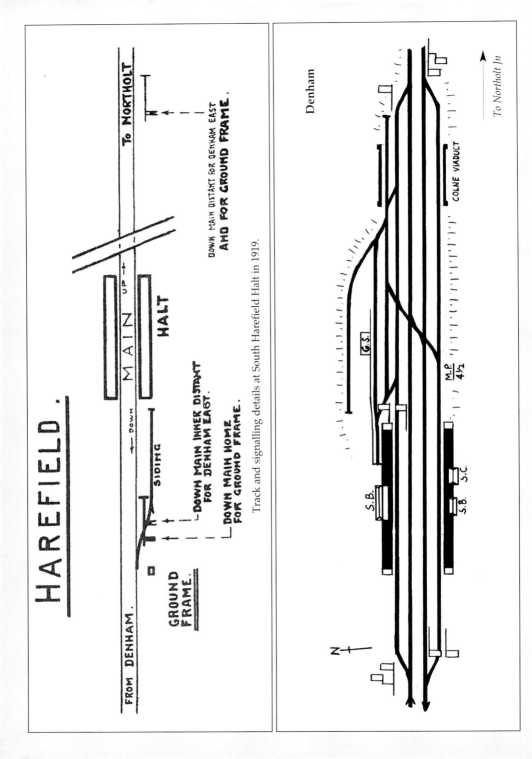

HAREFIELD.

FROM DENHAM.

To NORTHOLT

← DOWN

MAIN UP →

SIDING

HALT

GROUND FRAME.

DOWN MAIN DISTANT FOR DENHAM EAST AND FOR **GROUND FRAME.**

DOWN MAIN INNER DISTANT FOR DENHAM EAST.

DOWN MAIN HOME FOR GROUND FRAME.

Track and signalling details at South Harefield Halt in 1919.

Denham

G.S.

S.B.

M.P. 4½

S.B.   S.C.

COLNE VIADUCT

N

To Northolt Jn

who was responsible for ensuring that it was returned promptly to his counterpart at West Ruislip by the next available up train.

In the event, the hoped-for housing developments at Harefield never materialised, and passenger services were withdrawn from Harefield Halt with effect from 1st October, 1931. In the meantime, this obscure stopping place had been renamed twice, the name 'South Harefield Halt' having been adopted in May 1929, while in September 1931 it became simply 'South Harefield'. Goods facilities were retained after 1931, albeit for private siding traffic. A note in the 1938 Railway Clearing House *Handbook of Stations* reveals that the siding was used for the 'Peerless Wire Fencing Co.'s traffic only' (the siding closed in 1953).

Mr W.K. Mackenzie recalled that the siding was pressed into use in connection with a 'petrol unloading depot' during World War II, and it subsequently became a builder's plant depot. It appears that a short extension from the oil siding was laid on the trackbed of the abandoned East Curve, although it is unclear if this wartime facility ever formed a connection with the Anglo-American (later Esso) Oil Siding, with was brought into use in May 1942, and entered from a connection on the Uxbridge branch.

Denham

Running west-south-westwards, the line crosses the Grand Union Canal on a brick and concrete viaduct with nine elliptical arches (14 miles 17 chains). Eight of the arches have 47 ft spans, but the one over the canal is somewhat longer, with a length of 60 ft. The viaduct has a total length of approximately 198 yards. The canal which passes beneath this massive structure was incorporated as 'The Grand Junction Canal', in 1793, with powers for the construction of a waterway from the Thames at Brentford to Braunston in Northamptonshire. The first sod was cut in that same year, and the canal was opened throughout in 1805.

A quarter of a mile further on, at 14 miles 36 chains, a similar brick and concrete viaduct, with five arches, spans the River Colne - the boundary between the counties of Middlesex and Buckinghamshire. The Colne viaduct is 36 ft high, and its largest arch, over the river, has a span of 80 ft; the remaining arches have spans of 50 ft, the total length of this impressive structure being approximately 120 yards. From the viaduct, trains continue westwards into Denham station, 14 miles 64 chains from Paddington, and formerly the junction for branch services to Uxbridge High Street.

Opened, along with the rest of the Greenford to High Wycombe line, on 2nd April, 1906, Denham was a typical Great Western & Great Central station, with a spacious quadruple-tracked layout incorporating long up and down platform loop lines that afforded convenient separation between main line and local services. The up and down platforms were placed on the outside of the loop lines, enabling fast services to run through the station on the centre fast lines, while stopping trains were safely berthed on the platform roads. The goods yard, with three sidings and a lengthy headshunt, was situated to the east of the platforms on the up side of the running lines.

The main station building was situated on the up side of the line and, like other GW&GC buildings, it was a standard Great Western structure, with a low pitched, hipped roof and a projecting platform canopy. The main external walls were constructed of red brick, and the roof was covered in grey slate. Internally, the building followed a fairly typical Great Western arrangement, with a general waiting room in the centre of the structure, and gentlemen's toilets at the east (i.e.

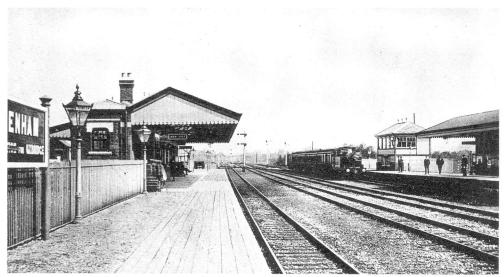

Denham station looking east around 1907, showing a 'Birdcage' 2-4-2T in the down loop. The word 'Junction' on the nameboard has been crossed out, suggesting that the Uxbridge branch had not yet been opened.   *J.M. Strange*

Denham station, looking along the down platform towards London; it is unclear if the GWR auto-trailers that can be seen alongside the up platform are some form of empty stock working – or could this be a very rare shot of a multiple steam railmotor formation?

John Alsop Collection

London) end; the ladies' waiting room and toilet occupied the intervening portion of the building, while booking office and staff facilities were grouped at the west end of the main block.

The canopy was supported on lightweight metal girders that projected from the top part of the main walling, the structure being extended at its west end to afford further protection for waiting travellers; this westwards continuation of the canopy also sheltered the subway steps in wet weather. The canopy was edged with typical Great Western 'V-and-hole' valancing. It is interesting to note that Denham's station buildings were supported on concrete piers buried deep within the embankment - which would otherwise have been unable to carry the weight of these substantial brick structures.

The up and down platforms were linked by a pedestrian subway, which descended below platform level at the western end of the station building. Unusually, this subway was in fact well above local ground level, the reason for this curious state of affairs being apparent when one realises that Denham station was built on a towering, 25 ft high embankment! The subway pierced the embankment roughly midway between track and ground level, and unsuspecting pedestrians were sometimes surprised to discover that, having descended the subway steps, they were still high above ground in the arch of an underline bridge.

Emerging from Denham's somewhat spectacular elevated subway, travellers found themselves in the down side station building. This was similar to its counterpart on the up platform, albeit smaller; waiting room facilities were again provided, and there was a generously-proportioned canopy with the usual Great Western 'V-and-hole' decoration. The down side building was built of red brick, with a grey, slated roof.

Other buildings at Denham included a standard Great Western hip-roofed signal box on the down platform, a small corrugated iron store on the up side, and various ancillary structures in the station approach. The signal box was a two-storey, timber structure, clad in horizontal weather boarding, and roofed with grey slate. It was heated by a stove, the chimney of which extended through the roof at the rear of the structure. The box was officially designated 'Denham Station Box' to distinguish it from 'Denham East Box' (the former West Junction box), just half a mile to the east.

In 1913, Denham booked 44,028 tickets, rising to 55,741 by 1931. In that same year, the station issued 892 season tickets, representing perhaps a further 53,200 individual journeys per annum (assuming that most season ticket holders were purchasing 3-monthly tickets and making five return journeys per week). By Joint Line standards, these figures are not particularly impressive, and it seems that in Great Western days Denham was one of the least busy stations between London and High Wycombe. Goods traffic was not particularly significant, only about 5,000 tons of freight being handled in an average year during the 1920s and early 1930s. A summary of Denham's traffic appears below.

Traffic dealt with at Denham

Year	Staff	Receipts (£)	Tickets	Parcels	Goods Tonnage
1923	15	10,167	53,624	11,559	7,281
1929	16	12,499	58,516	14,040	12,659
1935	14	17,077	55,722	29,020	10,939
1936	12	16,852	57,549	32,179	10,359
1937	14	15,930	58,119	32,202	8,396
1938	14	16,572	53,270	33,913	9,860

Great Western 'Pagoda' shelters at Denham Golf Club (opened in 1912). These characteristic buildings were still *in situ* in 1988.   *Lens of Sutton Collection*

A detailed view of the low level ticket office at Denham Golf Club on 4th October, 1982.
                                                        R.M. Casserley Collection

It will be noted that there was an apparent upsurge in goods traffic in 1935 and 1936. Much of this was in the form of incoming 'minerals' and 'general merchandise', which can probably be attributed to an influx of building materials for use during the construction of the nearby Denham Film Studios.

Denham village, still largely unspoiled, has featured in many of the films made at Denham Film Studios. The studios were constructed during the mid-1930s in rural surroundings about 300 yards to the north of the railway. They occupied a site that had formerly been owned by Lord Forres, and when completed, the new film studios, with their art-deco offices and huge, hangar-like buildings, were the 'biggest in the British Empire',

Railways featured in several Denham-made films, and in order to ensure greater realism, the studios had their own railway system, comprising a length of double track and a diverging branch. At least two locomotives were used for filming, the engines concerned being former Great Eastern Railway 'J15' 0-6-0s Nos. 7541 and 7835 - which presumably reached Denham via the GWR goods yard and a short journey by road. These ex-GER veterans featured as 'Russian' locomotives in the 1937 film *Knight Without Armour* - an epic love story set during the Russian Revolution and starring Robert Donat and Marlene Deitrich.

The presence of Denham Film Studios brought considerable activity to what would otherwise have been merely a quiet country station. There was no 'Green Belt' legislation during the 1930s, and it was clearly anticipated that Denham would eventually be absorbed into the burgeoning Greater London area. This assumption was implicit in the Central Line extension scheme, which had envisaged that Denham would be served by a frequent service of electric trains, in addition to GWR and LNER outer suburban services on the Great Western & Great Central Joint Line.

The proposed Central Line terminus would have been sited to the south of the main line station, on a parallel alignment to the GW&GC route, and presumably at a slightly lower level. Three terminal roads were planned, with two double-sided platforms between the three platform lines - the centre track having a platform face on two sides. As we have seen, the Central Line extension was not completed until after World War II, by which time the route had been cut back to West Ruislip. Denham was never developed as a suburban area, its rural character being protected by post-war Green Belt legislation.

Denham goods yard, and the sidings on the up side, were lifted in 1965, together with the central up and down fast lines, leaving only the outer platform roads and a crossover at the north end of the station *in situ*. Further rationalisation resulted in the closure of Denham signal box and abandonment of the crossover in June 1975, so that Denham is now only a shadow of its former self.

Denham Golf Club Platform

Entering pleasant open farmland, the line starts to climb up into the Chilterns on a ruling gradient of 1 in 175, before down trains reach Denham Golf Club Platform (15 miles 52 chains). Opened on 22nd July, 1912, this simple, wayside stopping place has retained its characteristic Great Western 'pagoda' shelters. The up and down platforms are formed of concrete segments, and a minor road passes beneath the line at the southern end of the station. As a 'platform', rather than a mere halt, Denham Golf Club boasted a small ticket office and a staff of two, the wage bill in 1936 being £256, against total receipts for passenger and parcels traffic of £1,203.

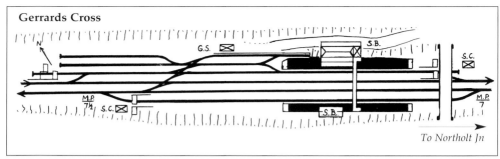

Gerrards Cross

G.S.

S.B.

S.C.

M.P. 7½

S.C.

S.B.

M.P. 7

To Northolt Jn

GWR railmotors at Gerrards Cross around 1910; steam railmotors were extensively used in the early days, but these interesting vehicles were later replaced by auto-trains.   *Real Photographs*

Gerrards Cross, looking north-westwards towards Princes Risborough on 14th June, 1958.

H.C. Casserley

Denham Golf Club's traffic returns were included with those from Denham until 1935, after which they were recorded separately. It is therefore possible to ascertain the level of passenger traffic dealt with at this minor stopping place, and in this context it comes as something of a surprise to discover that Denham Golf Club was much busier than stations such as Ardley or Bicester and, moreover, its bookings increased from 15,731 ordinary ticket sales and 349 seasons in 1936, to 20,990 ordinary tickets and 428 seasons in 1938.

Gerrards Cross

From Denham Golf Club Halt, the route climbs north-westwards on a rising gradient of 1 in 175, and crosses the River Misbourne on a viaduct with five arched spans of 51 ft (16 miles 33 chains). The Misbourne viaduct has a total length of 114 yards, and its height is about 60 ft above local ground level. Like other viaducts on this part of the Great Western & Great Central route, it is of composite construction, having concrete piers and abutments, faced with brickwork. The river was diverted for a distance of about 10 chains when the viaduct was built, in order to bring it at right angles to the railway.

A short distance beyond, trains cross the Chalfont Road on a further viaduct (16 miles 54 chains), with five 77 ft elliptical spans and a total length of 165 yards. Beyond, the railway enters Gerrards Cross cutting, which necessitated the removal of around 1,250,000 cubic yards of spoil when the railway was built. Gerrards Cross station (17 miles 34 chains) is situated in the middle part of the cutting, the rails at this point being around 45 ft below the original ground level. As they enter the station, trains pass beneath two towering, triple-arch bridges, the one nearest the platforms having a central span of 56 ft 3 in.

Gerrards Cross is another typical Great Western & Great Central Joint Line station, with standard Great Western brick buildings on both platforms and a quadruple-track layout. The main station building, on the up side, was unusual in that it was two storeys high, and as the station was situated in a deep cutting, its rear entrance was on the first floor. The station building was of the usual Great Western design, with a hipped roof and tall chimney stacks with 'oversailing' upper courses. A single-storey waiting room was sited on the down side, while a plate girder footbridge linked the up and down platforms. The small goods yard - now a car park - was on the up side.

In pre-Grouping days, the station was signalled from two standard Great Western signal boxes, known as Gerrards Cross East and Gerrards Cross West. Both were typical, brick-and-timber, hip-roofed boxes, with distinctive five-paned windows which were supposed to give the signalmen an unimpeded view. Boxes of this same general type were erected throughout the Great Western system from the early 20th century onwards, and they were utterly typical of the GW&GC Joint Line.

The East box was situated to east of the station on the up side, where two lines became four, while the West box was sited towards the west end of the down platform loop. Gerrards Cross East box was closed on 11th November, 1923, and the station was then signalled from the former West box, which remained in use until August 1990. This was an early GWR scheme of centralisation of signalling whereby points controlled by the box to be closed were operated electrically by the remaining box. A similar arrangement was introduced at Beaconsfield.

The passenger traffic handled here remained surprisingly healthy for many years, with approximately 135,000 ordinary tickets being issued every year, together with

A view of Gerrards Cross station from the station approach road on 14th June, 1958. Note the split-level station building.   *H.C. Casserley*

A detailed study of Gerrards Cross signal box.   *Mike Marr*

no less than 7,000 season tickets by the later 1930s. In 1929, 139,439 tickets were sold, together with 6,775 seasons, while in 1934 ordinary ticket sales amounted to 133,316, with 6,265 seasons. In 1938, the station issued 143,233 tickets and 7,014 seasons.

As Great Western season tickets were generally issued for periods of one, two, three, six or even 12 months, season ticket sales at Gerrards Cross may have amounted to as many as 420,000 return journeys per annum during the later 1930s (assuming that most customers had purchased three-monthly tickets and made 20 journeys each month). On this basis, it would appear that Gerrards Cross was one of the busiest commuter stations on the Great Western & Great Central Joint line.

Goods traffic on the other hand declined from over 20,000 tons per year during the pre-Grouping period, to around 18,000 tons per annum during the mid-1930s and just 14,000 tons towards the end of the decade. Incoming coal was the main source of traffic, although the station also handled a certain amount of incoming mineral traffic, 5,822 tons of 'other minerals' being received in 1931. By analogy with other local stations, most of this material was probably in the form of aggregates for use on the surrounding road system. Livestock traffic fell from 133 wagon loads in 1913 to 28 wagon loads in 1936 and just one wagon in 1938.

Gerrards Cross typically handled about 38,000 parcels and miscellaneous consignments per annum during the 1930s. In practice, the Great Western used the term 'parcels' to describe any small packages under 2 cwt in weight which were consigned by passenger train. 'Parcels traffic' therefore included luggage in advance, pigeons, poultry, eggs, laundry baskets and a variety of other items, as well as parcels and small packages. In addition, the station also dealt with about 1,200 tons of carted freight during the period under review, all of this traffic being collected or delivered by Great Western road vehicles within a defined cartage area.

In general, parcels or 'smalls' traffic was collected or delivered from Gerrards Cross, on the south side of the railway, and from Chalfont St Peter and Chalfont St Giles to the north - all of these places being within the station's free cartage area. Later, however, parcels for the Chalfont St Peter area were normally handled at Chalfont & Latimer station on the Metropolitan & Great Central route, while villages to the south of Gerrards Cross were served by GWR country lorries from nearby Slough.

The station retained its quadruple-tracked layout for many years, but work carried out in 1989-90 prior to resignalling resulted in an altered layout, with just two lines between the up and down platforms. At the same time, the down platform was rebuilt on a new alignment, while a reversing siding was installed to the west of the station on the up side. This new siding was brought into use on 13th August, 1990, together with a facing crossover between the up and down lines. The revised track layout enables trains terminating at Gerrards Cross to cross from the down to the up line in order to enter the siding and later return to London from the up platform.

Seer Green & Jordans

Accelerating away from the down platform at Gerrards Cross, trains continue their ascent on rising 1 in 254 gradients, and soon reach Seer Green & Jordans, a simple, two-platform station, 20 miles 10 chains from Paddington. There was no signal box at Seer Green, although an intermediate box known as Wilton Park (opened in 1914) was sited just 12 chains to the east of the station, on the up side of

Seer Green & Jordans was opened in 1915 to serve Beaconsfield Golf Links. The buildings were designed to harmonise with the nearby club house.   *Lens of Sutton Collection*

A platform view at Seer Green & Jordans, showing details of the plate girder footbridge.
R.M. Casserley Collection

the running lines; this box was replaced by intermediate block signals in February 1953.

Serving the adjacent Beaconsfield Golf Course, Seer Green has distinctive hip-roofed buildings on each side. The building on the up platform is slightly larger than its counterpart on the down side, and a footbridge provides pedestrian access between the two platforms. In addition to the golf course, the station serves two nearby villages. Jordans, about three-quarters of a mile from the railway, is the burial place of William Penn (1644-1718), the founder of Pennsylvania, while the picturesque village of Seer Green is about two miles to the north of the line.

When opened on 1st January, 1915, the station was known as 'Beaconsfield Golf Links', but as we have seen its name was subsequently altered to 'Seer Green (for Beaconsfield Golf Club)'. The name 'Seer Green Halt' was also employed during the GWR era while, to add to the confusion, British Railways changed the name to 'Seer Green & Jordans' in 1950. In recent years, this multi-named stopping place has been referred to as Seer Green.

Seer Green's traffic statistics were originally included with those from neighbouring Beaconsfield, but from 1934 onwards they were recorded separately. In that year, the station issued 35,737 ordinary tickets and 725 seasons; traffic continued to increase throughout the 1930s, and by 1938 Seer Green was issuing over 42,000 single or return tickets per annum. Sales of season tickets, meanwhile, had risen to as many as 900 a year, the station being busy enough to justify a staff of two.

Beaconsfield

The line levels off just beyond Seer Green, and then starts to fall at 1 in 460 as it runs due west towards the next station at Beaconsfield (21 miles 55 chains). Like Gerrards Cross, Beaconsfield station is situated in a chalk cutting, and it has the usual Great Western brick buildings. Rationalisation has resulted in the closure of the signal box, the abandonment of the goods yard, and removal of the up and down fast lines. As at Denham, all trains now use the outer platform roads.

In its heyday, Beaconsfield had been equipped with the usual quadruple-tracked layout, with up and down platforms on either side. The B474 road was carried across the line on a single-arch brick overbridge at the west end of the station, access to the platforms being by means of long approach roads on both sides. A single-span girder bridge crossed the line at the east end of the station, while the platforms were linked by a plate girder footbridge with corrugated iron roof coverings.

The main station building was situated on the up side, and this standard GWR hip-roofed structure contained the usual range of accommodation found at a station of intermediate size and importance. The booking hall was positioned near the centre of the building, with the ticket office to the left (when viewed from the platform). The ladies' waiting room and gentlemen's toilets were sited at the London end of the building, while the station master's office, parcels office and cloakroom, and a staff mess room were situated to the left of the ticket office at the Banbury end. There was, in addition, a newsagent's kiosk in convenient proximity to the booking office and waiting room.

Further accommodation for waiting passengers was available in another standard Great Western hipped-roof building on the down side. Internally, this structure contained a general waiting room, a ladies' waiting room and toilets for both sexes. Both buildings were constructed of brickwork, most of the bricks employed being a

A postcard view of Beaconsfield station, *circa* 1912, showing the up and down platforms, standard GWR station buildings and plate girder footbridge, and looking east towards London. A '36XX' or 'Birdcage' class 2-4-2T can be seen in the down platform, with its train of Dean clerestories. *Lens of Sutton Collection*

Beaconsfield station, looking east towards London, *circa* 1913, showing 'Birdcage' class 2-4-2T No. 3611 in the down platform with a train of Dean clerestory vehicles in crimson lake livery.
Lens of Sutton Collection

'A5' class 4-6-2T No. 69805 pauses at Beaconsfield with the 11.20 am Marylebone to Princes Risborough local working on 4th November, 1953.   *Brian W. Leslie*

A 'Western' class diesel heads through Beaconsfield on the up through line with a freight train in the 1960s. The standard GWR buildings and platform fittings show no sign of GCR influence, although in reality Beaconsfield's local train services were heavily geared towards Marylebone and the LNER!   *Nelson Collection*

Looking eastwards from the road overbridge at Beaconsfield during the 1960s.
                                                                                          Nelson Collection

bright, reddish-orange colour, though vitrified black bricks were used to create a contrasting effect. This form of construction is found on all parts of the 'New Line', red bricks being the predominant constructional material for stations, signal boxes, bridges and other structures.

The station was originally signalled from two standard Great Western hip-roofed signal boxes, which were known as Beaconsfield East and Beaconsfield West; both were sited on the down side of the running lines. The West box was taken out of use on Sunday 21st October, 1923, and the station was then signalled from the remaining East box, which was officially renamed 'Beaconsfield Signal Box'. The latter box was itself closed in December 1975, the through (fast) lines having been removed two years earlier in December 1973.

Prior to rationalisation in 1964, the goods yard, on the up side of the line, had contained four sidings, one of which was arranged as a reception loop while another loop siding passed through a brick goods shed. Two mileage sidings, at the rear of the yard, were used for coal or other full wagon load consignments. A long headshunt extended eastwards at the Paddington end of the yard, and a series of single slips provided a means of access between the down main or down platform lines and the goods yard. Goods traffic amounted, on average, to around 22,000 tons per annum during the mid-1930s, roughly half of this tonnage being in the form of incoming coal traffic.

Beaconsfield has always handled large numbers of passengers. In 1923, for example, 100,353 tickets were issued, while in the early 1930s the station typically dealt with around 135,000 bookings per year. There was, thereafter, a slight decline in the number of passengers, though by the mid-1930s Beaconsfield's tickets sales amounted to around 135,000 per annum. Of equal, if not greater significance, there were also about 3,500 ticket season sales during the later 1930s, the implication being that this Buckinghamshire station generated a significant amount of regular commuter traffic.

Like other GW&GC stations, Beaconsfield still has many traditional Great Western features, including station seats with 'GWR' displayed in their ironwork, and platform railings with distinctive lozenge-shaped spikes. The station was refurbished in connection with the 'total route modernisation' of the Chiltern Line, and like other stations on this part of the route, it remains in use as a busy suburban station, and a vital part of the local transport system.

Traffic dealt with at Beaconsfield

Year	Staff	Receipts (£)	Tickets	Parcels	Goods Tonnage
1929	17	40,856	140,269	37,000	23,580
1931	18	38,910	149,285	33,945	22,797
1935	18	32,194	128,982	33,778	24,664
1937	16	29,169	135,547	31,678	17,678
1938	16	28,391	133,423	30,126	16,130

'Bekonscot', the famous Gauge One model railway and village, is situated a short distance to the north of the station in Warwick Road. It was opened in 1929 after the owner's model railway had grown too big for the house, the name being a mixture of Beaconsfield and Ascot - the respective homes of the designer of the village and the designer of the railway.

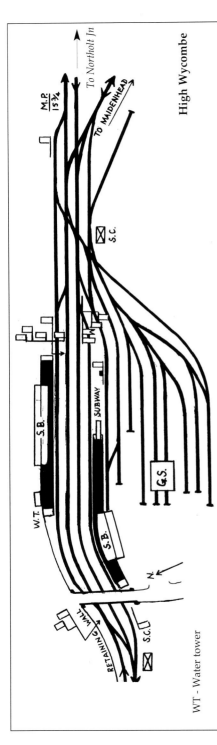

To Northolt In

M.P. 15¾

TO MAIDENHEAD

S.C.

High Wycombe

W.T.

S.B.

SUBWAY

S.B.

G.S.

RETAINING WALL

S.C.

N

S.C.

WT - Water tower

No. 359

GREAT CENTRAL

High Wycombe station on 2nd April, 1906, showing Robinson '9K' class 4-4-2T No. 359 in the up platform with 'the first Great Central train to High Wycombe'.

Lens of Sutton Collection

High Wycombe

Leaving Beaconsfield, trains run under the road overbridge, and through further cuttings. The 343 yds-long Whitehouse Farm tunnel is a little under two miles beyond. As mentioned in Chapter Two, this tunnel was the scene of an unexpected fall during the construction of the GW&GC Joint Line in 1902; the six men who were trapped and killed have a memorial in High Wycombe cemetery. The roof of the tunnel is only about 47 ft below local ground level.

Emerging into daylight once again, the line runs north-westwards along a ledge cut into the side of the Wycombe Valley, and the route of the original Wycombe Railway can be seen over on the opposite slope. Below, the A40 London to South Wales trunk road parallels both lines; originally a stage coach road the A40 became very busy in the post-war years, but now the M40 and M4 motorways have taken much of the through traffic away. There was, at one time, a signal box at Tyler's Green (24 miles 13 chains), but this isolated box, opened in 1914, was replaced by intermediate block signals in February 1953.

Sir Philip Rose's viaduct is only a short distance further on, at 24 miles 30 chains. This ornamental red and blue brick structure has three arched spans, and an overall length of 66 yards. It carries the railway over a picturesque valley and the carriage drive leading to Philip Rose's estate. Road and railway converge as they approach High Wycombe, some two miles from the tunnel, and trains then cross the 55 yds-long Gordon Road viaduct (26 miles 08 chains), which has three brick arches. With the abandoned Maidenhead branch now visible to the left, down workings enter High Wycombe station.

High Wycombe, 26 miles 44 chains from Paddington, has always been regarded as the principal intermediate station on the Great Western & Great Central Joint Line. Built on a restricted site, and on a reverse curve, High Wycombe has staggered up and down platforms, linked by a subway. Rationalisation has reduced what was, in the pre-Beeching era, a very complicated layout, to a basic double track arrangement, while goods sidings have been lifted to provided more space for commuters' cars. Nevertheless, the station is situated in a spectacular position above the red brick houses and furniture factories of High Wycombe, and the area retains much of its railway interest.

Railway development at High Wycombe began on 1st August, 1854, when the Wycombe Railway opened its single track branch from Maidenhead. As recounted in Chapter One, the first station was a typical broad gauge terminus with a 'Brunel' style train shed. This historic structure was adapted for use as a goods shed following the opening of a new station in 1864.

The second Wycombe Railway station was a through station on the northwards extension to Princes Risborough, up and down platforms being provided on either side of passing loop, together with a relatively spacious goods yard on the down side. The Wycombe Railway station building, which was also sited on the down side, was a single-storey structure with a low-pitched gable roof. A smaller building, of similar external appearance, was provided on the opposite platform, while the up and down sides were linked by an enclosed footbridge. The station was signalled from a gable-roofed signal box, sited to the east of the platforms on the up side of the running lines.

Some of the original Wycombe Railway infrastructure was retained when the station was enlarged and reconstructed during the early 1900s. The goods yard remained *in situ* and, as 'High Wycombe South Yard', it was developed as the town's main goods yard, dealing with general merchandise, small consignments, and similar forms of carted goods, including all forms of market and perishable traffic.

A detailed view of the down side station buildings at High Wycombe, *circa* 1910.

Author's Collection

A postcard view of High Wycombe station, showing the staggered platform layout that was necessary here because of the restricted site of the earlier Wycombe Railway station. The goods yard, which incorporated the town's original passenger terminus, can be glimpsed in the background.

John Alsop Collection

In addition, an entirely new goods yard known as 'High Wycombe North Yard' was constructed on a more spacious site, about three-quarters of a mile to the north of the passenger station. The North Yard was able to accommodate around 200 wagons, the intention being that 'timber, coal & coke, grain, bricks, stone, hay & straw, and all descriptions of merchandise & mineral traffic in full truck loads' would be concentrated in these new sidings. The new goods station was opened on 17th October, 1904.

The situation regarding the passenger station was more complicated, in that there was insufficient room for a quadruple-track layout with platforms on either side. A staggered platform arrangement was therefore adopted, a re-sited up platform being installed on a new site to the east of the original Wycombe Railway down platform. The up platform was equipped with extensive station buildings containing toilets, waiting rooms and other facilities for staff and passengers, while the main, down side building was entirely reconstructed in a matching architectural style, both buildings being standard Great Western red brick structures of the usual type.

The main station building measured approximately 120 ft by 20 ft at ground level. It was covered by a low-pitched gable roof that also formed the platform canopy, and there was, in addition, a small canopy at the rear. Walking into the building from the station forecourt, one immediately entered the booking hall and general waiting room, the ticket office being to the right, while the ladies' waiting room was sited to the right of the waiting room. The eastern end of the building contained a parcels office and cloakroom, together with additional staff accommodation, while the gentlemen's toilets were housed at the westernmost extremity of the structure.

In later years, the station master's office was housed in a small structure at the west end of the down platform, while a porters' mess room was sited immediately to the west. The former Home Guard hut on the up platform remained in use after World War II as a messroom for enginemen and goods guards.

There were, in all, three platform faces, the main down platform being augmented by an additional bay at its east end, for use by Maidenhead branch services. The three platforms were numbered in logical sequence from south to north, the branch bay being designated platform one, while the main down and up platforms became platforms two and three respectively. The up and down sides of the rebuilt station were linked by an underline subway while, on the north side, the enlarged station site was flanked by an enormous retaining wall that was said to have incorporated over a million and a quarter bricks when it was constructed during the early 1900s.

The remodelled station was controlled from three signal boxes, which were known as 'High Wycombe South Box', 'High Wycombe Middle Box', and 'High Wycombe North Box'. The South and Middle boxes were sited at each end of the station complex, while the North box controlled the North or 'New' yard to the north of the station. High Wycombe Middle box was closed in November 1972, though the North and South boxes survived until 1976 and 1991 respectively. All three cabins were standard brick-and-timber structures of the usual GWR type, with hipped, slated roofs and characteristic five-pane window frames.

The main goods shed was sited to the south of the main, down side station building. This was, historically, a structure of considerable interest insofar as it was in fact the original 1854 passenger station. The building measured approximately 244 ft by 60 ft at ground level, and it contained two loading platforms. The old station buildings remained in use as goods offices on the south side of this barn-like building, while the glazed end portions of the original 'Brunel' style gables could still be discerned; the timber roof trusses incorporated lateral tie beams and queen posts.

The internal loading platforms were equipped with three 1 ton 10 cwt hand cranes, two of these being on the south platform while one was on the north side. This former broad gauge structure was modified on several occasions during the course of its long, if somewhat obscure career. On 5th April, 1948, for instance, the building was modernised in connection with the introduction of the 'Zonal Collection & Delivery Scheme', the principal improvements put into effect at that time being the raising of the platform, the installation of an additional skylight, and modifications to the gas and electric lighting systems.

As mentioned earlier, the South Yard, which contained a large goods shed and other goods-handling facilities, dealt with 'smalls' traffic and general merchandise for traders and businesses in the local area, whereas the North Yard dealt mainly with larger consignments and through load traffic such as timber, military vehicles, iron and steel, coal and minerals, and furniture containers. In addition to its two goods yards, High Wycombe also dealt with private siding traffic from 'Gommes Siding', at the south end of the station, and 'Bellfield Works Siding', near the North Yard.

E. Gommes' siding, which served a furniture factory, was situated on the down side of the line, beyond the confines of the station near Gordon Road viaduct. It was installed under the provisions of a private siding agreement signed on 30th July, 1926 between the GWR and LNER companies and 'Ebenezer Gomme, Rupert Gomme and Edwin Gomme of High Wycombe'. The siding was linked to the down main line by a trailing connection, the siding points being worked from a 2-lever ground frame. The keys to the ground frame were normally kept in Beaconsfield signal box, and when a down goods train had to call at the siding, the guard would collect the keys from the signalman.

On arrival at the siding, the guard unlocked the ground frame and telephoned the signalman at High Wycombe South box, who then released the electric lock. When any necessary shunting operations had been completed, the guard re-set the points and telephoned the High Wycombe South signalman to say that the train was ready to leave. On arrival at the box, the guard handed the key to the signalman, who was responsible for ensuring that it was returned to Beaconsfield by the next available up train.

The siding was protected by a gate that was normally kept closed across the line. The siding bifurcated as soon as it passed the gate, the two parallel spurs thus created being able to accommodate eight (later nine) short wheelbase goods vehicles. A short headshunt extended westwards from the two main sidings, and this was long enough to hold another 10 wagons. There was, in addition, a run-off line on the GWR side of the gate to prevent runway wagons from fouling the main line. If necessary, Gommes Siding could also be served by trip workings from High Wycombe South Yard, but on these occasions a different operating procedure applied (*see below*).

Bellfield Works Siding was sited on the up side, and linked to the up running line by a single connection that trailed-in from the north-east near High Wycombe North box. The 1938 Railway Clearing House *Handbook of Stations* shows that this siding was at that time being used by Messrs Broome & Wade, though it also served the Associated Asphalt Company. The siding was brought into use on Thursday 26th January, 1928 under the terms of an agreement between the GWR and LNER companies and 'The Bellfield Works Ltd'.

Passing through a gate, the siding curved sharply northwards. It was single track, with a loop roughly halfway along its length; beyond this, two sidings continued through separate gates into Messrs Broome & Wade's iron foundry. In World War II, siding facilities were installed for use by the Ministry of Mines, the necessary authorization being granted on 7th August, 1941. In practice, the tight curve at the entrance to the siding seems to have caused difficulties when bogie vehicles were propelled into the works, and in December 1942 there was a request for 'four couplings, each 48 inches long, for use in connection with the working of warflats out of Messrs Broome & Wade's sidings'.

In steam days High Wycombe presented several operational problems in that it handled not only main line and local passenger services, but also terminating branch trains from the Maidenhead line and a multiplicity of goods workings. Light engine movements between the North and South (station) yards were another feature of pre-Beeching operation, and indeed a shunting engine was normally employed throughout the day on these duties. Further operating complexity stemmed from the presence of two sidings known as 'The Chalk Sidings', which were sited on the up side near the North Yard, and had been brought into use during World War II.

The June 1962 British Railways working timetable shows that a shunting engine was employed in the South Yard from 6.30 am until 11.00 am, and then ran to the North Yard at 11.05 am. It returned to the South Yard at 1.15 pm, and shunted until 3.25 pm before making further trips between the two yards. As Gommes Siding was situated about half a mile to the east of the station, there was also a requirement for light engine movements between this siding and the South Yard. Gommes Siding was normally shunted when the engine had returned to the North Yard.

When the shunting engine worked in Gommes Siding, it was necessary for the shunter in charge to inform the signalman in High Wycombe South box, who then sent a 'blocking back' signal to his counterpart at Beaconsfield (or Tyler's Green, if that box was in use). After the signal had been acknowledged and the block indicator placed at the 'Train on Line' position, the key to the Gommes Siding ground frame was handed to the shunter, who accompanied the engine as it propelled wagons eastwards along the down main line towards the siding. On these occasions, it was necessary for a brake van to be attached to the London end of the ingoing wagons, the shunter being required to ride in this vehicle.

The station was liberally-supplied with locomotive watering facilities, standard Great Western water cranes being sited at convenient places around the passenger station and goods sidings. There were columns between the main lines and loop lines at each end of the platforms, and at the east end of the South Yard. Further columns were sited to the west of the passenger station near High Wycombe Middle box, and in the North Yard. Water was fed from a GWR type 'stilted' water tower, which was sited at the west end of the up platform, and had a capacity of 22,500 gallons.

High Wycombe has always been regarded as the busiest station on the Great Western & Great Central Joint Line. Its passenger receipts were impressive, over 134,000 tickets being issued in 1913, while by 1931 - by which time the Great Depression had started to eat into railway receipts throughout the country - there were no less than 234,935 bookings, together with 5,886 season ticket sales, the latter equating to many thousands of individual journeys performed on a regular basis by large numbers of daily commuters. Passenger bookings declined during the rest of the 1930s, but with around 217,000 ordinary tickets and 4,200 seasons being sold per annum, the station remained very profitable.

Passenger traffic continued to increase after World War II, in line with rising affluence and a growing population in the High Wycombe area. In the latter context, one might mention that the town's population rose from 21,937 at the time of the 1921 census, to 40,000 by the end of World War II, and over 60,000 by the 1960s. The booking office receipts in 1961 were £184,635, and the number of tickets issued was 305,777. At the same time, the parcels office received 150,349 parcels and forwarded 169,142.

High Wycombe station looking south towards London, and showing the staggered up and down platforms.   *Brian W. Leslie*

Another view of the main, down side station buildings at High Wycombe, this time photographed from the station forecourt *circa* 1962.   *Lens of Sutton Collection*

In the early 1900s, the station handled about 112,000 tons of freight per annum, rising to 151,634 tons in 1929 and then decreasing to around 120,000 tons a year during the 1930s. Inwards traffic consisted mainly of timber and coal, while furniture products formed much of the station's outwards goods traffic. A similar pattern persisted into the British Railways era when, despite growing competition from rival forms of transport, High Wycombe continued to deal with about 100,000 tons of freight a year.

Prior to the cuts of the Beeching era, the station employed over 100 people in the goods and passenger departments, together with other employees in the engineering department. In 1923, the labour force comprised 84 people, though by 1937 this figure had risen to 114 by the addition of road motor drivers and other extra staff. In 1961, the passenger and goods departments employed 136 people including station master C. Day, goods agent G.C. Burgess, chief goods clerk K.F. Hudson, booking clerks R.W. Baines, A.E. Peddle, H.K. Harman and W.T. Chenery, ticket collector Mrs I. Hill, and foremen H. Rickards, G. Webb and J. Middleton.

In the early days of the Joint Committee, High Wycombe was served by expresses of both companies. but this practice had largely died out by the 1930s. Nevertheless. the station has always had a good train service - even after 1967, when the revised semi-fast workings then introduced all called here. The down-graded services introduced in May 1974 gave the station 45 up and 49 down workings daily, including the two remaining expresses, which put High Wycombe within half an hour of Paddington.

In addition, one or two dmu services omitted many intermediate stops between High Wycombe and Marylebone, and reached their destination in a little over 40 minutes - in other words almost as fast as the express which had a shorter journey to Paddington! In the mid-1990s, the station was served by around 50 trains each way, most of these being Marylebone to Banbury workings. The fastest train between High Wycombe and London accomplished its 28 mile journey in 33 minutes.

The reverse curves through the station had radii of 20, 25 and 40 chains, and for this reason there was a strict 35 mph speed limit in each direction. This meant that down workings were unable to gain speed prior to tackling the rising gradients beyond Saunderton. Realignment carried out in recent years has allowed the speed restrictions to be raised to 50 mph.

Track alterations carried out at High Wycombe as a result of 'total route modernisation' in 1990 included the removal of the up and down fast lines, the recovery of the remaining trackwork in the former South Yard, and the provision of two re-sited crossovers. The simplified layout incorporates up and down platforms and an additional bay on the down side. Platform two, the down platform, is signalled for reversible working in order that it can be used by terminating off-peak services that would otherwise have had to depart from platform three, on the up side. The bay platform also serves as a headshunt for a long siding on the down side that is in effect a remnant of the Maidenhead branch.

Traffic dealt with at High Wycombe

Year	Staff	Receipts (£)	Tickets	Seasons	Goods Tonnage
1923	127	150,899	272,875	1,636	109,833
1934	112	139,967	214,997	4,430	125,298
1935	114	128,259	218,920	4,379	118,905
1936	113	129,838	220,374	4,238	127,870
1937	114	130,456	217,972	4,122	124,502

West Wycombe was laid out as a quadruple track station, although only two lines were ever provided.   *Lens of Sutton Collection*

The down platform at West Wycombe around 1958, with the goods shed visible in the distance.
Lens of Sutton Collection

West Wycombe

Resuming their journey, present day trains pass beneath a skew girder bridge as they leave High Wycombe station, after which the Hughendon Road is crossed on an arched viaduct with four 46 ft spans and a total length of 77 yards (26 miles 78 chains). High Wycombe North box was sited on the up side of the line, just 9 chains beyond the viaduct, while the abandoned North Yard was on the left hand side of the running lines. Most of the sidings in this former mileage yard remained *in situ* until the 1980s, but they were finally taken out of use in April 1984. The railway is, at this point, heading in a north-westerly direction, while the rising gradient towards West Wycombe is at 1 in 175.

The A40, which has followed the railway for several miles, finally turns off on a more westerly course at West Wycombe, some two miles from High Wycombe. West Wycombe station (28 miles 63 chains), was closed to passenger traffic with effect from 3rd November 1958, and to goods on 4th February, 1963. It had a simple two-track layout, with its main buildings on the down side. The station was situated on a curve of 24 chains radius which, in steam days, had necessitated an overall speed limit of 45 mph.

West Wycombe had been opened by the Wycombe Railway on 1st August, 1862 and, as such, this former broad gauge station predated the Great Western & Great Central Joint Line by more than 40 years. It was, nevertheless, extensively reconstructed during the early 1900s, when a new up platform was built, together with a new station building on the down side. It is interesting to note that sufficient space was left between the up and down platforms to permit the installation of a quadruple track layout. In the event, the additional up and down fast lines were never laid, and there was, as a result, an unusually wide 'gap' between the up and down running lines.

The main station building, which replaced the earlier Wycombe Railway premises, was another standard Great Western structure. It differed slightly in relation to the GWR buildings erected at the London end of the GW&GC route, in that its gable roof extended forward over the platform in lieu of a separate canopy. Internally, this early 20th century structure contained the usual booking office, a waiting room, a ladies' waiting room, and toilets for both sexes. A corrugated iron extension at the west end of the main block served as a parcels office.

A subsidiary building was provided on the up side. Interestingly, this small, brick-built waiting room was slightly earlier than its counterpart on the down platform, having been erected around 1904, while the original Wycombe Railway building on the opposite platform was still in use. The up side building sported a hipped roof and a projecting canopy, and it incorporated a gentlemen's urinal in addition to waiting room facilities for southbound passengers. The up and down sides of the station were linked by a plate girder footbridge, which was never given a roof covering.

West Wycombe's track layout was comparatively modest in relation to most of the other stations on the GW&GC route. The goods yard, which was sited to the south of the platforms on the down side, contained just two sidings, one of these being part of the original Wycombe Railway infrastructure, whereas the other was added under the auspices of the Joint Committee. Both sidings were arranged as loops with connections at each end, while the inner siding was linked to the up and down running lines by trailing connections. Dead end spurs extended from each end of the two loop sidings, and one of these served a gable-roofed goods shed with an internal loading platform.

Other goods-handling facilities at West Wycombe included cattle pens, a weigh-house, and a 6 ton yard crane for use when timber, containers, or other large or bulky containers were consigned by rail. The station was signalled from another standard GWR signal box which was sited to the east of the platforms on the down side. As usual on the Great Western & Great Central route, this hip-roofed structure was of early 20th century origin, having been opened in 1905 to replace an earlier cabin that had been sited on the opposite side of the line. The signal box was closed in April 1966.

West Wycombe issued 19,101 tickets in 1903, the corresponding figures for 1913 and 1923 being 20,946 and 24,795 respectively. There was, thereafter, a severe decline in the number of ordinary ticket sales, although the fact that around 100 season tickets per year were issued during the 1930s would indicate that many regular travellers preferred to pay for their journeys in this convenient way. In 1935, the station issued 8,607 ordinary tickets and 103 seasons, while in 1937 7,899 tickets and 132 seasons were issued.

Although West Wycombe could hardly be described as a 'busy' station, the amount of freight traffic handled here was greater than one might, perhaps, have expected. In 1903, for instance, the station dealt with 14,495 tons of freight, including 4,303 tons of coal, 5,061 tons of 'general merchandise' and 5,123 tons of 'other minerals'. Similar amounts of traffic were handled throughout the 1930s, although in 1931 an upsurge in the amount of minerals received at the station meant that total goods traffic rose to 18,561 tons. At the end of the 1930s there had, however, been a noticeable decrease in West Wycombe's goods traffic, less than 10,000 tons being received or dispatched each year.

In practice, West Wycombe was used as a cartage centre for collections and deliveries over quite a wide rural area, and in this respect the station seems to have dealt with at least some of the traffic that would otherwise have been handled at neighbouring High Wycombe. In 1938, the GWR published an 896-page guide entitled *Towns, Villages & Outlying Works Etc, Served by the Great Western Railway*, and this large green volume listed all of the places served by the company, together with the mode of conveyance from the nearest station. Some of the information contained in this book is given in the following table, which shows some of the places served by road from West Wycombe station.

Some Typical Goods & Parcels Delivery Arrangements at West Wycombe, 1938

Location	Distance from Station	Delivery Arrangements
Beacons Bottom	2 miles	Carrier
Bolter's End	3½ miles	Carrier
Booker	2 miles	Cartage service
Bradenham	1½ miles	Cartage service
Cadmore End	4½ miles	Carrier
Frieth	6 miles	Carrier
Fingest	6 miles	Carrier
Hughendon	4 miles	No delivery arrangements
Stokenchurch	5 miles	Carrier
Totteridge	2 miles	Carrier
Walter's Ash	3 miles	Cartage service
West Wycombe	¼ mile	Free cartage service

Saunderton

Still heading towards the north-west, the railway enters a particularly narrow stretch of valley, with beechwoods on either side. To the left, the golden ball on top of West Wycombe Church tower can be seen projecting from a clump of trees high on a hill. It is said that Sir Francis Dashwood (1708-1781), the local squire, used the room inside the ball as a secret drinking den! The hill beneath the church contains the man-made tunnels known as the Hell Fire Caves, dug by Sir Francis in about 1753 to create work for unemployed labourers. The caves have associations with the legendary 'Hell Fire Club', and are now a popular tourist attraction.

Sir Francis is buried in St Lawrence's Church, which had been rebuilt, at his own expense, in 1763. This curious structure stands on top of a 600 ft hill, its golden ball being visible for miles around. Monuments to the Dashwoods and members of the so-called 'Hellfire Club' can be seen in the mausoleum that stands beside the parish church.

Ascending through the beechwoods, today's diesel multiple units traverse the most picturesque part of the whole route with little effort; the gradient here is rising at 1 in 164. Below, on the left-hand side of the line, traces of the original alignment of the old single track Wycombe Railway can still be seen while, further away, the impressive bulk of Bledlow Ridge dominates the western horizon. This section is particularly attractive during the Spring and Autumn months.

Passing the Chiltern village of Bradenham, with its memories of the Disraeli family, down trains soon reach Saunderton, 31 miles 42 chains from Paddington. 'This station', claimed the writer of *The Little Guide to Buckinghamshire* 'by its name, is calculated to be a snare to the unwary visitor' - the village of Saunderton being over three miles away! The station escaped closure during the Beeching period, but it is was, for many years thereafter, served only by peak hour services.

Saunderton predated the 'New Line' by a few months, the GWR Directors having authorised the erection of 'a new station to serve both passengers and goods traffic at Saunderton village ... about midway between West Wycombe and Princes Risborough on the Wycombe branch'. It was agreed that this new stopping place would incorporate 'up and down platforms, 400 ft in length, with station buildings, goods lock-up, station approach road, etc.' on the down side, and a 'waiting shed' on the up platform. The new works would also include a footbridge, a 'new loop crossing line', a 'siding with connections at both ends', signalling equipment and a signal box, the estimated cost being £6,016. The crossing loop came into use in September 1898.

When, in August 1899, the High Wycombe to Princes Risborough section was sold to the GW&GC, it was decided that the money that had already been expended on the new station would be charged to the Great Western & Great Central Railways Joint Committee. All subsequent expenditure was paid directly by the GW&GC, and thus, when finally opened for public traffic on 1st July, 1901, Saunderton became the first station to be brought into use under GW&GC auspices.

In its original form, Saunderton was a crossing place on the single track Wycombe branch, but this relatively new stopping place required very little modification in order to bring it up to full main line standards. The main station building was a standard Great Western hip-roofed structure, with tall chimneys and a full length platform canopy. When viewed from the platform, it contained (from left to right) a parcels office, a ticket office, the general waiting room, the ladies' waiting room and toilets, and a gentlemen's urinal.

The up and down platforms were linked by a covered footbridge, and a brick-built waiting room was provided on the up side. Unfortunately, the station was badly

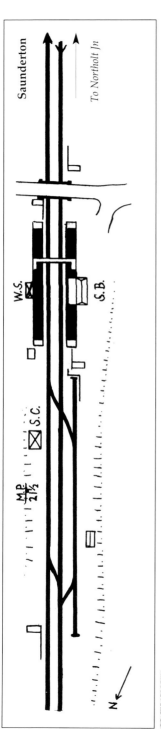

Saunderton

To Northolt Jn

W.S.

S.B.

MP 2½

S.C.

N

Saunderton station, looking north in the 1950s and showing the standard GWR buildings, signals and footbridge. This was one of the few two-platform stations on the GW&GC system.

Lens of Sutton Collection

SAUNDERTON

WAY OUT

Saunderton down platform on 20th December, 1970, showing the standard Great Western buildings. *Brian W. Leslie*

A detailed view of the up side waiting room at Saunderton, photographed in 1980. *Mike Marr*

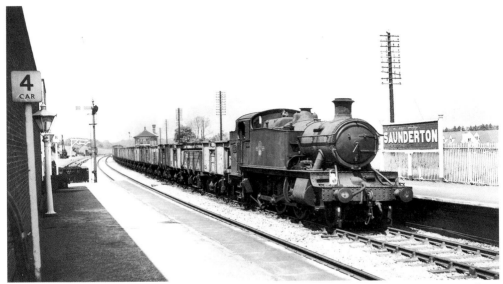

'61XX' class 2-6-2T No. 6167 drifts through Saunderton station with a train of 16 ton mineral
wagons.   *Nelson Collection*

The signal box at Saunderton, photographed on 20th December, 1970, was another standardised,
GWR hip-roofed design with a low-pitched hipped roof and distinctive five-paned window
frames.   *Brian W. Leslie*

'V2' class 2-6-2 No. 60911 passes Saunderton with the 12.15 pm Marylebone-Manchester (London Road) service on 27th December, 1958.   *Brian W. Leslie*

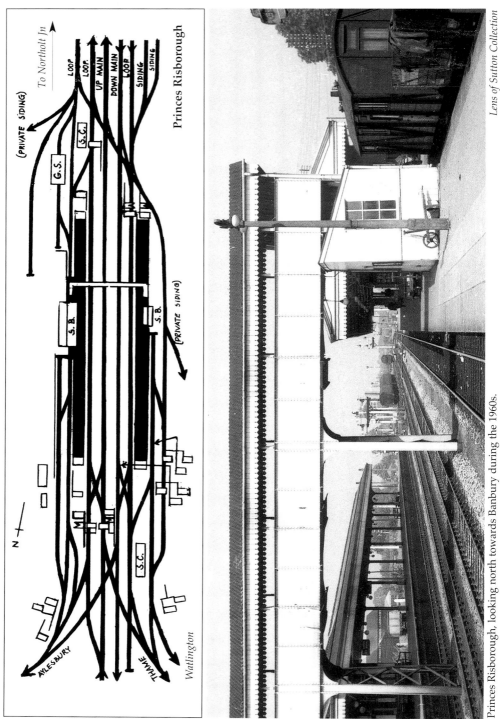

To Northolt Jn

Princes Risborough

LOOP
LOOP
UP MAIN
DOWN MAIN
LOOP
SIDING
SIDING

(PRIVATE SIDING)

S.C.

G.S.

S.B.

S.B.

(PRIVATE SIDING)

S.C.

N

AYLESBURY

THAME

Watlington

Princes Risborough, looking north towards Banbury during the 1960s.

Lens of Sutton Collection

damaged in an arson attack carried out by militant Suffragettes in March 1913, although the damaged structures were subsequently repaired. There was a modest goods yard to the north of the platform on the down side, its single siding being linked to the up and down running lines by trailing crossovers that obviated the need for facing points on the main line. The yard was equipped with a range of facilities, including coal wharves, cattle pens, an end loading dock and a weigh-house.

The station was signalled from a standard Great Western signal box of the now familiar hip-roofed design, this characteristic structure being sited on the up side of the running lines. In pre-Nationalisation days, the line between High Wycombe and Ashendon Junction had been maintained by the LNER, and perhaps for this reason Saunderton signal box sported LNER type nameplates, which were affixed to the ends of the cabin, rather than on the front - as would normally have been the case on a purely Great Western box.

In 1903, Saunderton issued 9,744 tickets while in 1923 11,191 tickets were sold. In the 1930s, the station typically issued around 4,000 tickets per annum, together with perhaps a dozen season tickets. Freight traffic was equally modest, 2,205 tons being recorded in 1903, while in 1923 just 2,309 tons of freight were handled, roughly half of this being in the form of coal traffic. In 1932, 6,041 tons of freight was dealt with, including 3,849 tons of incoming mineral traffic, most of which would probably have been aggregates for use in local road improvement schemes - a form of bulk freight traffic that would ultimately help rival forms of transport, to the detriment of the railway system.

Although Saunderton was never a particularly busy station, it managed to avoid closure during the Beeching period but, like most local stations, its goods yard has been abandoned, having been closed to goods traffic on 1st March, 1965. The signal box was closed in November 1975, while the main station building has now been replaced by a glazed waiting shelter. The GWR waiting room on the up platform has nevertheless survived, together with the now-roofless footbridge, which continues to provide a means of access between the up and down sides of the station.

Princes Risborough

Curving towards the north, the line reaches an area of bare chalk downs beyond Saunderton. This is the point at which the up and down lines part company for the next 2½ miles, and, coasting down off the Chilterns, trains often gain considerable momentum before coming to a stand in Princes Risborough station. In steam days, this section of the line saw much fast running, and the sight of a 'King' thundering down the single line, whistling all the way, was an unforgettable experience.

The down line follows the approximate course of the original Wycombe Railway, whereas the up line was constructed during the early 1900s to ensure an easier gradient for southbound workings. The up line passes through deep cuttings and an 88 yds-long tunnel, its gradient being 1 in 167, as opposed to 1 in 87 on the down line. The present down line is not entirely collinear with the earlier formation and, writing in the April 1906 edition of the *Railway Magazine*, Alfred Arthurton was intrigued to discover 'a third set of rails', which turned out to be 'the old line passing through a separate cutting between the two new tracks, and rejoining the old down line some chains distant'.

In its heyday, Princes Risborough, 34 miles 54 chains from Paddington, was a spacious, four platform station with additional bays for the Aylesbury, Oxford and Watlington branch trains. However, in its earliest days as a rural junction on the Wycombe Railway, the station had been a much simpler affair, with just one

The up side station buildings at Princes Risborough, photographed on a sunny afternoon in 1980.   *Mike Marr*

A detailed view of the up side station buildings at Princes Risborough, 1980.   *Mike Marr*

platform for passenger traffic on the up side and a single-siding goods yard sited immediately to the south. The running line bifurcated at the north end of the platform, with one single line running westwards to Thame, while the Aylesbury branch (opened in 1863) diverged north-eastwards; a short spur left the Aylesbury line and terminated in a dead-end bay behind the platform.

The original station building, opened in 1862, was a simple, gable-roofed structure with an open-fronted waiting area at its south end. The nearby goods shed was a classic broad gauge structure, similar to scores of other sheds found throughout the Great Western system on lines engineered by Brunel or his assistants.

This very simple station was modified in connection with the opening of the Watlington & Princes Risborough Railway in 1872. The principal alterations concerned the provision of a second platform and associated trackwork for branch traffic, the platform being sited on the down side of the original running line - which thereby became a 'through bay', with platform faces on each side. Further alterations were carried out in the 1890s, when the 'through bay' arrangement was replaced by a conventional layout incorporating up and down platforms and an additional face for Watlington services on the west side of the new down platform.

The Watlington branch platform had its own run-round loop, while similar run-round facilities were available for Aylesbury branch trains in the bay platform on the up side of the station. Other improvements put into effect towards the end of the 19th century included the provision of a covered footbridge and new signalling, and additional sidings.

Although, by the end of the 19th century, Princes Risborough had grown into a fairly complex junction station, it was decided that the existing accommodation was inadequate for main line traffic, and it was agreed that the station would be entirely reconstructed on a new site, about 100 yards to the south. Work progressed steadily during the early 1900s, and the new station was complete by the time that the Great Western & Great Central Joint Line was opened for public traffic on 2nd April, 1906.

The new track layout was an enlarged version of the usual GW&GC quadruple-track design, the main up and down platforms being served by loop lines on either side of the centre fast lines. The Aylesbury and Watlington branch bays were sited at the north end of the main platforms, while the main station building was sited on the up side. A subsidiary waiting room was constructed on the down platform, both of these buildings being standard Great Western red brick structures. The up and down sides of the station were linked by a fully-roofed girder footbridge, while the platforms were covered, for much of their length, by commodious canopies edged with characteristic GWR 'V-and-hole' valancing.

The platforms were numbered in logical sequence from one to four, platform one being the Watlington branch bay while platform two was the down main line; platform three, on the opposite side of the station, was the up main line, and platform four was the Aylesbury branch bay.

In its fully-developed form, the station was signalled from two hip-roofed signal boxes, which were known as Princes Risborough North and Princes Risborough South. The North box was situated to the north of the station between the running lines and the Watlington branch. It was of the usual GWR design, although the box was considerably bigger than most of its counterparts, the frame having more than 100 levers. The South box was positioned at the London end of the station, between the running lines and the goods yard.

As this part of the Great Western & Great Central route was, in later years, maintained by the LNER, the two signal boxes sported LNER nameplates at each

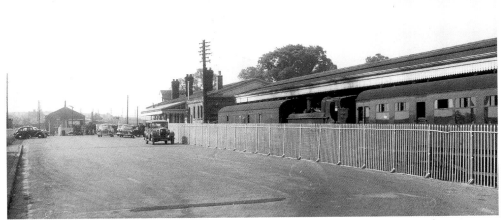

The up side station buildings at Princes Risborough, as seen from the station approach road on 4th June, 1960. The goods shed can be discerned in the distance, while '64XX' class 0-6-0PT No. 6429 occupies the Aylesbury branch bay.   *H.C. Casserley*

Collett '14XX' class 0-4-2T No. 1473 about to depart from Princes Risborough with the 11.15 am local passenger service to Aylesbury on 23rd July, 1973.   *H.C. Casserley*

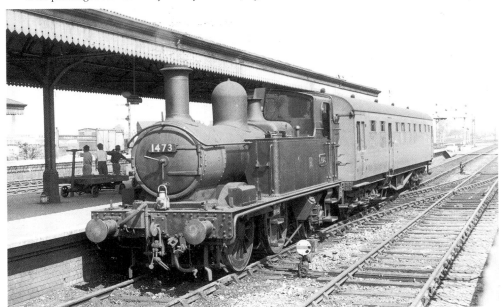

Large '51XX' class prairie tank No. 5101 is matched with named auto-trailer No. W220 *Thrush* while working the 2.30 pm local passenger service to Banbury on 26th May, 1962.

R.M. Casserley

'Hall' class 4-6-0 No. 5900 *Hinderton Hall* storms through Princes Risborough station on the centre fast road at the head of the 10.10 am Birmingham to Ramsgate service on 23rd July, 1955.

H.C. Casserley

Collett '57XX' class pannier tank No. 3608 passes through Princes Risborough with an up mixed freight working on 23rd July, 1955.   *H.C. Casserley*

Riddles class '9F' 2-10-0 No. 92092 toils southwards through Princes Risborough on 26th September, 1964 while hauling a heavy freight working from the Great Central line.
                                                                                                        Brian Stephenson

end, while many of the signals in and around the station were subsequently replaced by upper quadrant semaphores.

Princes Risborough goods yard was moved somewhat further to the south as a result of the rebuilding work carried out in the early 1900s. The new layout included a long reception siding, a goods shed road and a 'back' road for coal and other forms of mileage traffic. The goods shed, built in the early 1900s to replace the old Wycombe Railway shed, was a brick building with a low-pitched, gable roof. It measured approximately 63 ft by 42 ft at ground level, and incorporated a projecting office at the north end.

A private siding branched out from the goods yard towards the premises of Risborough Furniture Ltd, while another private siding on the down side served an extensive government establishment known as 'HM Forest Products Research Laboratory'. Both of these private sidings were in use by the early 1920s, and they remained *in situ* until the British Railways period, the furniture factory siding closing in 1966, while the Forest Research siding had been closed by 1971.

The station was, by that time, undergoing an inevitable rationalisation programme, resulting in the removal of the goods yard sidings and the closure of the down platform, so that all passenger facilities could be concentrated on the former up platform. Other work carried out at that time included the closure of Princes Risborough South box, and the installation of a new panel in the North Box, the new signalling system being brought into use in October 1968. At the same time, the line between Princes Risborough and Aynho Junction was reduced to single track, as described in Chapter Four.

In operational terms, Princes Risborough retained its importance after the singling of the line in 1968, in that it became the last crossing place before Bicester. For the next few years, northbound trains would sometimes wait for southbound workings to enter the up line before their northwards journeys could proceed, but as the rationalised station had just one through platform, it was necessary for down services to proceed beyond the confines of the passenger station in order that passing could take place on a short section of double track at the north end of the station; once the southbound train had entered the station, down workings could safely enter the single line. This situation pertained until March 1991, when the North box was closed, and control of the line was transferred to the Integrated Electronic Control Centre at Marylebone. As previously mentioned, Princes Risborough to Aynho Jn was eventually re-doubled, in two stages, in 1998 and 2002.

Although Princes Risborough was not as busy as the stations at the London end of the line, its passenger receipts were always relatively healthy. In 1913, just three years after the completion of the Bicester Cut-Off, the station issued 31,809 tickets and 122 seasons, while in the 1930s ticket sales amounted to about 50,000 per annum. There were, in addition, about 550 season ticket sales, while in 1938 the station issued 51,166 ordinary tickets and 670 seasons. Freight traffic fluctuated between 14,000 and 24,000 tons per annum over a 35-year period between 1903 and 1938, a gradual decline becoming evident after 1935, although coal traffic remained steady, and carted traffic was increasing.

Traffic dealt with at Princes Risborough

Year	Staff	Receipts (£)	Tickets	Parcels	Goods Tonnage
1903	12	8,489	24,565	10,294	21,889
1923	27	16,745	38,900	18,460	13,899
1936	28	18,070	50,633	23,606	17,364
1937	28	15,995	51,166	23,336	13,312
1938	29	17,091	49,252	22,566	14,647

A glimpse of Ilmer Halt during the early 1960s, showing the timber trestle platforms.
Lens of Sutton Collection

Haddenham station in the early 1960s, looking south towards London and showing the lattice girder footbridge and down side waiting room.   *Lens of Sutton Collection*

Chapter Seven

The Route from
Princes Risborough to Banbury

Leaving Princes Risborough down trains initially head northwards but, after a short distance, the route curves leftwards onto a north-westerly alignment as the railway falls gently towards the Vale of Aylesbury on a 1 in 200 descending gradient. Although, geologically speaking, the Vale is a low lying clay plain, it is far from flat, and for the next two miles the line runs through pleasant, rolling farmland, with an average elevation of about 227 ft above mean sea level.

Ilmer Halt

There were, at first, no stations between Princes Risborough and Brill & Ludgershall, but this situation was rectified on Monday 1st April, 1929, when the GWR opened a new halt at Ilmer, some 37 miles 31 chains from Paddington. This unstaffed stopping place was equipped with two short, timber trestle platforms, public access being arranged from the adjacent road overbridge. The halt was sited in a remote corner of Buckinghamshire, in convenient proximity to the tiny village of Ilmer, on the south side of the line, and within reasonable walking distance of Longwick, to the south-east.

Ilmer Halt was served by GWR local trains between Princes Risborough and Banbury, and its initial train service comprised four push-pull workings each way. There was, in addition, an LNER though service from Wotton to Marylebone at 8.15 am, and a down service from Marylebone to Wotton at 6.10 am. Although the halt had no provision for freight traffic, goods and parcels could be collected and delivered in the immediate vicinity by railway cartage vehicles from nearby Princes Risborough.

Sadly, Ilmer Halt became a closure victim in the early 1960s, and the last trains called at this isolated stopping place on Saturday 5th January, 1963. The timetable in operation during the final months of operation provided four up and five down services, with up trains to Princes Risborough at 7.19, 11.54 am, 2.54 and 7.08 pm, and down services to Banbury at 7.56 am, 12.36, 4.08 and 8.33 pm. Additionally, at 7.38 pm, the halt was served by the 6.24 pm down working from Marylebone to Brackley.

Haddenham

Maintaining its north-westerly heading, the railway passes over the A4129 Thame to Princes Risborough road on a steel girder bridge, beyond which the route continues towards Haddenham (40 miles 7 chains) on level alignments.

This station was, until its demise, very similar to its counterparts elsewhere on the Great Western & Great Central Joint Line. The familiar quadruple-track layout was again in evidence, with 400 ft platforms on either side. The minor road from Thame to Haddenham village crossed all four lines on a skew girder bridge at the south end of the station. The bridge was formed of steel girders resting on brick abutments, the single span being 56 ft 6 in. on the square, and 81 ft on the skew. The up and down platforms were linked by a single-span lattice girder footbridge.

Haddenham

N.

SIDING →

To Northolt Jn

W.B.

S.B.

G.S.

S.C.

The up platform and main station building at Haddenham, photographed on 15th April, 1956.

R.M. Casserley

In architectural terms, Haddenham resembled the other intermediate stations *en route* from London, although there were several minor differences, which could probably be explained by the fact that this part of the Great Western & Great Central Joint Line was maintained by the LNER. The footbridge, for example, was unlike those found elsewhere on the line, insofar as it had no roof covering, and was formed of slender, bow-string girders, with open lattice work.

The main station building was situated on the up platform, and there was a smaller waiting room on the opposite side. Both of these structures were of brick construction with gable roofs, the roof on the up side building being extended over the platform to form a verandah, whereas the subsidiary building on the opposite platform was fitted with a separate canopy. Photographic evidence suggests that both structures were originally of similar appearance, but at some stage in their careers they were altered - the likeliest explanation being that these changes took place under LNER auspices.

There was a three-siding goods yard to the north of the platforms on the up side, together with a goods headshunt. A further siding extended southwards from the up platform line, and there were two similar sidings at either end of the down platform line. One of the yard sidings ran into a 'van chute' or loading dock, while two further sidings at the rear of the goods yard were used for coal or other forms of mileage traffic. The goods yard also contained a cattle dock, a weigh-house and a 5-ton fixed yard crane. The signal box was sited immediately to the north of the down platform.

Like other stations situated in rural areas, Haddenham was originally lit by oil lamps, though paraffin vapour lamps were subsequently installed. On 12th February, 1952, it was agreed that electric lighting would be installed at the station at an estimated cost of £710, though in the event the final cost was £848, inclusive of a 'service charge'. The signal box controlled a mixture of lower quadrant and upper quadrant semaphores, another example of LNER influence on this northern section of the Great Western & Great Central Joint Line!

The station was well-sited in relation to Haddenham - a large village with an impressive Early English church - and the neighbouring village of Aston Sandford, which was about two miles from the railway. Haddenham was within the station's free cartage area, but a small charge was made for collections and deliveries in the Aston Sandford area. The station was not particularly busy, average bookings being about 3,250 per annum during the mid 1930s, although there were about 30-50 season ticket sales during the early part of the decade. In 1935, the station sold 3,316 ordinary tickets and 42 seasons, while in 1937 the corresponding figures were 3,241 ordinary ticket sales and 30 seasons.

Goods traffic was running at about 7,000 tons a year during the early 1900s, but this figure had halved by the 1930s, when Haddenham typically dealt with about 3,500 tons of freight per annum, including over 2,000 tons of domestic coal. There was a certain amount of livestock traffic, an average of 35 wagon loads being recorded each year between 1913 and 1938.

Haddenham was closed, along with most of the other stations north of Princes Risborough, with effect from Monday 7th January, 1963. As there was no Sunday service, the last trains ran on Saturday 5th January. Goods facilities lasted until the following September, and most of the goods sidings were lifted in 1965; the signal box was closed in April 1966.

In retrospect, the run-down and closure of this hitherto unimportant station was regrettable, insofar as nearby Thame was poised for a period of population growth and economic development. As Thame had also lost its direct rail link, it was

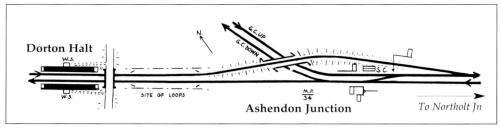

Ashendon Junction on 20th July, 1946, showing the typical Great Central style signal box, which was replaced in 1959 during a programme of track improvements. The girder bridge that can be seen in the distance carried the up Great Western line over the up and down Great Central tracks, which continued northwards to reach Grendon Underwood Junction and the GCR main line. *H.C. Casserley*

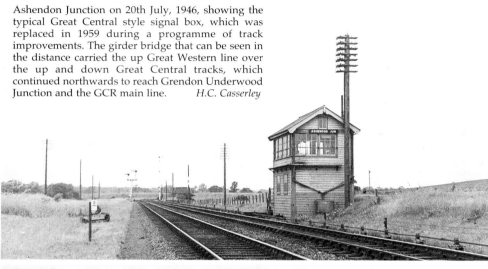

The short-lived signal box at Ashendon North, which controlled up and down running loops on each side of the Bicester Cut-Off.
Lens of Sutton Collection

decided that a new station, known as 'Haddenham & Thame Parkway', would be constructed on a new site at 40 miles 38 chains, about a third of a mile to the north of the original Haddenham station.

Funding for this £430,000 project was provided by BR, with contributions from Oxfordshire and Buckinghamshire county councils. The new station was officially opened on Saturday 3rd October, 1987, the historic nature of the occasion being underlined by the running of a special train, headed by Gresley 'A4' Pacific No. 4498 *Sir Nigel Gresley*. Regular public services commenced on the following Monday, 5th October.

The revived Haddenham & Thame Parkway station bore little resemblance to its predecessor, and although the new stopping place was staffed, its facilities were minimal, being confined to a single platform on the down side of the line. The uncompromisingly-modern booking office was linked to the platform by a sloping ramp, and there was ample room for commuters' cars in the adjacent car park. In recent years, Haddenham & Thame Parkway has become a two-platform station, a second platform having been added in connection with the re-introduction of double track working between Princes Risborough and Aynho Junction.

Ashendon Junction

From Haddenham, the route continues north-westwards. The A418 road from Thame to Aylesbury is carried over the line on a twin-arched brick bridge, beyond which trains cross the River Thame on the Chearsley (or 'Thame') viaduct, which has five brick arches, each of 40 ft span. The viaduct is about 33 ft above local ground level, and it has an overall length of approximately 80 yards.

As trains pass the site of Ashendon Junction (44 miles 4 chains), observant travellers may catch a glimpse of the trackbed of the abandoned Great Central line to Grendon Underwood Junction. This double track line formerly diverged northwards, passing beneath the flyover which once carried the up Great Western line over the up and down GCR tracks on a substantial girder bridge of the 'parallel boom' type, with a span of 53 ft. The junction was controlled from a gable-roofed signal cabin on the up side of the line, this all-timber box being of typical Great Central design.

The box itself was rebuilt in 1959, during a programme of modernisation designed to provide a better path for northbound Great Central line expresses such as the 'Master Cutler'. In connection with this modernisation scheme, the down line junction was slewed to provide a better alignment for the Great Central route, but this slewing had an adverse effect on the former Great Western line, and if over-enthusiastic drivers failed to observe the 50 mph speed limit, unsuspecting passengers were subjected to a disconcerting jolt as their trains negotiated the realigned pointwork.

Following the closure of the Great Central route in September 1966, the Ashendon to Grendon Underwood link was used for wind resistance tests; former gas-turbine locomotive No. 18100 (converted to experimental electric No. E2001) made some trips up and down the line, and was then parked for several months on the site of Akeman Street station. Coupled to two coaches, the locomotive had apparently been abandoned on a disused railway in the middle of nowhere - not surprisingly, it was known locally as 'The Ghost Train'!

Ashendon Junction signal box survived until September 1967, although, following a freight train derailment in November 1965, only the up Great Central line

Two companion views of Ashendon Junction, both taken on 20th July, 1946; the upper view is facing south towards London, while the lower view is looking north towards Grendon Underwood Junction.   *(Both) H.C. Casserley*

remained in use and, for this reason, the last regular trains could run in one direction only. The Ashendon Junction to Grendon Underwood line was soon lifted between Ashendon and Westcot Works, but a little-used connection was retained at the Grendon Underwood end.

Before leaving Ashendon Junction, it is worth recalling the occasion when, on a foggy Winter night in the 1950s, the signalman forgot that there was a relief train running in front of the regular 6.10 pm express from Paddington, which was in turn followed by the 'Master Cutler'. Thinking that the relief working was the 6.10 pm, he changed the points ready for what he thought was the 'Master Cutler', with the result that the 6.10 pm from Paddington thundered northwards onto the Great Central route. The Western Region driver was soon completely lost, and Mr W.K. Mackenzie (a regular traveller on the GW&GC Joint Line at that time) recalled that when the train reached Grendon Underwood the train crew asked the Grendon Underwood signalman where they were, and were promptly told 'But you *can't* be the Birmingham train' - a reply that surely deserves a place in railway folklore.

Passing from the Great Western & Great Central route near milepost 34, down trains reach the Bicester Cut-Off, and the speeding multiple units approach the now closed Dorton Halt. In the days when 'first generation' dmus were employed on the line, those travellers lucky enough to be in the front seats may have noted a slight widening of the trackbed immediately to the south of the halt. There were at one time up and down goods loops at this point, together with an attendant signal box known as Ashendon North, which had been brought into use on 4th April, 1910 when the Bicester Cut-Off was opened for through goods traffic.

It is possible that these loops were originally laid-in for contractor's use, although it is perhaps more likely that they were installed to increase line capacity during the early part of World War I. Whatever the reason, they were considered unnecessary, and lifted around 1917 - only a few years after the opening of the line! Ashendon North signal box survived until 1924, although, in a list of signal boxes dated 10th July, 1922, it was said to be 'closed until further notice'.

Dorton Halt

Continuing north-westwards, trains reach the site of Dorton Halt (45 miles 22 chains), which had been one of the new stopping places opened in the 1930s. In April 1937, *The Railway Magazine* reported that 'a new halt is to be provided by the GWR at Dorton, between Brill & Ludgershall and Haddenham stations, to serve an agricultural district with a population of 650 living in the villages of Dorton, Wotton, Chilton and Ashendon. The halt will have two platforms with shelters, and will be lit by electricity'. The halt referred-to was opened just two months later, on 21st June, 1937.

The infrastructure here was primitive in the extreme. The two platforms, each of which could accommodate barely one coach, were of earth-and-timber construction, and revetted with old sleepers and sections of bridge rail. The waiting shelters were simple timber sheds, access from the adjacent road overbridge being by means of sloping cinder pathways; at night, the platforms were lit by electric lights.

Like Ilmer Halt and Haddenham, Dorton Halt became a closure victim during the Beeching period, although to be fair to the British Railways hierarchy of the 1960s, it is unlikely that that this remote stopping place had ever generated much traffic. The last trains called here on Saturday 5th January, 1963.

Two views of Dorton Halt, both of which date from the 1960s.

(Both) Lens of Sutton Collection

The village itself can be seen to the left of the railway as trains pass the halt; a tiny place, Dorton once had pretensions to greatness by reason of its chalybeate springs - which were said to have therapeutic properties. A company was formed to promote 'Dorton Spa', and, during the 1830s, this venture could claim some modest success. If the railway had reached Dorton several decades earlier, it is possible that the village could have been developed. Unfortunately, by the time the railway was opened, the spa was abandoned and forgotten.

Brill & Ludgershall

Beyond Dorton, the railway enters a cutting, and Brill Hill, which rises to 694 ft on the left-hand side of the line, is hidden from view. Falling at 1 in 200, the line reaches the 192 yds-long Brill tunnel (46 miles 37 chains). The famous Brill branch of the Metropolitan Railway once crossed the main line in the vicinity of the tunnel; closed in 1936, this rustic by-way has left few visible remains - although the regular Brill branch engine, LT 4-4-0T No. 23, can be seen preserved in the London Transport Museum.

Emerging from the tunnel, down trains run through a further cutting and then pass beneath a road overbridge. Brill & Ludgershall station was immediately beyond. Another typical 'New Line' station, Brill, 47 miles 35 chains from Paddington and a little over three miles from Ashendon Junction, was the first station on the Bicester Cut-Off. It became unstaffed as early as 1956, and was closed to passengers on Saturday 5th January, 1963. In its final years of operation, the station was known as 'Brill Halt'.

Until its untimely demise, Brill & Ludgershall had been similar to neighbouring Haddenham. The layout incorporated up and down platform loops on either side of the centre fast lines, with a spacious goods yard to the north of the up platform. The station building, of standard Great Western design, was sited on the up platform, and there was a much smaller waiting room on the down side. The up and down platforms were linked by a roofed footbridge, and the platforms were fenced with tubular metal railings.

The goods yard was fully-equipped with a range of accommodation for dealing with coal, livestock and other forms of traffic. There was a small weigh-house, while the goods shed was merely a small, brick-built lock-up on the up platform. In addition to the up and down platform loops, there were at one time running loops for goods trains on each side, these facilities being arranged as extensions of the platform loops. The station was signalled from a large, hip-roofed signal cabin, that was sited towards the north end of the down platform. The signal box closed on 18th April, 1966 when the platform loops were taken out of use.

The station handled around 1,500 tons of freight per annum during the early 1900s, but this very modest figure had increased to 2,229 tons per annum by 1931, and 3,000 tons during the later 1930s. The main sources of traffic here were coal and general merchandise. Passenger bookings amounted to 2,624 in 1923 and 2,196 by 1930. Thereafter, Brill & Ludgershall normally issued around 1,800 ordinary tickets a year during the mid to late 1930s, together with around half a dozen season tickets. On average, cattle traffic amounted to 20 wagon loads each year during the period under review.

As its named implies, Brill & Ludgershall served the transport needs of two small villages, Ludgershall being sited a short distance to the north of the station, while Brill

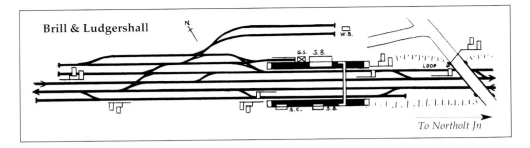

Brill & Ludgershall, looking south-east towards London during the 1960s. *Nelson Collection*

A detailed view of Brill & Ludgershall signal box *circa* 1912. *Lens of Sutton Collection*

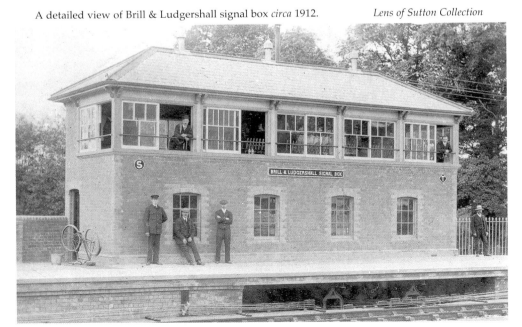

was a little under two miles to the south. Oddly, the 1938 *Book of Towns Villages & Outlying Works* indicates that Ludgershall was within the station's free cartage area, although there were apparently no collection or delivery arrangements for the inhabitants of Brill. In later years, following World War II, both villages were served by a 'Zonal Lorry' from nearby Bicester, which also called as necessary at Piddington and other neighbouring villages.

Blackthorn

From Brill the railway continues north-westwards into an area that is completely different to the Chiltern landscapes encountered earlier; there are fewer trees, and the pattern of settlement is much more dispersed. Pleasant enough in the spring and summer months, the region can become bleak and depressing in the depths of winter. With few trees to act as windbreaks, the line hereabouts is subject to drifts when it snows - indeed, during the Arctic Winter of 1963, the drifts were so deep that troops from nearby Bicester Ordnance Depot were called out to help railwaymen clear the line.

A mile from Brill, the railway enters Oxfordshire, and cuttings give way to embankments as the trains approach the site of Blackthorn station (50 miles 34 chains), closed to passengers with effect from 8th June, 1953, and to goods traffic in January 1955. The A41 road passes beneath the railway at the London end of the former station - its noticeably straight alignment underlying the fact that this is Akeman Street, the Roman road leading to *Corinium* (Cirencester) and *Aquae Sulis* (Bath). The plate girder bridge that carries the railway over this historic highway has a span of 69 ft.

Blackthorn was one of the few stations on the 'New Line' with only two lines between its platforms. The main station building was sited on the up platform, and there was a small waiting room on the down side, both of these structures being of the usual Great Western standard design. The up and down platforms were linked by a plate girder footbridge, and the station was signalled from a hip-roofed signal box at the Banbury end of the down platform. This was closed on 29th June, 1958.

There was formerly a three-siding goods yard on the up side, one of its sidings being arranged as a reception loop with trailing connections to the up and down running lines, while the other two were dead-end sidings for coal or other forms of wagon load traffic. Spurs extended from either end of the reception loop, and one of these terminated in a loading dock behind the up platform. The yard contained cattle loading docks, coal wharves and a weigh-house, but there was no yard crane.

Blackthorn was never a particularly busy place, its average passenger bookings during the period from 1913 until 1923 being around 2,000 tickets a year. Thereafter, the number of tickets issued at this Oxfordshire station declined from 949 in 1930 to 754 in 1936, and just 476 by 1938. The amount of freight traffic handled at Blackthorn varied from year to year though, on average, around 2,300 tons per annum were dealt with throughout the 1930s. In 1938, collection and delivery services in the immediate vicinity were carried out by a GWR 'country lorry', though after World War II parcels and smaller consignments were conveyed by a 'Zonal Lorry' from nearby Bicester.

In March 1946, Mr E.C. Varney of Chesterton, near Bicester, rented a coal wharf at Blackthorn measuring 60 square yards, at an annual rental of £3; the previous tenant, Messrs F. & G. Wright, had paid a rent of £4 10s. 0d. per annum for a wharf measuring 90 square yards.

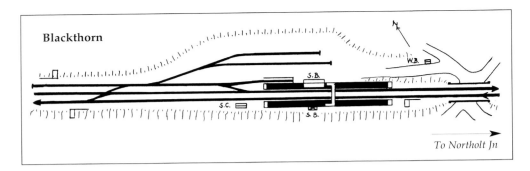

Blackthorn

To Northolt Jn

A postcard view of the two-platform station at Blackthorn, dating from the years before World War I. *Lens of Sutton Collection*

A post-closure view of Blackthorn station, showing the derelict facilities in 1958. *R.M. Casserley*

Bicester North

The railway is carried on almost continuous embankments for the next 2¾ miles, and passengers can obtain a good view of the rather flat, boring countryside of East Oxfordshire. To the left, Bicester Ordnance Depot can be glimpsed on the western horizon. The depot is still served by rail, and there are about 40 miles of track within the military complex. The 'main line' is around four miles long, and this military system has its own locomotives and rolling stock - some of which was, until comparatively recent years, of pre-Nationalisation and even pre-Grouping vintage.

There were at one time no less than 12 steam locomotives in operation on the Bicester Military Railway, the majority of them being 0-6-0 'Austerity' saddle tanks. The depot was also used as a central repair establishment for all army locomotives, but this work ceased in 1983 - by which time the 0-6-0STs had been replaced by a small fleet of 600 hp 0-8-0 diesel hydraulic locomotives. In 1978, the 0-8-0s were themselves replaced by 'Vanguard' 0-4-0 diesels, which are capable of being operated in multiple. One of the Bicester 0-6-0STs, No. 97 *Sapper*, is in service on the Kent & East Sussex Railway, where it is now No. 25 *Northiam*.

Approaching Bicester, the line crosses the former London & North Western Railway (LNWR) Buckinghamshire branch on a girder bridge with a span of 54 ft. This line predated the GWR line by many years, the section through Bicester having been brought into use on 1st October, 1850. In later years, the LNWR station was known as Bicester London Road to distinguish it from the GWR station, which became Bicester North. The former LNWR line lost its passenger services on Saturday 30th December, 1967, although a local service was officially reintroduced between Bicester London Road and Oxford on Saturday 9th May, 1987, with regular services commencing on Monday 11th May.

Bicester North, serving a picturesque, Cotswold style town, and the only 'urban' centre between Princes Risborough and Banbury, is 53 miles 31 chains from Paddington. The station is orientated from south-east to north-west, with its main buildings and the former goods yard on the down side. The platforms and goods yard (now a car park) are situated on an embankment, with a long approach ramp from the A421 road at the north end of the station.

Until the onset of track rationalisation at the end of the 1960s, the line through the station had been quadruple-tracked for a distance of about half a mile, the up and down platform loops being augmented by running loops and headshunts on each side. The up and down loops were both long enough to hold trains of 75 short wheelbase goods wagons, together with their locomotives and brake vans.

The station buildings at Bicester consist of a long range of standard Great Western red brick buildings on the down platform, together with a much smaller red brick waiting room on the up side. A GWR plate girder footbridge, once fully enclosed, links the two platforms. The main station building is similar to its counterparts elsewhere on the Bicester Cut-Off, in that its low-pitched gable roof is extended forward over the platform to create a full-length canopy. The subsidiary building on the up platform conforms to the usual hip-roofed design. Both of these structures are built of cheerful red brickwork - a form of construction found on all parts of the 'New Line'.

Bicester was clearly intended to be an important intermediate station, and to this end its main building incorporated a variety of facilities. These included, from left to right, a gentlemen's urinal, a ladies' waiting room, the booking office and general waiting room, a parcels office, a refreshment room, and additional staff

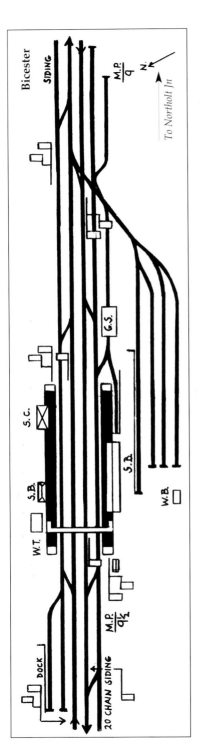

Bicester

SIDING

M.P.
9

To Northolt Jn

N.

S.C.

S.B.

W.T.

G.S.

S.B.

W.B.

DOCK

M.P.
9½

20 CHAIN SIDING

A general view of Bicester North station from the south end of the platform, showing the hip-roofed GWR-type signal box and other typical Great Western features.

Nelson Collection

accommodation. The refreshment room was notable in that its main, platform-facing windows displayed the Great Western Railway's heraldic crest in stained glass; in later years, the refreshment room found a new use as a taxi office.

Bicester is of course associated with the Bicester & Warden Hill Hunt. Although the famous 'Bicester Hunt' had been founded as long ago as 1778, its heyday coincided with the opening of the Bicester Cut-Off, and in this context it is no coincidence that Bicester station was so well-equipped. The Great Western Railway was an unashamedly patrician organisation, its Directors being drawn largely from the ranks of the landowning classes. Many of these gentlemen were enthusiastic horsemen, and hunt meetings held in GWR territory invariably attracted at least some of the company's own Directors, or members of their families.

The spacious station buildings at Bicester were sometimes used as changing rooms by members of the Hunt, and on one occasion the Prince of Wales wrote an appreciative letter to *The Great Western Railway Magazine*, thanking the company for the facilities provided during the previous hunting season.

Bicester's goods facilities were laid out on a relatively lavish scale. The goods yard was entered by means of connections from the down platform loop, and there was also a trailing connection from the up main line. Bicester was one of the few stations on the 'New Line' to have a goods shed, this structure being of timber construction, with an internal loading platform and a low-pitched gable roof. The goods shed siding continued north-westwards before terminating in a loading dock at the rear of the down platform, while four dead-end sidings were available for coal and other forms of mileage traffic. An additional horse landing was sited to the west of the platforms on the up side.

Bicester signal box was situated towards the London end of the up platform. It was again of standard Great Western design - albeit of all-wood construction, instead of the more usual brick-and-timber. It featured a hipped, slated roof, together with the usual five-pane high visibility windows. The box was closed on 27th October, 1968. Standard Great Western water cranes were positioned between the fast lines and the platform loops on both sides, both being supplied from a stilted metal water tower at the rear of the up platform. At night, the station was lit by gas lamps, while the platforms were fenced with tubular metal railings.

Despite the ample facilities provided for passenger and freight traffic, Bicester was not a particularly important station in terms of originating traffic. Indeed, during the 1930s, the station issued around 8,000-9,000 tickets a year, together with about 50 seasons. Freight traffic was equally sparse, only 9,198 tons of freight being handled in 1931 while, in the following year, this meagre total declined still further to only 5,624 tons. The absence of large scale freight traffic is surprising when one considers that Bicester was the site of an important aerodrome, though in practice this establishment was served by a siding connection from the LMS line, rather than the Great Western route.

Similarly, in World War II, Bicester Ordnance Depot was linked to the national railway system via a branch from the LMS line - with obvious ramifications in terms of traffic that might otherwise have been conveyed by the GWR. On the other hand, the station was one of the busiest on the line in terms of livestock traffic, an average of 333 wagon loads being handled each year over a 25-year period between 1903 and 1938.

A general view of Bicester North station, looking towards London on 27th February, 1957.

R.M. Casserley

Bicester North was the only station on the Bicester Cut-Off to have a goods shed, the building provided being of timber construction, as shown in the *circa* 1962 photograph.

Nelson Collection

Traffic dealt with at Bicester North

Year	Staff	Receipts (£)	Tickets	Parcels	Goods Tonnage
1913	8	4,892	10,376	n/a	5,270
1923	8	10,352	10,949	10,775	7,001
1930	8	12,332	10,833	15,209	10,588
1937	8	8,955	8,596	17,333	6,789
1938	7	8,707	8,321	15,894	5,709

In GWR days, the inhabitants of Bicester were served by a free cartage service, while nearby communities such as Stratton Audley (2 miles from the station), Launton (2 miles) and Chesterton (2 miles) were linked to the station by carrier services. This situation was transformed after World War II, when the collection and delivery arrangements for goods and parcels were much improved. In December 1948, Bicester became a 'sub-railhead' of Oxford under the 'Zonal' system, and for the next few years Bicester-based road vehicles provided collection and delivery services over a much wider swathe of countryside, encompassing Brill & Ludgershall, Blackthorn and Ardley.

Bicester had a staff of eight throughout most of the Great Western period, including porters, signalmen and clerical staff. In 1929, the station was placed under the supervision of the Bicester LMS station master although, by British Railways days, Bicester North had regained its autonomy. In 1961, for example, the station master was Mr C.W. Dealy, while others employed at Bicester North at that time included porters J.W. Smith, J.W. Bower and F. Hill, signalman W.J. Wickens, foreman D.C. Adams, chief goods clerk A.H. Tarrant, clerks G. Burton, R. Dossett and Mrs B. Houlihan, and motor drivers E. Smith and W. Coombs.

Following the singling of the line in October/November 1968, the simplified track layout consisted of a lengthy passing loop, which was worked from Princes Risborough North box. Two dead end sidings were initially retained, but one of these later succumbed to a further bout of 'rationalisation'. The remaining siding, which occupied the site of the former goods yard headshunt on the down side, was retained for engineer's use, but on occasions it also stabled crippled rolling stock.

Bicester's passing loop was initially intended only for emergency use, but in practice the loop was also used for crossing purposes after the singling of the line. In May 1988, for instance, the loop was regularly used by the 6.53 am, 10.06 am and 7.00 pm down services, which were routed into platform 2 (the old up platform), while southbound trains used the former down platform; both platforms are signalled for two-way working.

In spite of its simplified track layout, Bicester North remained a hive of activity throughout the remaining years of the BR era. In 1990 the GWR station buildings were extensively refurbished, £500,000 being expended on the provision of new platform surfaces, modern lighting and other improvements. The modernised station was officially re-opened on 10th December 1990, the ceremony being conducted by the Chairman of Oxfordshire County Council and 10-year-old schoolboy James Johnston, who inserted a piece in a giant jigsaw that was being assembled to mark the progress of the Chiltern Line modernisation scheme.

In its new form, the station building contained various amenities, including a spacious ticket hall and circulating area, a newsagent's, a Red Star parcels office, a taxi office, and accommodation for civil engineering staff. Further changes ensued in the early years of the 21st century when the second track was reinstated on the Bicester Cut-Off between Princes Risborough and Aynho Junction. The work was

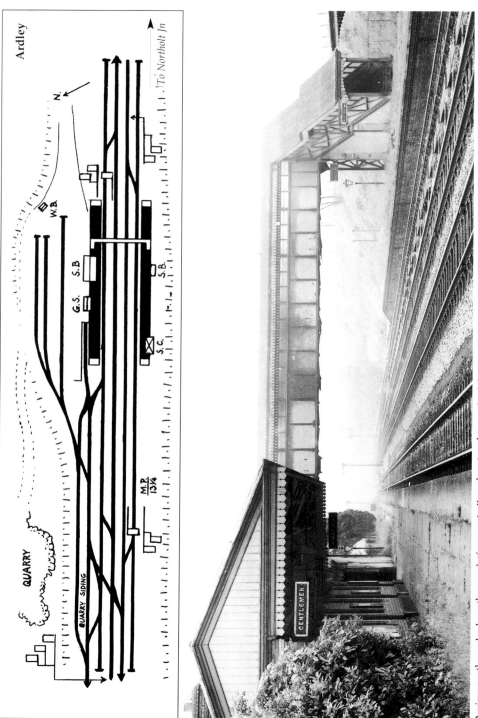

Ardley

QUARRY

QUARRY SIDING

W.B.

G.S.   S.B.

S.B.

S.C.

M.P.
13¼

N.

(To Northolt Jn)

A view southwards along the up platform at Ardley, showing the standard GWR red brick station building and plate girder footbridge.

CENTLEMEN

Nelson Collection

carried out in two stages, the second stage being completed on Monday 5th August, 2002 when double track working was brought into use between Bicester and Aynho.

In general, the re-doubling of the line entailed few track alterations at Bicester North. The engineer's siding at the London end of the station was retained, while a new siding was installed to the north of the platforms on the up side to facilitate the reversal of terminating trains. This siding, known as 'Bicester North Siding', is long enough to accommodate 8-car multiple unit trains, and it can also be used for stabling purposes. Crossovers are positioned to the north and south of the station, the lines through the platforms being signalled for bi-directional operation. The remodelled track layout is signalled with two and three aspect colour light signals, and fitted with Automatic Train Protection and Automatic Warning Systems.

Bicester North station is sited on the north-eastern side of the town which, as its name implies, originated in Anglo-Saxon times near the site of an earlier Romano-British settlement. In 1086, it was recorded as *Berencestra* in the Domesday Book - a reference, perhaps, to St Birinus, the 7th century Bishop of nearby Dorchester. Writing in the 1870s, Alfred Rimmer described Bicester as 'a very pleasant, old-fashioned town, situated about thirteen miles from Oxford'. Part of the town, he recorded, was known as 'Market End', and the other 'King's End', while there were many ancient buildings including the King's Arms Inn, the parish church of St Eadburg, and the remains of Bicester Priory.

In 1931, Bicester had a population of 3,109. This figure remained more or less static for several years, and by the end of World War II the town contained only 3,820 inhabitants. On the other hand, Bicester had by that time emerged as an important military centre, with the army firmly-established in and around the nearby villages of Ambrosden and Arncott, while the Royal Air Force maintained a significant presence at Bicester airfield, to the north-east of the station.

Opened towards the end of World War I, Bicester Aerodrome was extensively modernised in the 1920s. RAF Bicester's main wartime role was as an Operational Training Unit, No. 13 OTU having been formed in April 1940. Blenheims were associated with the airfield for much of the war, though Mosquitoes and other types also appeared. The station was transferred to Fighter Command in June 1943. Bicester remained an active military aerodrome until 1976, and thereafter its buildings were used as domestic accommodation for servicemen and their families.

Ardley

Accelerating away from Bicester, trains rumble across two road bridges, and then continue north-westwards along a long embankment. Some two miles from Bicester, the line enters a cutting and, climbing at 1 in 200, trains enter yet another type of landscape; having passed through the suburbs of London, the Chilterns, and then the Vale of Aylesbury, the railway finally comes to an extension of the Cotswold Hills. A subtle change has now taken place, and the surrounding farms and villages exhibit a noticeably 'West Country' appearance - an impression that is reinforced, not only by landscape and architecture, but also by the dialect of the local inhabitants.

Still running through cuttings, the route passes beneath several more overbridges, some of which are merely occupation bridges, while another carries the minor road from Bucknell to Middleton Stoney across the line.

A short distance further on, the line emerges briefly from its long cutting. A gated level crossing, known as 'Bucknell Crossing' (56 miles 31 chains) is provided at this

Ardley station, looking north towards Banbury during the 1960s.   *Nelson Collection*

A detailed view of the standard GWR hip-roofed signal box at Ardley, photographed *circa* 1962.
Lens of Sutton Collection

point. The crossing was improved in connection with the reinstatement of double track working in 2002, when 'non-slip' surfacing and self-closing gates were installed for the benefit of farm workers, horse riders and other road users. Telephones on each side provide a connection to the Marylebone IECC. The cuttings resume immediately beyond the crossing, after which present day trains pass under the A43 road bridge, and rush past the site of the now-closed Ardley station (57 miles 16 chains).

Ardley exhibited the usual 'New Line' characteristics, and facilities provided here included a four-track layout, together with a four siding goods yard on the up side; the main station building was also on the up side. Facilities on the down platform consisted of a small waiting room and a standard GWR hip-roofed signal box. Other items of interest at this typical early 20th century station included a small goods lock-up on the up platform, a fully-enclosed girder footbridge, and an additional siding on the up side to cater for local quarry traffic. The extensive track layout incorporated up and down platform loops, each of which could hold trains of 76 short-wheelbase goods vehicles.

The infrastructure at Ardley was virtually indistinguishable from that found elsewhere on the Bicester Cut-Off and the Great Western & Great Central Joint Line. The brick station building was of the 'large roof' type, while internally it contained a booking office, waiting room, ladies' waiting room and gentlemen's toilets. The goods yard was able to deal with coal, livestock, vehicles, machinery and general merchandise traffic.

The presence of quarries in the immediate vicinity ensured that freight was more important than passengers at this very rural station. In pre-Grouping days, Ardley issued about 3,800 tickets a year, falling to around 2,000 tickets per annum during the 1930s. In 1937, for instance, the station booked 1,923 tickets and 20 seasons. Freight traffic, on the other hand, increased from 4,878 tons in 1913 to 105,260 tons in 1929 and 123,357 tons by 1931 - the primary source of traffic being 'other minerals'. Coal traffic averaged about 2,000 tons a year during the mid-1930s, while the amount of general merchandise handled was rarely more than 300-600 tons per annum.

Ardley was closed with effect from 7th January, 1963, the last trains calling on Saturday 5th January. The signal box and refuge loops were retained until the singling of the line in 1968. There was a modest revival in the following year, when two new sidings were installed for quarry traffic on a new site to the south of the A43 road bridge. The sidings were sited on the down side, and entered by means of a connection that was facing to the direction of up trains; access from the main line was controlled from a ground frame. In the event, the quarry sidings had a relatively short life and they have now been removed.

Ardley itself - a small upland village - is situated above the cutting on the right-hand side of the line, while to the left one of the runways of RAF Upper Heyford came within a few yards of the railway. Opened in 1918, the aerodrome occupied a windswept site some 421 ft above mean sea level. It was the home of several squadrons during the 1920s and 1930s.

Many of the RAF squadrons stationed at Upper Heyford in pre-war years were bomber units; No. 10 Squadron, for example, remained at the station from 1928 until 1937. The aerodrome continued its association with bomber units during World War II, when it became the home of No. 16 Operational Training Unit (OTU). It is interesting to note that No. 16 OTU was at one time equipped with Handley Page Herefords - a rare version of the Hampden, which was built at Belfast and never saw

A view of Aynho Park Platform, *circa* 1963, showing the timber platforms and high level buildings.   *Lens of Sutton Collection*

A further glimpse of the up and down platforms at Aynho Park, which were 400 ft long. A red brick booking office was provided at road level on the up side.   *Lens of Sutton Collection*

operational service as a bomber. Other aircraft employed here included Ansons, Wellingtons and conventional Hampdens.

After the war, RAF Upper Heyford was, albeit for a short time, the home of a parachute training school, but in 1951 it became an American 'base'. By the 1970s this large aerodrome was being used by a force of approximately 90 F-111 fighter-bombers, which became a familiar sight above the rolling hills of North Oxfordshire. Upper Heyford was closed at the end of the Cold War, and at the time of writing its site is scheduled for redevelopment.

Aynho Park Platform

The cutting continues for two miles beyond Ardley, its maximum depth being around 50 ft. The cutting was driven through rock, much of which had to be blasted before it could be removed by steam navvies. The rock cutting leads to the 1,155 yds-long Ardley tunnel (59 miles 26 chains), which was constructed from four vertical shafts and one open end, and was completed and lined with brickwork in just 18 months. The tunnel is approximately 100 ft below local ground surface.

Emerging from the north portal of Ardley tunnel into the Cherwell Valley, the railway turns onto a northerly course, and with the older Oxford & Rugby line running parallel on the left, trains cross the spectacular Souldern No. 1 viaduct (60 miles 57 chains). This impressive structure has 18 semi-circular brick arches, each with a span of 40 ft; its total length is around 580 yards, and it stands 58 ft above local ground level. The first viaduct is followed, half a mile beyond, by a similar structure known as Souldern No. 2 viaduct. This second viaduct has 24 arches, each of 40 ft, and a total length of just under 400 yards; its maximum height is 51 ft.

Now heading due northwards, down trains cross the county boundary between Oxfordshire and Northamptonshire, and pass the site of Aynho Park Platform (61 miles 24 chains). This was a passenger-only stopping place, with high level platforms and a low level booking office on the road beneath. The platforms were of timber trestle construction, with hip-roofed waiting rooms on each side, both of these structures being timber-built with external framing. The booking office, in contrast, was built of red brick. The halt was closed with effect from 7th January, 1963.

Below, on the converging main line from Oxford, travellers could catch a glimpse of Aynho for Deddington station, which boasted a Brunel-designed station building. As the two stations were so close to each other, the Great Western treated them as a single entity, and placed them under the control of the same station master. Beyond the two Aynho stations, the down Bicester line crosses the older line on a girder bridge, and then descends to the same level before finally joining the Oxford & Rugby route at Aynho Junction (62 miles 33 chains). The down Bicester line converges with the down main line, while the up Bicester line leaves the up main line on a separate alignment.

The converging lines were controlled from a standard GWR hip-roofed signal cabin, sited on the down side of the Oxford & Rugby main line. The signal box was closed on 3rd April, 1992, the junction being controlled from Banbury South box. Running loops were originally installed beside the up and down Bicester lines, but these were removed by 1917. On the other hand, a new up loop was laid alongside the Oxford & Rugby line about 1912, so that the latter route became triple-tracked for a considerable distance - a situation that has pertained to this day. In steam days, the up running loop was able to hold trains of up to 138 short-wheelbase goods vehicles.

The interior of Aynho Junction signal box at around 10.30 pm on its final night of operation, Friday 3rd April, 1992. *Mike Marr*

Aynho Junction signal box, photographed at 8.00 am Saturday 4th April - the day after its closure. The signalmen employed in the box at that time included Aubrey Plasted, who had worked in the area for many years and lived in the neighbouring railway cottages; he had not been on duty on the last night, although he had worked the last full daylight shift. The box was demolished in 2002. *Mike Marr*

King's Sutton

Heading northwards along the Oxford & Rugby main line, down trains soon arrive at King's Sutton (63 miles 77 chains), where the disused Banbury & Cheltenham Direct line from Kingham once converged from the left. A few Marylebone-Banbury trains still call at this now-unstaffed station, which was opened on 1st December, 1873.

King's Sutton is a two-platform stopping place, with its main station building on the up side. There was formerly a small goods yard to the south of the up platform, together with a goods refuge siding on the opposite side of the running lines. The Banbury & Cheltenham branch converged with the Oxford & Rugby route by means of a double track junction at the south end of the station, while the up and down platforms were linked by a lattice girder footbridge. The nearby goods yard was equipped with coal wharves, cattle pens, an end-loading dock and a 2 ton hand crane.

The most interesting feature at King's Sutton was perhaps its ornate, Italianate-style station building. This single-storey structure (now demolished) sported a projecting canopy and a low-pitched, slated roof. The platform frontage was recessed to form a small covered waiting area, while three towering chimney stacks punctuated the gabled roof. This distinctive structure was constructed of contrasting red and black brickwork - the vitrified black bricks being used as horizontal string courses to relieve the otherwise plain wall surfaces.

Facilities for waiting passengers on the down platform were confined to a small, brick-built shelter with a single-pitch roof. There was no goods shed, as such, although an arc-roofed corrugated iron lock-up on the up platform was used for parcels and 'smalls' traffic. The station was, at one time, controlled from a signal cabin on the down side, but in 1884 this earlier box was replaced by a new signal box sited on the up side, near the junction with the Banbury & Cheltenham line (opened 1887). The latter cabin was itself closed in 1971.

Contemporary plans reveal that there was once an ironstone siding on the down side of the line, roughly on the site of the later refuge siding. Ironstone was conveyed from workings at neighbouring Adderbury on a narrow gauge tramway that crossed the Oxford Canal and the River Cherwell in order to reach the GWR main line. This method of transhipment was employed for several years, although the siding seems to have fallen out of use following the opening of Sydenham Sidings, on the Banbury & Cheltenham Direct line.

King's Sutton handled over 100,000 tons of ironstone per annum during the early years of the 20th century; in 1913, for example, the station dealt with 153,927 tons of freight, including 137,862 tons of minerals. Unfortunately, the Oxfordshire ironstone industry went into relative decline after World War I, and by the 1930s King's Sutton was dealing with no more than 3,000 tons of freight traffic per year. Passenger bookings, on the other hand, remained buoyant; in 1931 the station sold 29,345 ordinary tickets and 123 seasons, while in 1936 King's Sutton booked 28,626 tickets and 39 seasons.

The station was always much busier than the intermediate stopping places on the Bicester Cut-Off route. Its position on the GWR main line between Oxford and Banbury, and convenient commuting distance between those two places, ensured that it always attracted relatively large numbers of passengers.

Leaving King's Sutton, trains maintain a north-north-westerly heading for a distance of about four miles as they follow the Cherwell Valley towards Banbury. To the left,

Kings Sutton in the 1960s, looking southwards along the up platform, with the Italianate station building visible beyond the footbridge. The tiny weigh-house can be discerned behind the station building, while the signal box can be glimpsed on the far side of the overbridge.
Lens of Sutton Collection

Kings Sutton station, looking north towards Banbury on 7th October, 1972 after demolition of the main station building. *R.M. Casserley*

observant travellers can clearly see the sinuous Oxford Canal, which follows a parallel course along the valley towards Banbury. This 18th century waterway was incorporated by Act of Parliament in 1769, and opened between Hawkesbury Junction and Banbury in 1778, the engineers being James Brindley and Samuel Simcock. The canal was extended southwards to Oxford in 1789-90, the extension being, in effect, an improved River Cherwell - the actual riverbed being utilised for several miles.

Hurrying northwards along the Oxford & Rugby route, trains soon pass the site of Astrop Quarry Sidings, on the up side of the line, which had served nearby ironstone workings until their closure around 1923. The sidings were subsequently lifted, but Astrop Sidings signal box was retained in connection with long up and down running loops that had been completed in August 1908. Astrop Sidings box was a typical GWR hip-roofed cabin, which had replaced an earlier Victorian signal box on 5th April, 1907.

Banbury General

With the Oxford Canal still visible to the left of the line, northbound workings slow down for the approach to Banbury, and having crossed the county boundary between Northamptonshire and Oxfordshire for a second time, trains finally come to a stand in Banbury station (67 miles 38 chains). When opened to traffic on Monday 2nd September, 1850, Banbury had been little more than a branch line terminus, but when the Oxford & Rugby route was extended to Birmingham in 1852 the GWR station was elevated to main line status.

The evolution of Banbury station was a long and somewhat complex process. In its earlier guise, the station had featured a typical 'Brunelian' overall roof; the main buildings were on the down side, and the up and down platforms were linked by a lattice footbridge beneath the overall roof structure. The station was extensively remodelled at the end of the Victorian period, in order to deal with the additional traffic that was expected to flow to and from the Great Central system via the Banbury to Woodford line. These modifications were completed around 1903 - by which time Banbury had gained two additional bay platforms on the up side, and another at the north end of the down platform. The overall roof was retained, although additional up and down lines for goods traffic were installed to the east of the wooden train shed. The enlarged station had five platforms.

The Great Western rebuilt many of its larger stations during the 1930s, Taunton and Leamington Spa being notable examples. The company intended to reconstruct several more of its main line stations, including Oxford and Banbury, but World War II intervened before these plans could be put into effect. In the case of Banbury, the proposed rebuilding scheme was revived under British Railways auspices, and in September 1955 *The Railway Magazine* reported that BR was about to start work on a new Banbury station. Work was soon in full swing, and in July 1957 'the new Banbury General station' was said to be 'nearing completion'.

In connection with this scheme, an additional through track was laid along the west side of the main down platform - which thereby became an island with platform faces on either side. Extensive new buildings (which remain in use to this day) were built on the west side of the station, the main block being constructed of concrete with yellow brick infilling. The up and down sides of the station were physically connected by a massive, 40 ft wide overbridge with two spans, one of which was 30 ft wide, while the other had a width of 50 ft.

Although Banbury station had once boasted a Brunel-style overall roof, this structure had been removed by the time that this photograph was taken on 27th October, 1956. The bay platform visible to the right of the picture was used by Great Central local services to and from Woodford Halse.   *R.M. Casserley*

A general view of Banbury General station, looking north towards Birmingham on 27th October, 1956. The austere canopies seen in this photograph were erected following the removal of the overall roof, but they did not last for very long as the station was extensively rebuilt in 1957.
                                                                                                         R.M. Casserley

The booking hall was situated on the down side, and a wide staircase gave access to the footbridge, which was large enough to contain waiting rooms and a refreshment room. The platforms were covered, for much of their length, by substantial pre-cast concrete canopies, supported on concrete beams placed at 20 ft intervals. The completed station was, at the time of its completion, regarded as a startlingly-modern edifice - although in retrospect it could be argued that this predominantly brick-built structure now has a distinctly 'period' appearance.

Banbury's goods handling facilities were laid out on a generous scale. The original goods yard, containing a goods shed for 'smalls' traffic and mileage sidings for coal and other forms of wagon load traffic, was sited to the south of the passenger station on the up side of the running lines. There was a short, end-loading dock at the north end of the down platform, while a number of additional goods loops and sidings were available on the up side. The up side facilities were considerably extended during the early 1900s, when up and down goods lines were provided, together with two loop sidings and a number of dead-end sidings.

The original goods facilities were expanded at various times, notably during the early 1900s in connection with the Great Central line from Woodford & Hinton. The GCR line joined the Great Western route at a point known as Banbury Junction, 1 mile 14 chains to the north of the passenger station. A marshalling yard with seven (later eight) parallel sidings was installed alongside the GCR route at Banbury Junction, and further sidings were sited on each side of the Great Western line. On 22nd July, 1931, the Great Western opened an additional marshalling yard on the up side of the line between Banbury station and Banbury Junction, this new facility being known as Banbury Hump Yard.

The Banbury to Woodford Halse line was the most northerly of the four links between the Great Western and Great Central systems, and it was used by through freight and passenger trains from the North and Midlands. London traffic, however, utilised the Great Central main line or the High Wycombe route. (Thus the Banbury to Woodford line complemented, rather than rivalled, the Ashendon to Grendon Underwood link.)

Banbury was served by the London & North Western Railway, as well as the GWR, the former Buckinghamshire Railway terminus at Banbury Merton Street having been opened on 1st May, 1850. Merton Street station and goods yard was sited to the east of the GWR station.

One of the goods sidings at Merton Street continued north-westwards, beyond the limits of North Western property, to form a useful connection between the LNWR and GWR stations, while another connecting line diverged from the Great Western station in order to serve Banbury Gas Works. The latter siding formed an end-on connection with a corresponding LNWR siding - although the resulting link was hardly suitable for through running.

Banbury GWR station was controlled from two standard hipped-roof signal boxes, both of these being sited on the down side of the running lines. They were known as Banbury South and Banbury North, the South box being situated at the south end of the platforms whereas the North box was sited immediately to the north. Banbury Junction box was a third cabin just 1 mile 7 chains to the north of the station, while Banbury Merton Street station was controlled from an LMS type box.

With over 100,000 passenger bookings a year during the pre-Grouping period, Banbury was by any definition a very busy station. Sales of ordinary tickets averaged around 120,000 per annum during the 1930s, while at the same time season ticket sales reached 430 in 1936 and 561 by 1938. Goods traffic rose from 52,507 tons

Banbury station, looking north towards Birmingham on 14th July, 1977, and showing the new station buildings provided under British Railways auspices. These main buildings were of reinforced concrete construction with infilling of yellow brickwork. The platforms were connected by a massive footbridge, some 40 ft in width, which was large enough to accommodate a refreshment room and other facilities; the rebuilt station has remained in use until the present day.   *H.C. Casserley*

A further view of the rebuilt Banbury General station, looking south towards London in the early 1960s.   *Lens of Sutton Collection*

in 1903 to as much as 578,339 tons in 1929. Much of this traffic was in the form of ironstone and, as such, it was subject to severe fluctuations over the years. In 1935, for instance, the amount of goods traffic being dealt with had dropped to 90,172 tons - which was, however, still a very appreciable figure.

Traffic dealt with at Banbury

Year	Staff	Receipts (£)	Tickets	Parcels	Goods Tonnage
1913	101	59,996	137,018	67,716	65,183
1930	176	187,764	148,196	95,496	519,690
1936	200	114,339	123,440	115,033	98,621
1937	210	119,318	120,044	120,814	97,461
1938	219	119,318	116,568	119,088	84,414

Banbury formerly boasted two engine sheds, the original Great Western shed being a modest single-road structure on the up side of the station, while the neighbouring London & North Western depot was a three-road structure. The opening of the Great Central line and the Bicester Cut-Off led to a vast upsurge in activity at Banbury, and it was therefore decided that the small shed on the up side would be replaced by a much larger depot on the opposite side of the running lines. Work on the new motive power depot commenced in 1907 and the shed was completed in the following year.

A report printed in the *Great Western Railway Magazine* stated that the new facilities were handed over to the Locomotive Department on 6th September, 1908. The depot incorporated a standard Great Western straight road shed measuring approximately 210 ft by 66 ft at ground level. The new building was of brick construction, with a double gabled roof that was swept down on its west side to cover a 210 ft range of offices. The shed contained four terminal roads with the usual inspection pits, while the adjacent turntable was of 66 ft diameter.

Banbury shed was considerably enlarged during World War II, when an additional coaling stage and several extra sidings were added to help deal with the demands of wartime operations. Plans to construct a four-road extension alongside the existing shed were not implemented, although two covered ash shelters were erected beside the enlarged coaling stage to hide the glow of discarded firebox ash from enemy aircraft. Appropriately, for wartime structures, the ash shelters were painted in a disruptive 'camouflage' livery, similar to that applied to many other buildings during the 1939-45 conflict.

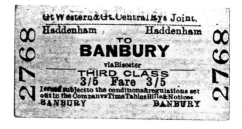

At the end of the war, Banbury had a large locomotive allocation, including numerous 4-6-0 mixed traffic engines and 2-8-0 heavy freight locomotives. On 31st December, 1947 the allocation included 22 'Hall' class locomotives or other 4-6-0s, 27 '28XX' or 'WD' 2-8-0s, 10 moguls, four '2251' class 0-6-0s, one '56XX' class 0-6-2T, two '14XX' class 0-4-2Ts and 15 pannier tanks.

Southbound Great Central trains changed engines at Banbury, and the shed was therefore used by GCR as well as GWR locomotives. Indeed, in the last months of the Great Central main line, Banbury became the main 'London' depot for all GCR services following the closure of Cricklewood shed (which had itself replaced Neasden).

The use of this former GWR depot, which was almost 69 miles from Marylebone, is of interest insofar as it meant that Banbury became one of the last former Great Western steam depots in existence In theory, Banbury should have been shut by January 1966 following the end of steam power on the Western Region, but Banbury was, at the time, a London Midland Region shed, and therefore exempt from the Western Region 'steam ban'. Steam power - in the form of Stanier '5MT' 4-6-0s, '8F' 2-8-0s and BR Standard classes - lasted until the final closure of the Great Central main line in September 1966.

Banbury itself could be seen to the north and west of the railway stations, but there was little for inquisitive visitors to see. Much of the town was of Victorian origin - including the famous 'Banbury Cross', which was erected in 1859 in imitation of an original Eleanor Cross that had been torn down in 1612. In earlier times, the town had boasted several interesting old buildings including a castle and a Medieval parish church, but most of these historic structures were swept away during the 17th and 18th centuries. The castle was dismantled after the Civil War, whereas the church was blown up with gunpowder in 1790 to avoid the expense of restoring it.

Banbury engine shed looking south *circa* 1944: note the wartime camouflage scheme.
BR/OPC Joint Venture

Chapter Eight

The Branch Lines

The 'New Line's' branches have already been mentioned, albeit briefly, in connection with the construction and opening of the main GW&GC route. As we have seen, only the Aylesbury branch was jointly owned, but the Oxford, Watlington, Maidenhead, Uxbridge and Ealing lines were nevertheless off-shoots from the main route, and it would be appropriate to add further details of these other branches before describing the Aylesbury line. The Maidenhead, Oxford and Watlington routes will not be examined in any great depth, but the Uxbridge High Street and Ealing lines were more intimately connected with the 'New Line', and they will therefore be studied in somewhat greater detail.

The High Wycombe to Maidenhead Line

The opening of the Joint Line in 1906 effectively severed the old Wycombe line north of High Wycombe and south of Princes Risborough. The High Wycombe to Maidenhead section then became a 9 mile 68 chain link between the 'New Line' and the original Bristol main line, with intermediate stations at Cookham, Bourne End, Wooburn Green, and Loudwater, and a short dead-end branch from Bourne End to the Thameside resort of Great Marlow. Some trains nevertheless continued to run from Paddington to High Wycombe, Princes Risborough or Oxford via Maidenhead, and to that extent the opening of the GW&GC route had curiously little effect on the pattern of train services between Maidenhead and High Wycombe.

The July 1947 edition of *Bradshaw's Guide* shows a weekday service of 13 up and 14 down workings between Maidenhead and High Wycombe, most of these being through services to and from Paddington. In September 1963, there were 11 up and 13 down trains, together with a number of additional workings between Maidenhead, Bourne End and Marlow, or High Wycombe, Bourne End and Marlow. By 1969, however, the basic train service had been cut to just 7 up and 8 down workings between High Wycombe and Maidenhead, with a handful of short distance services between High Wycombe and Bourne End. The southern end of the line, in contrast, was served by 18 up and 19 down trains between Bourne End and Maidenhead.

Although a few trains continued to run from either Oxford or Aylesbury to London via the Maidenhead line, they were not - in recent years at least - necessarily advertised as through workings, and latterly only one weekday train (the 2.01 pm from Maidenhead to Aylesbury) continued northwards beyond High Wycombe, returning at 3.36 pm. On Saturdays, there was an additional through working from Maidenhead to Aylesbury at 6.31 am, with a return service from Aylesbury at 7.36 am. All such workings came to an end on Saturday 2nd May, 1970, when the Bourne End to High Wycombe section was closed to all traffic.

Thereafter, all trains ran to and from Marlow, with an intermediate reversal at Bourne End, and the Maidenhead line could no longer be classed as a branch of the GW&GC Joint Line. The 5¼ mile section between Bourne End and High Wycombe was subsequently lifted, and the last links with the 'New Line' were thereby severed.

The Maidenhead to High Wycombe line was classified as a 'Dotted Red' route under the GWR system of colour-coded engine weight restrictions. This meant that it

Cookham station, on the High Wycombe to Maidenhead line, looking north towards High Wycombe around 1960.   *Lens of Sutton Collection*

Loudwater station, on the High Wycombe to Maidenhead line, looking south towards Maidenhead in the 1960s.   *Lens of Sutton Collection*

could be traversed by most Great Western locomotive classes, although 'Hall' class 4-6-0s and other larger engines were subjected to a 20 mph speed restriction. In general, the branch was worked by the usual range of GWR London Division locomotives, including '61XX' class 2-6-2Ts, '14XX' class 0-4-2Ts and '57XX' class 0-6-0PTs. After dieselisation, the route was normally worked by Pressed Steel class '117' diesel multiple units - the Western Region equivalents of the visually-similar class '115' sets employed on the GW&GC main line.

In its later years, this single line route was operated by electric train token, with intermediate crossing places at Cookham, Bourne End and Loudwater. The railway ran northwards from its junction with the GWR main at Maidenhead. A small station at Boyne Hill was closed as long ago as 1871, but on 5th July, 1937 a simple halt was opened at Furze Platt (1 mile 22 chains) to serve the northern suburbs of Maidenhead.

Continuing northwards, down trains reached open countryside, and soon arrived at Cookham (2 miles 74 chains), which had been a two-platform station until the removal of its crossing loop in 1969. The Wycombe Railway type station buildings were sited on the up platform, and there was a level crossing immediately to the north; the platforms were linked by GWR type plate girder footbridge. Leaving Cookham, trains passed over the level crossing and approach the River Thames. Cock Marsh, a low lying meadow on the south bank of the river, was crossed by a 44 yds-long viaduct, while the Thames itself was spanned by a 160 yds-long bridge; both of these bridges were originally made of timber.

Bourne End, the principal intermediate station, was immediately beyond the two bridges at 4 miles 33 chains. Three platforms were provided here, the down platform having an additional bay for use by terminating branch trains from the Marlow line. The station buildings, on the down side were, like their counterparts at Cookham, of Wycombe Railway vintage, and dated back to 1854; the adjacent goods shed was a typical 'Brunel' style timber structure, while the up and down platforms were linked by another Great Western style covered footbridge.

Bourne End, a scattered settlement to the east of the railway, was once famous for its cardboard mills, one of which specialised in making the circular tops of Victorian stovepipe hats! Leaving Bourne End, down trains passed over a level crossing and, heading north-eastwards on a rising gradient of 1 in 80, they soon reached the next stopping place at Wooburn Green (5 miles 63 chains). The infrastructure at this wayside station consisted of a single platform and two-siding goods yard, both of which were sited on the up side of the running line; a minor road crossed the single line on the level immediately to the north of the platform.

After Wooburn Green, the railway curved onto a north-westerly alignment for the approach to High Wycombe. Loudwater, the penultimate station (7 miles 20 chains), was a two-platform station with its main station buildings on the up side and a level crossing at the north end of the platforms. The station building was another Wycombe Railway structure, the original portion being of traditional brick-and-flint construction, although the two-storey station master's house at the north end of the building had been considerably extended in later years. The nearby goods yard contained four main sidings and a headshunt at the south end.

From Loudwater, the route ran north-westwards into High Wycombe station (*qv*), the final approach being along the south side of a narrow valley, which provided good views of the Great Western & Great Central main line as the converging routes entered the station on different alignments. Although the route between High Wycombe and Bourne End has been severed for many years, the remaining portion

Thame looking west towards Oxford during the 1960s, and showing the classic Brunelian-style train shed.   *Lens of Sutton Collection*

Morris Cowley station facing west towards Oxford around 1960.   *Lens of Sutton Collection*

of the line between Maidenhead and Bourne End has remained a busy suburban route, with a service of around 22 trains each way, many services being extended through to Marlow after reversal at Bourne End.

The Princes Risborough to Oxford Route

The history of the Princes Risborough to Oxford line parallels that of the Maidenhead route; worked as a branch after the opening of the GW&GC route, it was an 18 mile 48 chain single track railway, connecting the New Line to the Old at Kennington Junction, 2 miles 28 chains to the south of Oxford. The line was single track throughout, and in its final years the route was worked by electric train token. Stations were originally provided at Bledlow, Thame, Tiddington, Wheatley and Littlemore, while additional stopping places were later opened at Towersey, Horspath, Iffley and Morris Cowley - the latter station being built to serve the Morris car plant.

The line left Princes Risborough in a west-north-westerly direction, with the Watlington branch running parallel to the left. Soon, however, the latter route diverged south-westwards, while the Oxford line ran more or less dead straight towards the first intermediate stopping place at Bledlow (1 mile 51 chains). This was merely a wayside station, with its platform and single siding goods yard on the down side of the line, and a level crossing to the east. The station building incorporated a single-storey booking office and a two-storey station master's house, the house portion being arranged at right angles to the booking office wing.

Beyond, the route continued west-north-westwards, and having crossed the county boundary between Buckinghamshire and Oxfordshire, trains reached Towersey Halt (4 miles 32 chains), which had been opened by the GWR on 5th June, 1933. The single platform was sited on the up side of the line, in convenient proximity to Towersey village. Thame, the principal intermediate station between Princes Risborough and Oxford, was only a mile and a half further on, at 5 miles 53 chains. Thame was a passing station, with up and down platforms on either side of a crossing loop, its Wycombe Railway station building being sited on the up side.

Sidings were available on both sides, the main goods yard, with its characteristic 'Brunel' style goods shed, was sited on the up side, while an additional loading dock was provided at the rear of the down platform. The station buildings were of Wycombe Railway vintage, but the most impressive feature of the station was perhaps its gable-roofed train shed which, like the nearby goods shed, was a classic Brunelian design. The up and down platforms were linked by a covered footbridge at the west end of the train shed, and the station was signalled from a gable-roofed signal box sited to the east of the platforms on the down side.

Continuing westwards from Thame, trains reached Tiddington (9 miles 65 chains), a wayside station with its single platform and two-siding goods yard on the up side; the station building was an austere, timber-framed structure clad in vertical matchboarding. From Tiddington, the single line maintained its westerly heading, the A40 road being crossed on a skewed alignment on a massive, twin-span girder bridge. Wheatley, the next stopping place (13 miles 13 chains) was about two miles further on. Up and down platforms were provided here, the main station building and two-siding goods yard being on the up side, while the signal box was sited to the east of the station on the down side. A minor road was carried across the line on a single-span stone bridge at the west end of the platforms.

The station building was, like many others on the Maidenhead to High Wycombe and Princes Risborough to Oxford lines, of Wycombe Railway origin. It was a single-storey, gable-roofed structure with an open-fronted waiting area at the east end. These buildings were of interest in relation to the GW&GC main line insofar as they were very similar to the original buildings at High Wycombe, West Wycombe and Princes Risborough - the Wycombe Railway having adopted a unified architectural style on its lines between Maidenhead, Oxford and Aylesbury.

From Wheatley, the railway proceeded south-westwards, and after passing through the 520 yds-long Horspath tunnel, down trains reached Horspath Halt (14 miles 68 chains). This unstaffed stopping place was opened on 1st February, 1908, closed in 1915, and re-opened on 5th June, 1933. Beyond, the railway continued to Morris Cowley (16 miles 10 chains). The station was opened on 24th September, 1928 and, as its name implied, it served the adjacent Morris Motors car factory; confusingly, Morris Cowley station occupied the site of an earlier halt known as Garsington Bridge, which had been opened on 1st February 1908, and closed as a wartime economy measure in 1915. Although Cowley was originally surrounded by open countryside, the presence of the huge Morris and Pressed Steel factories ensured that it was eventually subsumed into a sprawling urban area on the eastern fringes of Oxford.

However, as the railway approached Littlemore (17 miles 47 chains) there was an illusory feeling of rural tranquillity. Littlemore station had, at one time, handled car parts for Morris Motors and steel plate for John Allan, together with the usual range of coal, minerals, livestock and general merchandise traffic. The single platform was sited on the down side; it boasted a standard Great Western brick station building that resembled those on the GW&GC main line. There were several sidings, including a rail link to the neighbouring County Lunatic Asylum that left the goods yard by means of a wagon turntable. Leaving Littlemore in a north-westerly direction, and passing the site of Iffley Halt (1908-1915) some ¾ mile further on, trains soon reached Kennington Junction (18 miles 48 chains), where the single track branch from Princes Risborough converged with the Didcot to Oxford main line. As the line approached the junction, it crossed the River Thames on a bow-girder bridge (18 miles 27 chains).

Having joined the main line, trains ran northwards for another two miles passing, *en route*, the wartime marshalling yard at Hinksey, and then Oxford's main goods yard. Finally, after crossing the Botley Road on a plate girder bridge, trains came to rest in Oxford station, where the 20 mile 76 chain journey from Princes Risborough came to an end.

The line - a 'Red' route - was often used for diversions when the main Oxford to London line was under repair, and as we have seen, some through suburban trains were routed to Paddington via Thame and Princes Risborough. There were, in general, around four such workings each way, together with a number of purely local workings between Oxford and Princes Risborough. In addition, short-distance services operated between Princes Risborough and Thame, and to and from Morris Cowley, where the car factories generated a significant amount of workmen's traffic as well as very large amounts of freight traffic.

The Thame route was closed to passenger traffic from 7th January, 1963, and it was later severed between Morris Cowley and Thame. The remaining stubs continued to carry goods traffic, the Morris Cowley to Oxford section being used by car trains, while at the eastern end of the line, goods trains still ran from Princes Risborough to a rail-linked oil terminal at Thame. Sadly, this useful source of bulk freight traffic came to an end in 1991, following the completion of an oil pipeline. The last train left Thame on 17th April, 1991, behind class '47' Co-Co No. 47295.

Meanwhile, at the western end of the route, the section of line between Kennington Junction and Morris Cowley has continued to function as a rail link for car export traffic. There have, from time to time, been suggestions that all or part of the intervening section between Morris Cowley, Thame and Princes Risborough might be re-opened for passenger traffic. A renewed link between Princes Risborough and Oxford would enable Chiltern Railways to serve a whole new range of destinations, and introduce an element of competition on the lucrative Oxford to London route.

Much of the infrastructure on the abandoned parts of the line has remained in place, although the tunnel at Horspath has recently found a new role as a secure home for bats. As such, it would probably impede attempts to re-open the railway, as local conservationists now regard the tunnel and its associated cuttings as a major wildlife conservation area.

The Watlington Branch

On 25th July, 1864, a company known as the Wallingford & Watlington Railway was incorporated by Act of Parliament, with powers to build a railway commencing on the GWR main line at Cholsey, and terminating in Upper Moor Meadow, Watlington. Unfortunately, the company was unable to complete its scheme throughout to Watlington, and in the event the line progressed no further than Wallingford. Spurred on by this apparent failure, a group of local landowners sought Parliamentary consent for an 8 mile 69 chain branch from Princes Risborough, and the 'Watlington & Princes Risborough Railway' Act received the Royal Assent on 26th July, 1869.

The Watlington to Princes Risborough branch was opened on Thursday 15th August, 1872. This simple, single track line was initially worked by the Watlington & Princes Risborough Railway Company as an independent concern, but in 1883 the undertaking was purchased by the GWR. The railway was then worked as a typical Great Western branch line, with a service of around four trains each way. The May 1946 timetable shows up trains from Watlington at 7.25, 8.42, 11.30 am, 3.10 and 7.15 pm, and down workings from Princes Risborough at 10.22 am, 1.55, 5.48 and 8.02 pm. The single line was worked by train staff on the 'One-engine-in-Steam' system.

At Watlington, the railway terminated in a single platform station with a run-round loop, three goods sidings, a carriage siding and an engine spur. The station building was a distinctive 'H-plan' design with a central block and two gabled cross-wings, while the nearby goods shed was a wooden, barn-like structure. Intermediate stations were provided at Aston Rowant and Chinnor, and halts were subsequently opened at Bledlow Ridge, Wainhill, Kingston Crossing and Lewknor Bridge. In the mid-1930s the branch stations issued approximately 16,000 tickets per annum, while goods traffic amounted to about 40,000 tons a year - much of this being generated by Chinnor Cement Works.

After an uneventful life, the line was closed to passengers with effect from Monday 1st July, 1957, the last trains being run on Saturday 29th June. Goods traffic lingered on for another four years, but further retraction took place with effect from Monday 2nd January, 1961, when freight services were withdrawn from the section of line between Chinnor and Watlington. The final goods train from Princes Risborough to Watlington was run on Friday 30th December, 1960, motive power being provided by Ivatt class '2MT' 2-6-2T No. 41272.

'74XX' class 0-6-0PT No. 7441 waits in the down bay platform at Princes Risborough with a
Watlington branch train, *circa* 1960.   *Lens of Sutton Collection*

Chinnor station *circa* 1958, showing the single platform and station building, with Chinnor lime
works visible in the background.   *Lens of Sutton Collection*

The route survived as far as Chinnor in connection with the cement works, which had originated as long ago as 1908, when William Elijah Benton, a mining engineer from Acton, had started a lime-burning business. Cement manufacturing commenced in 1919, and the cement works subsequently developed into a major complex - its 175 ft high chimneys being visible for miles around. The remaining stub was 3 miles 57 chains in length, and worked on the one-engine-in-steam principle with a round train staff, coloured black. The main source of rail traffic was coal for the rotary kilns, about 61,000 tons being consumed per year during the 1970s, together with about 15,000 tons of gypsum.

This modest line was classified as an 'Uncoloured' route under the GWR system of locomotive weight restrictions, which meant that it could be worked only by the smallest and lightest engines. The diminutive '2021' class 0-6-0PTs worked on the route for many years, though in later years an easing of weight restrictions allowed the larger and more powerful Collett '57XX' class 0-6-0PTs to be used, despite their 50 ton weight. No. 4650 worked the last passenger train on 29th June, 1957.

The branch was worked by somewhat unusual motive power after the withdrawal of passenger services, in the form of Worsdell 'J15' class 0-6-0s from the former Great Eastern Railway! Two of these veteran locomotives - Nos. 65390 and 65405 - were transferred from Cambridge in 1957 and sub-shedded at Aylesbury for service on the Watlington goods trips. An earlier attempt to employ former GER 'J68' class 0-6-0T No. 68650 on the branch was unsuccessful because the engine had insufficient tank capacity.

The first diesel types to be employed on the route were the North British class '22' Bo-Bos, but following their untimely demise the Chinnor cement trains were typically worked by class '31' A1A-A1A, such as Nos. 31269 and 31258. Another diesel type seen on the Chinnor coal trains were English Electric class '20' Bo-Bos, which worked in pairs on a twice-weekly train of hopper coal wagons from the East Midlands. The last train ran on 20th December, 1989, when class '47' Co-Co No. 47258 worked the last loaded coal train, conveying imported coal from Newport Alexandra Docks to Chinnor.

Following the demise of freight services, the Chinnor to Princes Risborough line was identified as an ideal candidate for preservation, and a group was formed to take over the line as a private railway. By the end of 2000, the Chinnor & Princes Risborough Railway was operating over three miles of line between Chinnor and Thame Junction, although trains were unable to run into the bay platform at Princes Risborough. In 1998, the C&PR began work on the reconstruction of a Chinnor station building, the still-extant building at Watlington being used as a model for what was in effect an entirely new structure.

Like other preserved railways, the Chinnor line has been worked by a range of locomotives and rolling stock in recent years, the core fleet of three or four diesel engines being augmented by visiting locomotives from other preserved lines.

The Uxbridge High Street Branch

The short branch from Denham to Uxbridge had a long pre-history, beginning in the 1850s when the Oxford Worcester & Wolverhampton Railway had attempted to build its London Extension via Thame, Denham and Uxbridge. As we have seen, the OW&WR schemes were unsuccessful, but there were, thereafter, a variety of projects which, if completed, would have placed the town of Uxbridge on an important north-to-south main line.

An early view of the high level station buildings at Uxbridge High Street; note the covered stairway down to street level. This style of building, with its cantilevered roof, was erected all over the GWR system from about 1900 (usually in brick).   *Lens of Sutton Collection*

A post-closure view of Uxbridge High Street, taken on the occasion of a special railtour on Sunday 26th September, 1954. This tour of London Division branch lines was organised by the London Railway Society and it left Kensington Olympia at 2.00 pm travelling outwards via High Wycombe and returning via Maidenhead, with trips along the branches to Uxbridge High Street, Marlow, Windsor and Brentford Dock.   *R.M. Casserley Collection*

The Uxbridge & Rickmansworth Railway, for instance, hoped to build a connecting link between the London & North Western system at Rickmansworth and the Staines & West Drayton Railway, thereby opening-up a through route between the LNWR and London & South Western systems that would (hopefully) have been independent of the Great Western. In the end, the Great Western itself began work on a modest branch from Denham to Uxbridge, the necessary powers having been obtained in 1898, and amended in 1899. The construction of this short line was undertaken by Messrs R.W. Pauling & Co, as an adjunct to their main Northolt to High Wycombe contract.

The line, as finally authorized on 1st August 1899, was defined as:

A Railway (No. 4), 3 miles and 2.35 chains in length, commencing in the Parish of Hillingdon West in the Urban District of Uxbridge in the County of Middlesex, by a junction with the Uxbridge Branch Railway of the Company, and terminating in the Parish of Harefield in the County of Middlesex by a junction with Railway No. 1 authorised by the Great Western Railway (Additional Powers) Act 1897.

Initially, the Great Western had intended to continue the line southwards to join the earlier Uxbridge Vine Street branch, with the apparent aim of completing an outer suburban 'ring' between the Birmingham and Bristol main lines. It was also decided that the junction with the GW&GC route near Denham would incorporate a triangle, in order that some Uxbridge workings would be able to proceed from Paddington to Uxbridge via the new main line, and return along the old route through West Drayton (or vice versa). To facilitate this mode of operation, the 1899 Act provided consent for an east-to-south curve at the north end of the line, which was described as:

A Railway (No. 5), 2 furlongs and 6.76 chains in length, wholly in the Parish of Harefield in the County of Middlesex, commencing by a junction with Railway No. 4 by this Act authorised, and terminating by a junction with Railway No.1 authorised by the said Act of 1897.

From an engineering point of view, the Uxbridge branch presented few problems. The authorized route from Denham was relatively flat, and generally speaking the meadowlands of the Colne Valley provided an ideal course for the new branch. There were, however, one or two minor problems in relation to the multiplicity of waterways in the Uxbridge area - the Colne having several channels at this point. It was, in consequence, necessary for several streams to be diverted, while at the Denham end of the line a large area of land had to be drained before construction of the major earthworks could be started.

In Uxbridge, the proposed route necessitated some significant bridge works, and there were fears that certain much-loved local landmarks would have to be demolished in connection with the new works. One of the threatened properties was an ancient dwelling known as 'The Old Treaty House'; built around 1570, this venerable structure had been used as a meeting place between opposing Royalist and Parliamentary delegations towards the end of the First Civil War in 1645, and having escaped many threats of destruction, the house had lasted more or less unscathed until the early 1900s.

In 1903-04, it seemed likely that the railway builders would finally demolish the property, but in the event the Old Treaty House was spared, and in 1905 John Firth recorded that the house had 'just escaped the embankments of the new Great Western line'. A large plane tree on the site of the proposed station at Uxbridge was less fortunate, and on 13th July, 1906 this 200-year-old specimen was felled by J. Lavender of Ruislip; it is on record that the unfortunate tree was 70 ft high, and had a girth of 17 ft.

It was envisaged that the proposed branch from Denham to Uxbridge would converge with the existing line from West Drayton in Uxbridge Vine Street goods yard, the original terminus at Vine Street being replaced by a new through station at High Street. This would, in turn, have entailed the closure of Vine Street station, and on 7th November, 1903 *The Locomotive Magazine* suggested that this earlier station would 'be used for 'goods traffic only'. In May 1904, however, the same magazine painted a slightly different picture, in which Vine Street would be retained for passenger services that terminated at Uxbridge and did not use the 'new loop line' from Denham:

> The loop, which is three miles long, skirts the town of Uxbridge on the west and joins the existing line between Uxbridge and West Drayton Junction, on the Great Western main line, in Uxbridge goods yard. By means of this loop, another circular suburban service from Paddington will be possible. There will be a new station at Uxbridge, at the bottom of the High Street; but the present terminal station, built by Brunel for the broad gauge, will be retained, though it will not be used by the trains performing the circular service.

There was, in fact, considerable indecision *vis-à-vis* the Uxbridge scheme, and in 1904 the Great Western announced, that it was 'not proposed to connect the new line to the existing branch from West Drayton' for the present. The reason for this change of plan was probably connected, at least in part, with the promotion of a rival Metropolitan branch from Harrow to Uxbridge, which was opened as a steam-worked route on 4th July, 1905, and electrified from 1st January, 1905. The appearance of this new line, with its fast and frequent services to central London, called into the question the entire GWR scheme - while further competition stemmed from the opening of an electric tramway from Southall.

These new rail and tramway links posed a very serious threat to the GWR's position in Uxbridge, and it seems that the company decided to complete the Denham to Uxbridge line as a simple, dead-end branch in the first instance. Accordingly, on 1st May, 1907, the line was opened to public traffic as a two mile double track branch from Denham to Uxbridge High Street, the train services on this modest suburban line being worked exclusively by steam railmotor cars.

In the early years, these vehicles ran from Ealing to Greenford and thence on to Denham, from where, after reversal, they continued over the Uxbridge High Street branch. In 1909, many services were extended northwards to Gerrards Cross, which thereby became a useful interchange point for passengers travelling from Uxbridge to High Wycombe or other GW&GC stations beyond Denham.

The new railmotor services were fully integrated with the rest of the Great Western's local services, and in the next few years the Uxbridge High Street branch functioned as part of a wider GWR suburban network that was worked by Southall-based railmotors. It was hoped that these relatively cheap local services would be able to compete effectively with the burgeoning Metropolitan system for traffic to and from London, and the Great Western management anticipated that a profitable suburban traffic would subsequently develop.

There were still hopes that the Denham to West Drayton loop scheme could be completed in its entirety, and in this context it is interesting to note that the extension from Uxbridge High Street station reached an advanced state of completion. Unfortunately, the Denham and Uxbridge areas were slow to develop as residential areas, and in any case, people wishing to travel daily between Uxbridge and London already had a wide choice of trains on the Uxbridge Vine Street and Metropolitan routes. In these circumstances, the Great Western Directors reluctantly concluded that Uxbridge High Street would remain the end of the line from Denham, and the extension to Vine Street was formally abandoned.

Having failed to become part of the hoped-for Denham to West Drayton loop line, the Uxbridge High Street branch settled down to become a very rural 'feeder' to the busy GW&GG main line. Traffic receipts were, from the very outset, disappointing, and in 1913 the annual takings at High Street station amounted to only £847. To put this miserable figure into perspective, it is worth pointing out that the corresponding receipts from neighbouring Vine Street station amounted to £19,120. GWR traffic returns show that, in the year under review, Uxbridge High Street booked just 22,341 tickets; in that same year, Vine Street station issued 120,000 tickets.

In May 1914, a small goods yard was opened at High Street station, but World War I intervened before this new facility could be fully developed. Indeed the war brought little extra traffic to the branch, and its passenger service was suspended altogether in January 1917. The line was eventually re-opened, as a single track route, in May 1920 - much of its original double track having been requisitioned by the Army during the recent conflict.

In its new, single-track guise, the Uxbridge High Street line managed to eke out a meagre existence for several more years, but passenger services were finally withdrawn from 1st September, 1939. The line was, at the end, worked by conventional push-pull auto-trains, the steam railmotors having been withdrawn in the 1930s. In its final years as a passenger station, Uxbridge issued around 10,000 tickets a year and handled about 5,000 tons of coal or other goods. Occasional consignments of roadstone sometimes boosted these modest figures but, in general, the Uxbridge High Street branch must be seen as one of the Great Western's less successful single track branch lines.

Freight services survived for another 14½ years, and the small goods yard at Uxbridge High Street found a useful role as a coal yard. Meanwhile, in World War II, an Anglo American Oil Company siding was installed on the trackbed of the abandoned east-to-south curve at Denham.

Denham, the junction for most Uxbridge High Street services, had no bays for terminating branch trains, but its spacious four-track layout ensured that there was plenty of room for both main line and branch traffic. Leaving Denham's up platform, Uxbridge branch trains passed the three-road goods yard and, running on the up platform loop line, they then crossed the River Colne on the five-arched Colne viaduct (30 chains). The up and down platform loop lines rejoined the two main running lines just a short distance further on (37 chains).

Trains gained the up main line before crossing the Grand Union Canal viaduct (49 chains). Denham West Junction signal box was situated near the Denham end of the viaduct; this box was later renamed 'Denham East'. The branch proper began at Denham West Junction, which was a little way beyond the viaduct at 54 chains; at this point, trains left the Great Western & Great Central Joint Railway and entered purely Great Western property - the Uxbridge High Street branch being something of an anomaly in that it was a branch of the GW&GC line that never came under the control of the Great Western & Great Central Railways Joint Committee.

Rounding a sharp curve, Uxbridge trains passed a GWR 'mushroom' water tank, that was surprisingly isolated in the midst of open countryside. Nearby, a twin-boiler steam pumping station supplied water for Ruislip water troughs; a sleeper-built chute was provided so that coal for the pumping engine could be unloaded by manual labour. The pillar tank is said to have been used occasionally by Great Central locomotives - which sometimes ventured onto the branch in order to take water, as there was a general paucity of watering points on the Great Western & Great Central main line.

The northern-most extremity of the Uxbridge High Street branch remained double-tracked for a few chains after the remainder of the line was singled, but the two lines soon converged into a single running line, the junction between the double and single track sections being some 60 chains from Denham.

Continuing south-eastwards around the west-to-south curve, branch trains reached the site of Denham South Junction, at 1 mile 2 chains. This junction was later revived as 'Harefield Branch Ground Frame', the ground frame in question being needed to control access to the Anglo-American (later Esso) oil depot that was constructed on the site of the abandoned east-to-south curve in 1942. It is interesting to note that, although the branch was classified as a 'Yellow' route under the Great Western system of route restrictions, large locomotives such as the BR Standard class '9F' 2-10-0s were (in theory, at least) allowed to work into the oil depot, subject to a strict 15 mph speed restriction.

Having taken up a southerly heading, the route descended gradually towards Uxbridge on a ruling gradient of 1 in 175. The scenery, on this section of the line, was pleasant, rather than spectacular; the branch followed the Grand Union Canal and the two branches of the River Colne through a verdant landscape of lush meadowlands while, to the east and west, wooded hillsides provided a satisfying backdrop to these pastoral surroundings.

Some half a mile from Uxbridge, the route forked; to the right, a half-mile gradient dropped below the level of the main running line to terminate in a two-road coal yard, while to the left the main passenger line continued southwards on a long embankment before coming to an end in Uxbridge High Street station, 2 miles 56 chains from Denham.

The terminus was a single platform station, with a run-round loop and two longish spurs - in effect a residual section of the original double track. The wooden platform was on the up side of the line, and it could accommodate five or six bogie vehicles. The main high level station building was a timber structure, with prominent external framing, and a large roof that projected over the platform in lieu of a separate canopy. Internally, this building provided the usual booking office, waiting room and toilet facilities. A covered stairway at the south end of the platform descended to ground level, and having walked down these stairs travellers found themselves in Uxbridge High Street.

The line ended abruptly beyond the station, although until 1922 a plate girder bridge had remained as evidence of the proposed extension over Oxford Road, which if completed as planned, would have reached Vine Street station. A tea room and other facilities were built into the openings of the bridge, these low level station buildings being of typical Great Western 'standard' design.

When first opened, Uxbridge High Street had been fully signalled, but when the line re-opened after singling it was worked on the 'One Engine in Steam' principle, the train staff being held in Denham East box while High Street signal box was reduced to ground frame status. The low level goods yard, on the west side of the passenger station, was able to handle coal and wagon class traffic only. It had two sidings, and these were arranged as a loop. There was (1938) no yard crane, loading docks or cattle pens, and facilities chiefly consisted of an array of sleeper-built coal wharves; a standard GWR loading gauge spanned the line near the northern exit from the yard.

In 1956 the rusting, weed-grown tracks into High Street passenger station were finally taken out of use, and a new run-round loop was constructed half a mile up the branch for the benefit of surviving freight trains. About two years before this, in September 1954, the branch had been traversed by a former GWR diesel railcar - and it is believed that this enthusiasts' special was the very last passenger train to use the redundant passenger station.

The 1962 Western Region working timetable provides a useful glimpse of freight train operation on the Uxbridge High Street line during its declining years. There was, by that time, just one daily freight working, which left Southall at 6.10 am and reached Uxbridge at 8.16 am. After shunting the coal sidings, the train returned to Denham at 9.18 am, and having shunted Denham goods yard the service finally terminated at Southall at 1.00 pm. Motive power, in these last years, was usually a '45XX' 2-6-2T, one of the engines known to have appeared on the route being No. 5564. A 15 mph speed limit applied throughout from Denham.

Goods traffic to and from Uxbridge High Street ceased in the early part of 1964, although the line into the oil depot near the former south loop junction remained officially open for a further 12 months. By the end of 1965 this too, had succumbed, and Denham East signal box was taken out of use in December of that year.

Today, the course of the Uxbridge High Street branch can be followed for at least part of its route, and a good view of the trackbed can be obtained from the A40 viaduct near Denham. Elsewhere, part of the former branch has been converted into a nature reserve, while at Uxbridge the station site has been redeveloped. On a footnote, it is interesting to recall that the train staff used on the Uxbridge branch was later employed on the Princes Risborough to Chinnor line. It was clearly stamped 'UXBRIDGE HIGH ST-DENHAM EAST', and had probably been in use since the de-signalling of the branch after World War I.

The Greenford to Ealing Loop

In contrast to the unsuccessful Uxbridge High Street branch, the Greenford to Ealing line remains in use as a busy passenger and freight line. Built as a link between the GW&GC and the Bristol main line, this two and a half mile double track railway was first used in June 1903 in connection with the agricultural show mentioned in Chapter Two. Trains originally ran outwards from Paddington to Park Royal, providing a 20 minute service frequency during the show period from 23rd until 27th June.

Regular passenger services began on 1st May, 1904, and on 1st October a line running westwards from Greenford East Junction to Greenford station was brought into use. When, on 2nd April, 1906, the GW&GC main line was opened throughout to High Wycombe, the Ealing to Greenford branch came into full use as a connection between two important Great Western trunk routes.

Steam railmotors were extensively used in the early years and, by making use of triangular junctions provided at each end of the Greenford loop, these vehicles were able to take various combinations of route. In general, however, most workings ran from Ealing to Greenford and beyond via West Ealing and Greenford West loop. Ealing Broadway eventually became the usual eastern terminus, but in the west many workings ran over the Great Western & Great Central main line in order to reach Denham or Gerrards Cross.

Castle Bar Park Halt, which served an adjacent Great Western sports ground, was opened as an intermediate stopping place on 1st May, 1904, and Drayton Green Halt

A *circa* 1950s view of South Greenford Halt, showing the familiar GWR 'pagoda' shelters.
Lens of Sutton Collection

A single unit railcar, hauling a driving trailer, enters South Greenford.
Lens of Sutton Collection

was added on 1st March, 1905; a third halt, at South Greenford, was opened on 20th September, 1926. Suburban development was, by that time, well under way, and in the next few years the district served by the Greenford loop became a heavily built-up suburban area. Meanwhile, the steam railmotors had been replaced by push-pull auto-trains, though a high-frequency service was still maintained.

The Central Line extension had far-reaching consequences for the Greenford loop, in that the former Great Western station at Greenford lost most of its passenger services in 1947-48, and the Greenford to Ealing auto-trains were then diverted into the new 'Underground' station. This meant that the branch service ceased to connect with main line services at its northern end, and it became instead a dead-end line worked from Ealing Broadway.

Goods traffic was not affected, and the Greenford Loop continued to carry a variety of freight workings via the triangular junctions at Greenford and West Ealing; many of these services were inter-regional trains from the Southern Region to the London Midland Region or the Eastern Region (or vice-versa). Similarly, car sleepers and other specialised workings ran via Greenford and Ealing until the run-down of the Great Central and GW&GC routes during the 1960s.

In the 1980s, the Greenford Loop retained a busy local service, with around 35 dmu trips each way daily on Mondays to Fridays, and only a few less on Saturdays. Goods traffic was less healthy, but air-braked company trains continued to use the line, together with empty coaching stock workings and parcels services. In May 1988, Paddington replaced Ealing Broadway as the eastern terminus for Greenford workings.

Collett '14XX' class 0-4-2Ts or '54XX' class auto-fitted 0-6-0PTs were the usual forms of motive power during the steam era, but after the dieselisation of Paddington suburban services the Western Region introduced a small fleet of double-ended motor brake seconds. These were able to operate as single railcars, but in practice they often ran in conjunction with an unpowered single-ended driving trailer second. These units were built in 1960-61 by the Pressed Steel Company of Linwood, and they were designated class '121', while a series of visually- similar vehicles manufactured by the Gloucester RC&W Co. in 1958 were designated class '122'.

With the demise of the 'classic' slam-door multiple unit types in recent years, services on the Ealing to Greenford branch are normally worked by class '165' two-car sets from the Thames Trains fleet (now First Great Western).

Departing from Paddington, present-day trains run westwards along the Great Western main line to West Ealing, from where they diverge north-westwards onto the Greenford Loop at West Ealing Junction. Rounding a 28 chain curve, the route continues to Drayton Green Junction; here, the double track West Curve from Hanwell East Junction converges from the left. Drayton Green (45 chains) is just two chains further on.

Passing beneath Bridge Road, trains enter a cut-and-cover tunnel that has replaced an open cutting (in order that new housing developments can be built on top). About two minutes later, the multiple units arrive at Castle Bar Park (1 mile 2 chains). Like Drayton Green, this is a simple, two-platform halt with red brick shelters in place of the GWR 'pagoda' sheds originally provided. The up and down platforms are connected by a footbridge.

From Castle Bar Park the line continues northwards, and crossing the Brent viaduct, trains reach an area of golf clubs and playing fields. South Greenford (1 mile 63 chains), the last of the intermediate stopping places, occupies an exposed position on top of an embankment. When opened, it had been equipped with Great Western 'pagoda' sheds on each platform, but these relatively robust corrugated iron huts were later replaced by vulnerable glass 'bus stop' shelters.

Drayton Green Halt on the Greenford loop, looking towards Greenford; the GWR 'Pagoda' sheds have now been replaced by modern BR-built red brick shelters.   *Lens of Sutton Collection*

Collett '14XX' class 0-4-2T No. 1446 and auto-trailer No. 181 form the 1.22 pm local passenger service from Greenford to Ealing, photographed at West Ealing on 14th June, 1958.

H.C. Casserley

Departing from South Greenford, trains cross the six-lane Western Avenue on a large girder bridge; below, extensive traffic jams can usually be seen stretching away on both sides. At Greenford South Junction, the East Loop diverges north eastwards; still used by freight workings, the loop was singled in 1970. Running on the West Loop, Greenford locals curve north-westwards to enter the London Transport station. The loop becomes single as it nears the station, then divides into two, with a northerly fork passing beneath the Central Line to reach the Greenford West Junction, and a southerly arm leading into the London Transport station.

Ealing locals pass under the northbound London Transport line, and then ascend to platform level between massive retaining walls. The terminal platform is sandwiched between the up and down Central Line tracks - the LT station having an island layout. Here, 2 miles 37 chains from West Ealing, the Greenford branch comes to an end in an 'Underground' station perched high above ground, with escalators that convey travellers up to rail level!

The Aylesbury Branch

The Aylesbury branch, a single track country branch line, 7 miles 18 chains long, and connecting the GW&GC and Metropolitan & Great Central joint lines was, in the 1860s, and again in the 1890s, the scene of much skirmishing between rival railway companies. Authorized on 28th June, 1861 and opened on 1st October, 1863, it was worked as a branch of the Wycombe Railway, which meant, in effect, that it was an integral part of the Great Western broad gauge system. In 1868, the line was extended northwards by the Aylesbury & Buckingham Railway which, though built with financial help from the London & North Western Railway, chose to be worked by the rival Great Western company!

The Princes Risborough to Aylesbury branch was narrowed to facilitate through working in 1868, and for the next 23 years the Aylesbury branch and the Aylesbury & Buckingham line were worked as a 19½ mile-long branch from Princes Risborough. The line connected with the LNWR Buckinghamshire branch at Verney Junction, and it is interesting to record that as there was no connection with the standard gauge at its southern end until the Wycombe Railway 'main line' was narrowed in 1870, the standard gauge rolling stock used on the Aylesbury line had to be delivered via London & North Western metals.

In 1891, the Aylesbury & Buckingham company was taken over by the Metropolitan Railway, and when, in the following year, the Metropolitan main line reached Aylesbury, the Aylesbury line became part of the Metropolitan's extended northern route from Baker Street. This was the line which the Great Central hoped to use in order to reach London, but as we saw in Chapter One, the Metropolitan and Great Central companies were soon at loggerheads over this arrangement.

Aylesbury station, meanwhile, remained the property of the Great Western (along with the rest of the branch to Princes Risborough) and when, in 1898, the Great Central and Great Western companies were preparing their new alliance, the Great Central attempted to send coal trains southwards via the Aylesbury branch.

Perversely, the Metropolitan Railway refused to allow Great Central traffic over its line until the London Extension was fully open throughout its length, and faced with this kind of spiteful intransigence, it became clear to the GCR Directors that the Aylesbury branch could not be utilised as the main northern link between the Great Western and Great Central systems. The Joint Committee was therefore forced to build an entirely

A useful view of Monks Risborough & Whiteleaf Halt from the rear on 4th June, 1960.
H.C. Casserley

The single platform and waiting shelter at Monks Risborough & Whiteleaf Halt, photographed
around 1962.   *Lens of Sutton Collection*

new line between Ashendon Junction and Grendon Underwood, and the Princes Risborough to Aylesbury line was never brought up to main line standards.

The branch did, on occasions, carry main line traffic; the formal opening of the GCR London Extension in March 1899 meant that the troublesome Metropolitan could no longer object to Great Central traffic passing over its line, and from August 1899 until the opening of the Great Central line from Culworth Junction to Banbury in June 1900, coal trains ran southwards via Princes Risborough and High Wycombe.

In general, the line was subject to weight restrictions, and this meant that it was only used by main line trains in real emergencies. Classified by the GWR as a 'Blue' route, the heaviest Great Western 4-6-0s were barred from the line. Curiously, 'B1' class 4-6-0s and 'Black Five' 4-6-0s were allowed onto the route, subject to a strict 20 mph speed restriction, but in practice they only appeared in emergencies. In November 1965, for example, 'Black Five' 4-6-0 No. 44965 headed the 5.15 pm Nottingham to Marylebone semi-fast working over the branch, following a derailment at Aylesbury.

The normal motive power in steam days was a Collett '14XX' class 0-4-2T and a single auto-trailer, with '61XX' class prairies on through trains to Paddington. Collett '54XX' class 0-6-0PTs were used instead of the auto-fitted 0-4-2Ts at various times, while former Great Central classes sometimes appeared at the head of local passenger workings. In the 1950s, the daily goods train was normally worked by an 'N5' class 0-6-2T or a Robinson 'Pom-Pom' 0-6-0.

In the mid-1950s the Aylesbury to Princes Risborough branch was served by around a dozen trains each way, some of these being through workings to Marylebone, while others ran through to Paddington via High Wycombe and Maidenhead. A similar pattern or operation persisted for many years, and by June 1962 there were still 12 up and 11 down trains, many of these being through workings between Aylesbury and Marylebone. Goods traffic was conveyed by an early morning down service that left Paddington at 2.05 am (MX) and Old Oak Common at 2.55 am (MO), and arrived at Aylesbury at 5.52 am. A return working left Aylesbury at 9.07 pm.

In the 1970s, there were very few trains on the Aylesbury branch, and most local commuters clearly preferred the faster, more frequent services provided on the Metropolitan & Great Central route. The May 1971 public timetable shows just five up and nine down workings on weekdays and two up and three down on Saturdays, though this meagre service had been increased to 14 up and 12 down trains by May 1993.

The Aylesbury branch curves away from the up bay platform at Princes Risborough, and runs along the foot of the Chilterns for the first three or four miles. Monks Risborough & Whiteleaf, the first stopping place, is only 1 mile 29 chains from the junction; it was opened, as a simple halt with minimal facilities on 11th November, 1929. The single platform was sited on the up side, and a wooden shelter afforded scant comfort for the occasional traveller. The halt has remained in operation, its modest facilities being completely renewed as part of the Chiltern Line modernisation scheme, being moved 6 chains further north on 13th January, 1986.

Heading in a north-easterly direction, the trains reach Little Kimble the principal intermediate station, which is 2 miles 71 chains from Princes Risborough. This passenger-only station has its platform on the up side of the single running line. It was opened on 1st June, 1872, and is now an unstaffed halt, although its station building survives as a private dwelling. It is a simple, rectangular structure, with a gable roof and a small canopy.

Falling at 1 in 50, the line turns onto a more northerly course, and heads away from the hills towards Aylesbury. Marsh Lane Level Crossing, a mile and a half beyond Little Kimble, is the only public level crossing on the entire GW&GC system.

Little Kimble station, photographed in 1957, on the jointly-owned single track branch to Aylesbury; the quaint building was a relic of the original Wycombe Railway.

Brian W. Leslie

A general view of Little Kimble, *circa* 1960s, showing the single platform and station building.
Lens of Sutton Collection

As the trains approach their destination, they pass the site of South Aylesbury Halt (6 miles 41 chains), a relatively short-lived stopping place that was opened on 13th February, 1933 and closed in June 1967. The halt consisted of a single platform, again on the up side of the running line, together with an open-fronted waiting shelter and a single nameboard. At night, the platform was lit by oil lamps.

Turning on a westerly heading as they approach their destination, trains come to rest in the platforms at Aylesbury (7 miles 18 chains). Aylesbury station now has three platform faces - the down platform being an island with tracks on either side. A two-road engine shed once stood on the west side of the platforms, while the goods yard was sited to the north of the platforms on the up side. Loading docks and further sidings were situated to the south of the platforms.

When, in 1892, the Metropolitan Railway reached Aylesbury, its double track main line had to execute a sharp 'S' bend in order to gain the platforms. This bend was notorious, and in December 1904 it was the scene of an accident in which a down newspaper express derailed itself and was then hit by a southbound train. Finally, and at a cost of about £9,000 the curve was ironed out in 1907.

The present station has been remodelled on several occasions, and the red brick, 'Norman Shaw' style station building, with its tiny cupola, is obviously a product of the 20th century. The original station building, which had stood on the same site, was similar to that at Little Kimble, only bigger, while the original track layout differed from the present arrangement in that the Princes Risborough line was then the 'main line'.

Amusingly, Aylesbury must have been one of the most jointly-owned stations in Britain, as it was shared (after 1907) by two joint committees; cast metal signs used to carry the heading 'GREAT WESTERN & GREAT CENTRAL RAILWAYS JOINT COMMITTEE METROPOLITAN & GREAT CENTRAL JOINT COMMITTEE' - a mouthful if ever there was one. Further evidence of the joint nature of operations at Aylesbury could be found in the engine shed, which often housed a small, but eclectic assemblage of locomotives. In the 1950s these typically included one '61XX' class 2-6-2T, one '14XX' class 0-4-2T, one 'L1' class 2-6-2T, two 'N5' class 0-6-2Ts, one class '4MT' 2-6-4T and two class '4MT' 2-6-0s.

Important changes were put into effect at Aylesbury in 1990, when a new maintenance depot was constructed on a 'green field' site to the north-west of the station. This incorporates several stabling sidings and a three-road maintenance building, the latter structure being approximately 375 ft long and 134 ft in width; internally, two of its tracks are equipped with servicing pits and one has lifting equipment to facilitate heavy maintenance work on today's class '165' and '168' multiple units.

The introduction of the class '168' fleet led to a change in the management arrangements at Aylesbury Turbo depot, whereby control of the site was handed over to ADtranz under a partnership agreement with Chiltern Railways. The depot was formally transferred on 15th September, 1996, on which date all of the shed staff became ADtranz employees. The deal covered maintenance of the class '165' units as well as the class '168' sets, the idea being that ADtranz would guarantee that sufficient numbers of trains would be available for operation each day.

In a recent development, it was decided that the two-car class '165' unit that had been employed on the Aylesbury to Princes Risborough line would be replaced by a refurbished class '121' single unit railcar, so that the modern two-car set could be released for service elsewhere. A veteran class '121' unit was therefore added to the Chiltern Railways fleet, its special status being underlined by the provision of a distinctive overall blue livery scheme.

Situated on the southern outskirts of Aylesbury, South Aylesbury Halt was opened in 1933 to serve new housing developments although, sadly, it attracted comparatively little traffic and was closed with effect from 5th June, 1967.   *Lens of Sutton Collection*

A postcard view of Aylesbury station, *circa* 1912, looking south towards London with the engine shed visible in the right background.   *Lens of Sutton Collection*

Aylesbury station around 1958, showing the bay platform and loading docks on the up side.
Lens of Sutton Collection

Western Region '61XX' class 2-6-2T No. 6151 stands alongside the island platform on the down side at Aylesbury with a suburban service from Paddington. *Lens of Sutton Collection*

Aylesbury station in the 1970s, looking southwards along Platform Two in the direction of London.   *Lens of Sutton Collection*

A view along Platform One at Aylesbury *circa* 1958, showing the two-road locomotive shed.
                                                                Lens of Sutton Collection

An assemblage of motive power at Aylesbury on the occasion of an open day at the Turbo depot on 25th April, 1992. Locomotives on display include class '59' Co-Co No. 59005 *Kenneth J. Painter*, class '50' Co-Co No. 50031 *Hood* and 'Deltic' class '55' Co-Co No. D9016 *Gordon Highlander*.   *P.G. Barnes*

Envoi

Viewed against the sorry shambles of the 'Last Great Privatisation', the achievements of Chiltern Railways are remarkable. The story of the GW&GC Joint Line has, in truth, been a case of rise and fall, followed by an unexpected renaissance. The restoration of two-hour schedules on a double track main line has completed the transformation of a neglected route, and offered a realistic alternative to the former London & North Western route between Euston and Birmingham. Indeed, it seems likely that, with sufficient advertising, more and more travellers could be attracted from Euston to the former GW&GC route.

Although journey times are still marginally longer than those on the West Coast Main Line, Chiltern fares are cheaper, the trains are less crowded and they arrive on time. Moreover, customers who turn up on the day of travel are able to purchase reasonably-priced 'walk-on walk-off' tickets with few of the irritating restrictions that discourage travellers on the rival route from Euston to Birmingham New Street.

At the time of writing the GW&GC route is worked as part of a longer-distance route between Marylebone, High Wycombe, Banbury, Birmingham Snow Hill and Kidderminster. Other services run between London, High Wycombe and Aylesbury, giving travellers an excellent choice of trains at the southern end of the route. Paddington is still shown in the timetables as a possible destination and in the December 2005-June 2006 timetable just the 5.26 am (SX) from Aylesbury and 12.55 pm (WSX) from Paddington run between Paddington and South Ruislip. In practice, the Old Oak Common to South Ruislip link comes into its own during emergencies, or when the Marylebone route is closed for routine engineering work.

On 28th February, 1999, for instance, Chiltern Line services were diverted into Paddington because of engineering work, bringing class '168' units into the Great Western terminus for perhaps the first time. More recently, on the weekend of 26th-27th April 2003, services were again diverted into Paddington station while engineering work was carried out at Marylebone.

Appendix

Principal Locomotive Classes used on the GW&GC Joint Line 1906-1990

GWR classes 1906-61

'Saint' class 4-6-0
'Star' class 4-6-0
'Atbara' class 4-4-0
'County' class 4-4-0
'de Glehn' Compound 4-4-2s
Dean 'Armstrong' class 4-4-0s
Dean Goods 0-6-0s
'63XX' class 2-6-0s
'28XX' class 2-8-0s
'47XX' class 2-8-0s
'Metro' class 2-4-0Ts
'36XX' Birdcage class 2-4-2Ts
'County Tank' 4-4-2Ts
'54XX' class 0-6-0PTs
'14XX' class 0-4-2Ts
'King' class 4-6-0s
'Castle' class 4-6-0s
'Hall' class 4-6-0s
'County' class 4-6-0s
'61XX' class 2-6-2TS
'74XX' class 0-6-0PTs
'94XX' class 0-6-0PTs
'97XX' class 0-6-0PTs

GCR/LNER Classes 1906-58

Robinson Atlantic 4-4-2s
Robinson 'B2' class 4-6-0s
Robinson 'Director' class 4-4-0s
Robinson 'A5' class '4-6-2Ts
Robinson 'O4' class 2-8-0s
Robinson 'C13' class 4-4-2Ts
Robinson 'C14' class 4-4-2Ts
Robinson 'J11' class 0-6-0s
Gresley 'A3' class 4-6-2s
Gresley 'V2' class 2-6-2Ts
Thompson 'B1' class 4-6-0s
Thompson 'L1' class 2-6-4Ts

LMS Classes 1958-66

Stanier class '5MT' 4-6-0s
Stanier class '4MT' 2-6-0s
Fairburn class '4MT' 2-6-4Ts

BR Classes 1958-1990

Steam
Standard class '4MT' 2-6-4Ts
Standard class '4MT' 2-6-0s
Standard class '9F' 2-10-0s

Diesel
Class '47' Co-Cos
Class '52' 'Western' Co-Cos
Class '43' 'Warship' Bo-Bos
Class '22' Bo-Bos
Class '31' A1A-A1As
Class '37' Co-Cos
Class '50' Co-Cos
Class '08' 0-6-0s

Sources and Further Reading

The main primary sources for this study were found in the rail transport section of the University of Leicester Library, the Oxfordshire County Record Office, and the National Archives. At the same time, a wealth information was obtained from material in private collections, and in the historic newspaper collections of local libraries. The following Acts or plans were among those consulted at various times:

Acts of Parliament
The Great Western Railway Act 1835; 1897; 1898; 1899
The Great Western & Great Central Railways Act 1899
The Ashendon & Aynho Railway Act 1905
The Wycombe Railway Act 1847; 1852; 1857; 1861; 1862; 1865
The Uxbridge & Rickmansworth Railway Act 1896

Deposited Plans in Oxfordshire County Record Office
The Oxford & Brentford Railway, 1852 (PD2/57)
The London & Mid Western Railway, 1853 (PU2/6U)
The London, Buckinghamshire & West Midland Junction Railway
The London, Buckinghamshire & East Gloucestershire Railway (PD2/99 & 127)
The London & South Wales Railway 1895 (PD2/127)
The Great Western & Great Central Railway (PD2/134)
The Ashendon-Aynho Railway (PD2/139)
The Wycombe Railway (PD2/80)

Also Ordnance Survey sheets (various) and RAF Topographical charts. Other important sources of information included *The Oxford Mail*, *The Oxford Times*, *The Railway Magazine*, *The Railway Modeller*, *Railway World*, *The Meccano Magazine*, *Bradshaw's Shareholders' Manual & Guide*, *The Locomotive Magazine*, *The Great Western Railway Magazine*, *The British Railways Magazine*, *The Engineer*, *The Railway Engineer*, *The Western Region London Division News*, *The Bucks Herald*, *The Railway Times*, *Steam Days* and the *Great Western Railway Journal*.

The following list of books and articles is by no means exhaustive, but it may be of interest to those seeking further information on the GW&GC Joint Line or its connections.

Ahern, J.H., The Watlington Branch, *Model Railway News*, August and September 1950.
Allen, Cecil J., *British Atlantic Locomotives* (Ian Allan, 1968).
Allen, Cecil J., London-Birmingham, *Railway World*, June 1967.
Allen, Cecil J., Great Central Train Services of 1905, *Railway World*, March 1965.
Allen, Cecil J., *Great Western* (Ian Allan, 1962).
Allen, Cecil J., British Locomotive Practice & Performance, *The Railway Magazine*, February 1954.
Allen, Cecil J., British Locomotive Practice & Performance, *The Railway Magazine*, July 1961.
Atherton, Alfred W., Opening of the New Route to the North and North-West, *The Railway Magazine*, April 1906.
Atherton, Alfred W., The Great Western Railway's New Route to the North and North-West, *The Railway Magazine*, May 1910.
Baker, R.M.G., The Metropolitan & Great Central Joint Line, *The Railway Magazine*, June-July 1960.
Barnes, Alan, Tales of Bell, Book & Booking Boy, *Great Western Railway Journal* No. 40, Autumn 2001.
Behrend, George, *Gone With Regret* (Jersey Artist Ltd, 1964).
Bolger, Paul, *BR Steam Motive Power Depots: ER* (Ian Allan, 1982).
Bonnett, Harold, Minerals to Chinnor, *The Railway Magazine*, August 1979.
Brabant, F.G., *The Little Guide to Oxfordshire* (Methuen, 1906).
British Railways, *Public & Working Timetables*, *Permanent Way Alterations, Signalling Instructions, Etc.*
Cannan, Joanna, *Oxfordshire* (Robert Hale 1952).
Casserley, H.C., *Britain's Joint Lines* (Ian Allan, 1968).
Clark, R.H., *An Historical Survey of Selected Great Western Stations* (OPC, 1976).
Coles, C.R.L., Memories of the Great Central, *The Railway Magazine*, July 1954.
Coles, C.R.L., By Rail to Wembley Stadium, *The Railway Magazine*, May 1959.
Cooke, B.W.C., British Railways Diesel-Electric Pullman Trains, *The Railway Magazine*, August 1960.

Cooke, R.A., *Track Layout Diagrams of the GWR and BRWR* (Section 26), 1992.

Copsey, John, Risborough South in the 1930s, *Great Western Railway Journal* No. 29, Winter 1999.

Copsey, John, Postwar Traffic Working on the Thame Branch, *Great Western Railway Journal* No. 27, Summer 1998.

Cormack, J., & Pigott, N., The Great Railway Sale is Over, *The Railway Magazine*, April 1997.

Cummings, John, *Railway Motor Buses & Bus Services* (OPC, 1980).

Dow, George, *Great Central*, Vols I & II, *passim*. (Locomotive Publishing Co.)

Edwards, D., & Pigram, Ron, *The Final Link* (Midas, 1982).

Farr, Keith, Centenary of the Great Central, *The Railway Magazine*, March 1999.

Farr, Keith, Monarchs of the Rails, *The Railway Magazine*, June-July 2002.

Firth, John B., *The Little Guide to Middlesex* (Methuen 1906).

Fraser, Maxwell, *Companion into Buckinghamshire* (Methuen 1935).

Freezer, Cyril, Aylesbury, *Railway Modeller*, November 1959

Gadsden, E.J.S., Last Rights on the Great Central, *Railway World*, November 1966.

Goudie, Frank W., Railways to Uxbridge, *Railway World*, October 1982.

Gourvish, T.R., *British Railways 1948-73: A Business History* (Cambridge University Press, 1986).

Great Western Railway, *Traffic Dealt with at Stations & Goods Depots*, (National Archives RAIL 253/45); *Towns, Villages, Outlying Works etc* (1938); *Working & Public Timetables, passim; Station Accounts Instruction Book* (1929).

Harris, Michael, Special Traffic - The FA Cup, Wembley & Special Trains, *Steam Days* No. 142, June 2001.

Harrison, Ian, *Great Western Railway Locomotive Allocations for 1921* (Wild Swan Pub. 1984).

Healy, John M.C., *History of the Chiltern Line* (1992).

Holcroft, H., *An Outline of Great Western Locomotive Practice 1837-1947)* (Ian Allan 1957).

Holden, John, *The Watlington Branch* (OPC 1974).

Hughes, Geoffrey, *LNER* (Ian Allan 1986).

Jackson, Alan A., Central Line to the West, *Railways South East* No. 1, 1987.

Jackson, Alan A., North-West from Ealing, *The Railway Magazine*, September, October 1959.

Jackson, Alan, Brent Valley Railcars, *Railway World*, May 1979.

Jenkins, Stanley C., *The Oxford Worcester & Wolverhampton Railway* (Oakwood Press 1977).

Jenkins, Stanley C., West London Link, *The Railway Magazine*, April 1982.

Jenkins, Stanley C., The Uxbridge High Street Branch, *Great Western Railway Journal* No. 1, Winter 1992.

Jenkins, Stanley C., The Uxbridge High Street Branch - A Little Known Line, *Railway World*, March 1984.

Kapur, Ian, The Line that Fought for a Future - and Won, *The Railway Magazine*, June 1992.

Karau, P., & Turner, C, *The Marlow Branch* (Wild Swan Pub 1987).

Karau, P., & Turner, C., *Country Branch Line* (Wild Swan Pub 1998).

Lee, Charles E., British Named Express Trains, *The Railway Magazine*, August 1958.

Lee, Charles E., *The Metropolitan Line* (London Transport 1972).

Lee, Charles E., *Seventy Years of the Central* (London Transport 1970).

Lee, Charles E., The Metropolitan in its Prime, *The Railway Magazine*, February 1963.

Lee, Charles E., Diamond Jubilee of the Twopenny Tube, *The Railway Magazine*, July 1960.

Lyons, Eric, *An Historical Survey of Great Western Engine Sheds* (OPC 1972).

MacDermot, E.T., *History of the Great Western Railway* 2 vols. (GWR 1927).

Machell, G., Railway Development at Aylesbury, *The Railway Magazine*, November, December 1955.

Marsden, Colin J., Towards Network 2000, *The Railway Magazine*, August 1991.

Marsden, Colin J., The 'Blue Pullmans', *The Railway Magazine*, May 1994.

Marsden, Colin J., Travelling in Luxury, *The Railway Magazine*, September 1994.

Marsden, Colin J., New Generation Multiple Units, *The Railway Magazine*, November 2000.

Marsden, Colin J., New Train Orders, *The Railway Magazine*, November 2002.

Mee, Arthur, *Oxfordshire* (Hodder & Stoughton 1945).

Mowat, C.L., The Wycombe Railway, *The Railway Magazine* 1933.

Nock, O.S., *Fifty Years of Western Express Running* (Edward Everard 1954).

Nock, O.S., Requiem for the Great Central, *The Railway Magazine*, April 1974.

Nock, O.S., *The Great Western Railway in the 20th Century* (Ian Allan 1964).

Nock, O.S., *The History of the Great Western Railway*, Vol. III (Ian Allan 1967).

Nock, O.S., British Locomotive Practice & Performance, *The Railway Magazine*, March 1963.

Peacock, Thomas B., *Great Western London Suburban Services* (Oakwood Press 1970).

Peaty, Ian P., Stout Work: The Railways of Arthur Guinness & Son Ltd, Park Royal, *Railway Bylines*, May 2000.

Pevsner, N., *The Buildings of England: Buckinghamshire* (Penguin 1960).

Pevsner, N., *The Buildings of England: Middlesex* (Penguin 1951).

Pigott, Nick, The Death of Railtrack, *The Railway Magazine*, December 2001.

Potts C.R., *Oxford to Princes Risborough - A GWR Secondary Route* (Oakwood Press 2004).

Potts, W., *A History of Banbury* (Banbury Guardian 1958).

Pound, Peter, *Lyons Centenary Booklet* (1994).
Robbins, Michael, Railways & Railway Schemes in Uxbridge, *The Railway Magazine*, May 1956.
Robbins, Michael, The Size of the Tube, *The Railway Magazine*, February 1959.
Robbins, Michael, *Middlesex* (1953).
Roscoe, E.S., *The Little Guide to Buckinghamshire* (1903).
Semmens, P.W.B., *The Heyday of GWR Train Services* (David & Charles 1990).
Semmens, P.W.B., Up for the Cup, *The Railway Magazine*, May 2003.
Semmens, Peter, 'Blue Pullmans', *The Railway Magazine*, February 1997.
Shannon, Paul, Bicester: In the Military Style, *The Railway Magazine*, December 1992.
Sherwood, J., & Pevsner, N., *The Buildings of England: Oxfordshire* (Penguin 1974).
Sikes, R.C., Geology of the Acton & High Wycombe Railway, *The Great Western Railway Magazine*, 1904.
Smith, Michael J., God's Wonderful Electrics, *The Railway Magazine*, February 1990.
Thompson, Mike, High Days at Aynho Junction, *Steam Days* No. 157, September 2002.
Treby, Edward, Railways & the British Empire Exhibition, *The Railway Magazine*, May 1974.
Tuplin, W.A., The Sir Sam Fay Class: A Reappraisal, *The Railway Magazine*, April 1955.
Tuplin, W.A., *British Steam Since 1900* (David & Charles 1969).
Turner, Chris, Uxbridge High Street: A Follow-Up, *Great Western Railway Journal* No. 10, Spring 1994.
Walker, Colin, Farewell to the Marylebone-Manchester Expresses, *The Railway Magazine*, March 1960.
Warren, F.C., The New Main Line to the North, *The Great Western Railway Magazine*, 1910.
Widdowson, Keith, 'Travels over the London Extension', *Steam Days* No. 180 August 2004.
Williams, Ethel Carleton, *Companion into Oxfordshire* (Methuen 1935).
Williams, Kenneth, *Just Williams* (J.M. Dent 1985).

Index